OPERATION CHOWHOUND

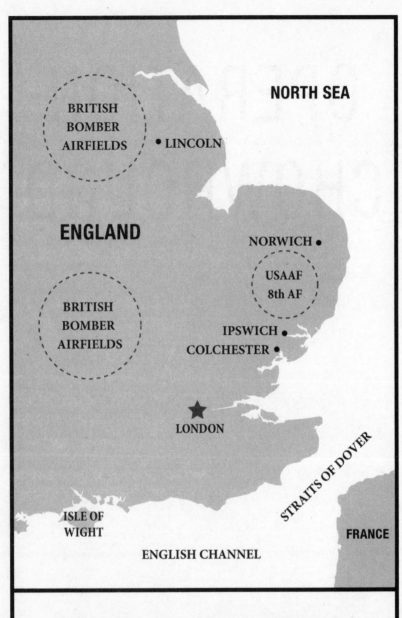

**ALLIED HEAVY BOMBER AIRFIELDS,
EASTERN & CENTRAL ENGLAND,**
April-May, 1945

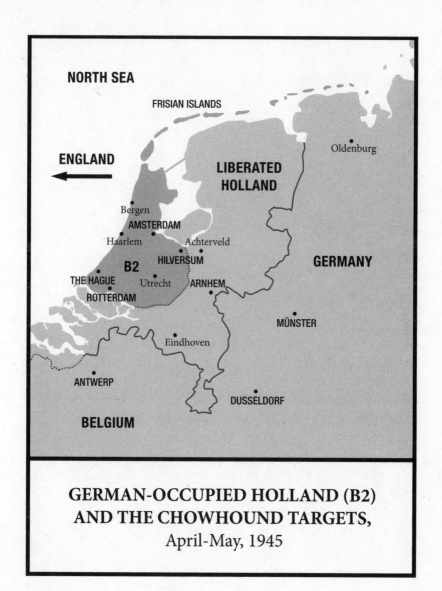

GERMAN-OCCUPIED HOLLAND (B2)
AND THE CHOWHOUND TARGETS,
April-May, 1945

OPERATION CHOWHOUND

THE MOST RISKY, MOST GLORIOUS US BOMBER MISSION OF WWII

STEPHEN DANDO-COLLINS

palgrave
macmillan

OPERATION CHOWHOUND
Copyright © Stephen Dando-Collins, 2015.
All rights reserved.

First published in 2015 by PALGRAVE MACMILLAN® TRADE in the
United States—a division of St. Martin's Press LLC, 175 Fifth Avenue, New
York, NY 10010.

Palgrave® and Macmillan® are registered trademarks in the United States,
the United Kingdom, Europe and other countries.

ISBN: 978-1-137-27963-7

Library of Congress Cataloging-in-Publication Data

Dando-Collins, Stephen.
    Operation Chowhound : the most risky, most glorious US bomber mission of
WWII / Stephen Dando-Collins.
       pages   cm.
    Includes bibliographical references and index.
    1. World War, 1939–1945—Food supply—Netherlands. 2. Food relief,
American—Netherlands—History—20th century. 3. Survival and emergency
rations—Netherlands—History—20th century. 4. United States. Army Air
Forces. Air Force, 8th—History. 5. B-17 bomber—History—20th century.
6. World War, 1939–1945—Aerial operations, American. 7. Netherlands—
Economic conditions—1918–1945. I. Title.
D802.N4D36   2015
940.53'1—dc23

                                                                                    2014028702

Design by Letra Libre, Inc.

First edition: February 2015

10 9 8 7 6 5 4 3 2

Printed in the United States of America.

CONTENTS

ACKNOWLEDGMENTS

For their help my grateful thanks go to my publisher Karen Wolny; my New York literary agent, Richard Curtis; and to Eric Heijink, creator of the Operation Manna website in the Netherlands. Also to James Mutton of the 95th Bomb Group Heritage Association in the UK.

And, as always, my special thanks goes to my wife, Louise, who keeps me flying high.

PREFACE

The Berlin Airlift of 1948–49 would be splashed large across the pages of history as an amazing eleven-month-long Cold War operation in which the governments of the West, led by the United States, who, under the code name of Operation Vittles, flew in ton after ton of food and other vital supplies to the people of Berlin after the Soviets cut the city off from supply by land.

Yet three years earlier, in the dying days of the Second World War, there had been a remarkable and heroic precedent for that successful airlift. This was a massive operation involving upward of 900 heavy bombers a day at its height. Over ten days, thousands of air and ground crew delivered 11,185.7 tons of food to the starving 3.5 million Dutch in Nazi-occupied Holland. This was an operation driven by two determined American generals, Dwight D. Eisenhower and his deputy, Walter Bedell Smith, who, in the face of political wrangling in Britain and the United States, opposition even in Holland and with just a verbal promise from the Nazis that they would not fire on Allied aircraft involved in the operation, were determined to send the bombers of the US 8th Air Force and Britain's 2nd Tactical Air Force over Holland, dropping food without parachutes from just a few hundred feet, day after day.

Over the winter of 1944–45—called the Hunger Winter by the Dutch—and up to the end of the war in May 1945, 25,000 Dutch civilians in Nazi-occupied Holland died from starvation. The majority of these victims were in the cities and were the most vulnerable—the youngest and the oldest in the population. Newborn babies figured high among the death totals. The German occupiers had enough food to last them many months. Not only were they were not sharing their food stocks with the millions of Dutch civilians under their control, they cut off electrical power to the population over the winter. As the Dutch froze and starved, they resorted to eating tulip bulbs and stripping their homes of doors and other woodwork for firewood.

In Britain, exiled members of the Dutch royal family and the Dutch government begged the Allies to save their people from looming disaster. British Prime Minister Churchill prevaricated. In the United States, President Franklin D. Roosevelt, himself of Dutch descent, ordered food relief for the Dutch but died just days after doing so. For a month, his order was not acted upon. In the end, to get the ball rolling, the Supreme Allied Commander, General Eisenhower, had to act on his own initiative. And the Nazi governor of German-occupied Holland, Dr. Arthur Seyss-Inquart, worried about saving his own skin and disobeying Hitler, finally ordered occupying German forces in the Netherlands not to fire on the low-flying bombers taking part in the mercy mission. But would disgruntled German troops obey such an order?

The Americans called their part of this mission Operation Chowhound. The British called their part Operation Manna. Between them, in late April and early May 1945, Operations Manna and Chowhound delivered desperately needed food to the Dutch from the air as 120,000 German troops, including men of the dreaded SS, stood by and watched with their fingers on the triggers of their guns—and sometimes gave in to the temptation to open fire on the bombers.

With 2015 bringing the seventieth anniversary of this previously unsung episode in American wartime history, this book is intended to bring to light the details of how this operation came about, and to bring to light the personalities behind its conception and difficult implementation. Men like Eisenhower and Bedell Smith, and the officer to whom they gave the job of planning the air drops, Briton Andrew Geddes, as well as the American, Canadian, Australian and British airmen whose stories appear in these pages.

Then there are people such as a young Audrey Hepburn, the future Hollywood star, who, as a teenager, was one of the starving millions under the Nazi jackboot in Holland. Future best-selling Canadian author Farley Mowat went on a crazy behind-the-lines mission just as Operation Chowhound was at a delicate stage of negotiation with the Nazi governor. And James Bond creator Ian Fleming, himself a spy, was charged by Churchill with giving a security clearance to the man pushing for the air drops from the Dutch side—German-born Dutch royal Prince Bernhard—while unaware that the prince was keeping past Nazi connections a secret.

This book also tells the stories of Dutch people who struggled to feed their families during the Hunger Winter of 1944–45. By necessity, many of those doing the dangerous work of stealing food from the Germans or going on missions to the countryside in quest of food were children. In fact, the youth of key participants in this drama is what struck me most when researching this book.

Not only the children of Holland were involved. I was reminded of the youth of the American airmen who flew on Operation Chowhound and who flew throughout the Second World War. These were predominantly boys of nineteen, twenty and twenty-one who were put in charge of B-17 Flying Fortresses and sent over Hitler's Europe to bomb the Nazis into submission. And then they were expected to fly over Holland at 300 feet and drop food to the Dutch people—in the face of German guns and without a signed truce in place. No wonder so many of these aircrew went on hair-raising low-level buzz flights over Holland after making their food drops!

Above all, this book salutes the courage and determination of the many people who made Operation Chowhound succeed, on the ground and in the air. Long may they be remembered.

1

NAVIGATOR ELLIS B. SCRIPTURE'S PRAYER

This was madness! Sitting at the navigator's table behind the bombardier in the nose of a B-17 Flying Fortress bomber, Major Ellis B. Scripture, or "Scrip" to his fellow members of the United States Army Air Force (USAAF), looked ahead through the Plexiglas nose and shuddered.[1] The flat earth of Holland was flashing by beneath the bomber, uncomfortably close as the B-17 hurtled along at 120 knots just a few hundred feet above the ground. A mistake by the pilot, or a German antiaircraft shell, could spell the end for all on board—they were way too close to the ground to bail out and survive.

B-17s were built to bomb from close to 30,000 feet, not to clip the treetops like this! But here they were, hundreds of mighty American bombers, flitting over German-occupied territory as if out on a sightseeing trip, with nothing more lethal in their bomb bays than Hershey bars, cigarettes, margarine and coffee. Operation Chowhound it was called. This operation in the first week of May 1945 had been touted as a mercy mission. That's why Scrip hadn't hesitated to follow the example of his long-time commander and close friend Lieutenant Colonel Griffin

"Grif" Mumford and volunteer for this sortie, leaving the comfort and protection of their offices at 3rd Air Division Headquarters at Elveden Hall in the picturesque English county of Suffolk.

Scrip and Grif had been in the first cadre of the 95th Bombardment Group aircrew to arrive in England in 1943. Grif, a squadron commander with the 95th, and Scrip, his navigator, had flown together on the group's first combat mission over a Nazi target and on plenty of dangerous missions together since. When Grif was promoted to group command pilot, Scrip moved up to group navigator. They'd gone together to air division HQ, where Grif was now director of operations and Scrip was head honcho in the navigation department as division navigator.

Grif Mumford was legendary in the USAAF and famous back home in the States. The stubborn, independent and determined native of West Texas had made his name in March 1944 by leading the first US bombing raid on Berlin, Hitler's capital. Reichsmarshall Hermann Goering, number two in the Nazi hierarchy and chief of the Luftwaffe, the German air force, had been boasting for years that no bombs would ever fall on Berlin. "If an enemy bomber reaches the Ruhr," Goering had declared back in 1939, "my name is not Hermann Goering. You can call me Meier [the German equivalent of Smith]."[2]

Well, Allied bombers had reached the Ruhr. And British aircraft were bombing Berlin, primarily by night because it was less risky, but to negligible effect and with punishing losses. Before the United States entered the war, Dr. Goebbels' Propaganda Ministry had published English-language editions of German military magazines in America that showed pictures of Berlin's monstrous flak towers and boasted of the thousands of antiaircraft guns and hundreds of fighters that protected the city. In February and March of 1944, the US 8th Air Force had set out to prove that mass air raids against Berlin in daylight could succeed despite those daunting defenses. But bad weather had forced the cancellation of one attempt after another. Finally, on March 4, a total of 850 B-17s had taken to the English skies, bound for the "Big B"—Berlin. Midway into the mission, as the weather began to close in, squadron after squadron received a recall message by radio, and hundreds of bombers turned around and went home. But Grif Mumford ignored the recall.

Mumford was flying as group commander in *I'll Be Around*, as its crew had named the B-17G piloted by Lieutenant Alvin Brown. The airplane's radio operator reported that the recall message had not entirely followed the rules set down for these messages and wondered if the Germans on the ground had sent it in an attempt to break up the attack. Mumford, flying in the copilot's seat for the historic mission, had calculated that they were halfway to the target. He knew that German radar had been tracking them ever since they'd appeared in the skies over the Continent. He also knew that, based on their flight path, Luftwaffe fighter controllers on the ground would be scrambling squadrons of Messerschmitt 109s and Focke-Wulf 190s to meet them before they reached Berlin and to intercept them on their way back—likely anticipating that they would fly the same route out that they had flown coming in.

But the flight plan for this mission against the Big B called for a different return route, going south via heavily defended Frankfurt. Reckoning that it was just as dangerous to turn back and fly into waiting fighters as it was to continue on course, Grif Mumford decided to use his discretion as group commander pilot and fly on. As twenty-eight other B-17s followed his lead, Grif Mumford flew on to Berlin. Short of the target, twenty German Me-109 and Fw-190 fighters had come hurtling down out of the heavens, cannons blazing, knocking one B-17 from the sky on their first pass. But before the German pilots could return for another pass, they were jumped by several squadrons of American P-51 Mustang long-range fighters that had decided to accompany the bombers to the target after also ignoring the recall order.

In the ensuing dogfight, future famed jet test pilot Chuck Yeager bagged his first German aircraft on the way to becoming a fighter ace. Overall, the P-51s had the worst of it on that day, with twenty-one of their number being shot down for fourteen Luftwaffe fighter losses. But the intervention of the P-51s prevented the German fighters from again attacking the bombers. The Mustang pilots had done their job. The bombers reached the target. As they came over Berlin at 29,600 feet, 2,500 radar-controlled heavy antiaircraft guns on the ground opened up on the twenty-nine B-17s above the clouds. Grif Mumford would recall that the black clouds of exploding flak shells were so thick that it looked as if he could walk on them. Four of the bombers were knocked down by the flak. But the remainder had dropped forty tons of bombs on "impregnable" Berlin before turning for home.[3]

Tough, uncompromising commander of the 3rd Air Division Brigadier General Curtis LeMay had been waiting for Mumford and the other survivors of the mission when they landed back at Horham in Suffolk. The general had come to berate Grif for disobeying the recall order, but hordes of reporters had gotten to the air station ahead of the general. Word had leaked out that the USAAF had bombed Berlin, and the press was hungry for heroes. Among the newsmen were a reporter and photographer from *Life* magazine. Three weeks later, Grif Mumford and the crew of *I'll Be Around* were on the front cover of *Life*, with Grif hailed as the man who had bombed Berlin. "Old Iron Pants" LeMay hadn't torn strips off Grif. Instead, he gave him the Silver Star and recommended a Presidential Citation for the entire 95th Bombardment Group, which was duly awarded by President Franklin D. Roosevelt.

Everyone wanted to fly with Grif after that, but he was kept out of the skies and at the planning table for much of the rest of the war. When he did get a chance to fly, he always took Scrip with him. Most recently, it had been flying a B-17 to liberated Paris. That had been fun. But this Chowhound flight was different. For a change, the American bomber pilots would be saving lives, not taking them. At least, that was the plan. With Hitler dead on April 30, having committed suicide in his Berlin bunker, and the war in Europe expected to end any day with a German capitulation, Grif was determined to make one last contribution. And he couldn't think of a better way to do it than to fly desperately needed food to 3.5 million starving Dutch civilians in the Nazi-occupied west of Holland, an area that took in all the major cities of the Netherlands, including Amsterdam, Rotterdam and the capital, The Hague.

The problem was that this part of Holland was still in the hands of 120,000 well-armed German troops, including some of the tough Waffen-SS who had stopped the Allied advance into Holland at Arnhem the previous autumn. That bloody rebuff of the push into Holland had fated the bulk of the Dutch people to remain under Nazi control and to fight a battle of their own, against starvation.

As lead navigator in the lead aircraft, Ellis Scripture was looking down at towns and villages and seeing joyous Dutch men, women and children out in the open, waving their hands and Dutch flags at them—risking arrest by the Germans, who had outlawed Holland's flag and national anthem. Scrip saw German troops down there, too—armed, watching the Americans fly over. And quick-firing antiaircraft guns that traversed to follow the bombers' course.

This was worse than bombing Berlin. At least then you knew that the Germans were going to fire at you, and you had the advantage of height and the cover of escorting fighters. Thankfully, there was no longer a threat from German fighters in Holland's skies; not since the Luftwaffe's disastrous Operation Baseplate in January had resulted in the loss of hundreds of Me-109s and Fw-190s over Holland and Belgium. Allied air supremacy was total, and both sides knew it. German soldiers told a black joke about the failure of Hermann Goering's Luftwaffe to protect them in these dying days of the war. "If you see an aircraft with silver wings," they said, "it's the American air force. If it has gray wings, it's the British air force. And if it has no wings, it's the Luftwaffe."[4]

Just the same, when flying at such low altitude, the risk of being brought down by ground fire was acute. And there were tens of thousands of enemy guns down there! The 50-caliber machine guns on B-17s were loaded and ready to return fire should the Germans on the ground open up on them. But if the Germans did open fire, there would be little chance for a lumbering, low-flying bomber. Even a lucky rifle bullet from a German soldier disobeying orders could be enough to down a B-17 flying at this altitude. Would the Nazis keep their word and refrain from firing? Could you trust a Nazi? Could an American take a Hitlerite's word for anything? Was this a giant trap, a cunning and elaborate plan to lure hundreds of American aircraft into a nest of antiaircraft guns that would knock them all out of the sky? Would Operation Chowhound become Operation Turkey Shoot?

Ellis B. Scripture, thinking of his family back home, and thinking how close death might be on this day, remembered words from a Native American prayer.

When I'm dead cry for me a little
Think of me sometimes, but not too much
Think of me now and again as I was in life
At some moment that is pleasant to recall
But not for long
Leave me in peace and I shall leave you in peace
And while you live let your thoughts be with the living.[5]

2

HITLER'S SECRET AGENT

Adolf Hitler, the fuehrer of Nazi Germany, waited for the prince to cross the room to join him.

Coming to a halt several yards from the fuehrer, and, clicking his heels together, Prince Bernhard of Lippe-Biesterfeld gave the fascist salute. "Heil Hitler!" he cried.

Hitler responded with his usual casual salute, raising his right hand a little, then nodded for the twenty-four-year-old to approach, extending his hand for Bernhard to shake, which he did—in a most fawning manner as far as Hitler was concerned. It was the summer of 1936, and Bernhard was paying the fuehrer a farewell visit before setting off to Holland for the official announcement of his engagement to Princess Juliana of the Netherlands in September. He was going with Hitler's blessing—a German prince marrying into Dutch royalty, becoming the husband of the heir to the throne of the Netherlands, suited the fuehrer's plans for extending German influence.[1]

To Hitler, and to many Germans, the Dutch were almost as good as Germans. Historically, they had come from the same Germanic roots east and north of the Rhine. In fact, Hitler felt that the Dutch would make very good SS men. Six years after this 1936 meeting with Bern-hard, Hitler would declare over dinner one evening, "A race like the Dutch, which has shown itself capable of organizing a magnificent Far Eastern air service and which produces a host of first-class seamen, can easily be taught to assimilate the military spirit. One must not lose faith in the essential soundness of the race, for sound it certainly is."[2]

As for the German who was setting off to become prince consort of the future queen of the Netherlands, Hitler was less impressed. At the same 1942 dinner where he extolled the Dutch, Hitler would recall his 1936 meeting with Bernhard. "When, before his marriage, he came to pay me a farewell visit, he cringed and scraped like a gigolo," he would tell his staff.[3]

But Hitler was convinced that manipulating the Dutch would be easy with Bernhard on the throne beside Juliana. In the fuehrer's opin-ion, the prince was "an absolute imbecile oaf." Hitler was to say that his view of Bernhard would be reinforced when, to his amusement, several days after arriving in the Netherlands, the prince told the Dutch press, "In my heart, I have always felt myself a Dutchman!"[4]

Hitler would have known that Bernhard had been a member of the Nazi Party, and was likely to have known that he'd also been a mem-ber of a branch of Heinrich Himmler's SS.[5] To his dying day, Bernhard would deny any links to the Nazi Party or its apparatus. "I was never a Nazi," he was to declare.[6] He was lying. It was the convenient lie of many Germans who had joined the Nazi Party and Nazi organizations to further their careers in the 1930s.

Under the Nazi government, it became compulsory for German boys to join the Hitlerjugend, the Hitler Youth, and for girls to join the female equivalent, the Bund Deutscher Mädel. But it was not compul-sory to join either the Nazi Party or the Schutzstaffel, the dreaded and elite SS, which had begun life as Hitler's bodyguard. Documents that did not come to light until more than seventy years later show that, while studying at Berlin's Humboldt University, the former Friedrich-Wilhelm University, in the early 1930s, Bernhard had been a member of the Deutsche Studentenschaft, a Nazi student fraternity; had joined the Nazi Party and its paramilitary wing, the brown-shirted Sturmabteilung, or SA; and been a member of the Reiter-SS, the SS's cavalry corps, spending part-time hours in the SS garage pandering to the love of powerful cars that would come to the fore in later life.

After graduating from Humboldt University with a law degree in December 1934, Bernhard had been employed by the giant German industrial conglomerate IG Farben and sent to the headquarters of its French operations in Paris. IG Farben had been created in 1920 following the First World War via the combination of chemical companies Bayer, BASF, Hoechst and five smaller companies, becoming the largest business concern in Germany, and, by some reckonings, the fourth largest in the world. In Paris, Bernhard took up the appointment of salesman with IG Farben, a role he carried out with considerable success, later becoming secretary to the company's French board, performing these duties until his marriage to Princess Juliana in 1937. A 1976 American magazine report would state that, during the Nuremberg Trial of IG Farben directors in 1947–48, verbal testimony had come out that a special secret Nazi overseas intelligence unit had been set up within IG Farben, and that Prince Bernhard was a member of this unit and undertook spying duties for the German government while working for the company in Paris.[7] No documentary evidence was to come forth to support this claim. However, in December 1945, Colonel Bernard Bernstein, General Eisenhower's chief financial adviser and Director of the US Group Control Commission for Germany's Division of Investigation of Cartels and External Assets, delivered a damning report on IG Farben to US Congress.

According to the report compiled by Bernstein and a large team of US investigators, "Without IG Farben, World War II could not have been possible."[8] Bernstein was referring in part to the company's industrial output, but also to its vast espionage contribution to Germany's war effort. "Farben was a Nazi agency for worldwide military and economic espionage," said Colonel Bernstein. His report detailed how IG Farben set up a secret economic and political intelligence unit known as N.W.7 within the company, with its headquarters at IG Farben's head office in Berlin. Executives at IG Farben offices around the world were required to submit intelligence reports every month to N.W.7 in Berlin about everything ranging from foreign armaments factory locations to shipping movements, local political machinations to foreign economic statistics. N.W.7 fed masses of this information to the German military high command from 1929 until war's end.[9]

N.W.7's field agents were called "IG Verbindungsmanner."[10] The company's sales executives such as Prince Bernhard were able to travel extensively and visit militarily sensitive locations without raising suspicion, and there can be little doubt that Bernhard was among the Verbindungsmanner and was one of the executives required to submit monthly intelligence reports to N.W.7 while he worked for IG Farben. The secret of the company's extensive spying activities was not revealed until interrogation of IG Farben personnel after the war, although no records identifying agents such as the prince were ever unearthed.

In 1995, Dutch researcher Gerard Aalders found documents that suggested that Prince Bernhard had been a member of the SA and Nazi Party, but located nothing conclusive.[11] Nonetheless, in 2002, Dutch investigative journalist Philip Droge published in Holland the book *Bernhard, Master of Spies: The Intelligence Career of Prince Bernhard*, in which he repeated the earlier assertion that Bernhard had been a spy within IG Farben, adding the claim that Bernhard continued to act as a spy for the Nazis for years and was active in that role at least until late 1944 and the Battle of Arnhem. These claims were not backed by documentary evidence, only speculation and anecdotal evidence that was far from compelling.

Hard evidence was, however, to emerge of Bernhard's membership in the Nazi student organization and in the Nazi Party and SA—something he always denied. In 2010, following five years of research for a doctoral thesis, Dutch historian Annejet van der Zijl wrote of Bernhard's Nazi background after unearthing the prince's Deutsche Studentenschaft membership card in the Humboldt University archive. Not only was the card signed by Bernhard, it referred to his membership in the Nazi Party and the SA, and also mentioned his nonpolitical memberships—a flying association and a tennis club.[12] It turned out that he did not resign Nazi Party membership until 1937. His letter of resignation, which ends with the words "Heil Hitler," found its way into Washington's National Archives.[13] Bernhard never revealed his Nazi Party membership to his bride to be or his future mother-in-law, but he did tell them up front that he had been a member of the Reiter-SS, explaining that away as a necessary way to help him through university.[14] He would continue to lie to them, and to the rest of the world, about his Nazi background, for the remainder of his life.

As soon as he arrived in Holland in 1936, Bernhard took Dutch citizenship and set out to counter criticism of him in Dutch newspapers such as the influential *Het Volk*, which declared that "It would be better if the future queen had found a consort in some democratic country rather than in the Third Reich."[15] The prince soon overcame the criticism, charming the Dutch by always speaking Dutch in public and being warm and witty whenever meeting the Dutch people. His marriage to Juliana in January 1937 proved widely popular with the Dutch, even if Adolf Hitler did send a congratulatory telegram. The German government would even claim the marriage cemented an alliance between Holland's House of Orange and Germany, a claim that Queen Wilhelmina did not hesitate to publicly scotch.

The queen had Bernhard appointed a captain with the Royal Dutch Hussars, a cavalry unit within the Dutch army, and with talk of war in the air he did several courses at the Dutch army's War College in 1939. When German forces invaded the Netherlands in May 1940, he armed himself with a machine gun and took charge of the guard at the Soestdijk Palace, at Baarn in the province of Utrecht, where he lived with his wife and two young daughters. When the British government invited the queen to evacuate to England, Bernhard declared that he wanted to stay and fight the invaders. But Queen Wilhelmina was adamant that, to avoid falling into Nazi hands, all members of the royal family would escape to England. This they did, aboard the British destroyer HMS *Codrington*, with the queen taking just a single suitcase with her as her family sailed from the Dutch port of IJmuiden. Against the queen's orders, Bernhard shortly afterward slipped back into Holland to attempt to resist the Germans, but, seeing that the Netherlands had been swiftly occupied and that organized resistance was impossible at that time, he returned to England and joined Wilhelmina's staff in London as her liaison officer with the British government.

In June 1940, Bernhard's wife the Crown Princess Juliana accepted, with her mother's encouragement, an invitation to relocate from London to the safety of Canada. The invitation came from Juliana's British cousin Princess Alice, whose husband, the Earl of Athlone, was serving as governor general of Canada at the time. Off sailed Juliana aboard the Dutch navy cruiser *Sumatra*, taking along the couple's two daughters, two-year-old Beatrix and ten-month-old Irene. Bernhard would visit his wife and children in Canada several times over the next four years, but Juliana would not return to Britain until the fall of 1944.

Bernhard, now on his own in England, began to foster friendships among the British elite.

3

THE SUSPECT PRINCE IN THE
WORLD OF JAMES BOND

I t was the early evening of a fine autumn day in the first half of October 1940 when Ian Fleming stepped from his parked car on a street in the inner London residential area of Lincoln's Inn.[1] This was the same Ian Fleming who, little more than a decade later, would become renowned as the creator of the literary world's most famous spy, James Bond. In 1940, Fleming was a commander with Britain's Royal Navy, just as James Bond would be in Fleming's books. Like Bond, Fleming's naval rank disguised his true role as a spy. A very senior and influential spy.

The tall, suave Fleming crossed the pavement and entered one of the eighteenth-century residential buildings lining the neat streets— the British call such buildings blocks of flats. Striding across the impressive entry foyer, Fleming trotted up the elegant 200-year-old staircase to the door of the flat occupied by London *Daily Express* reporter Sefton Delmer and his wife, Isabel. Delmer was aware that Fleming was involved with Britain's secret intelligence services, although he didn't know to what extent. The previous year, both men had been part of an official British government trade delegation to Moscow. Fleming had gone under the guise of reporting for the *Times* of London, but during the delegation's stay in Russia, Delmer had worked out that his fellow journalist had a more covert purpose.

With kisses from Isabel and a handshake from her husband, Fleming was admitted to the large flat to join the Delmers' other dinner guests. Leonard St. Clair Ingrams and his wife, Victoria, were there. Ingrams was undersecretary of state at Britain's Ministry of Economic Warfare, and Fleming had cultivated his friendship. Two attractive young women were also dinner guests. One was Martha Huysmans, daughter of Camille Huysmans, mayor of Antwerp and chairman of the lower house of the Belgian parliament before he and his family escaped to England in May ahead of the Nazi invasion of the Low Countries. The other female guest was Anna McLaren, a pretty British girl who had joined the Delmers to escape from France earlier in the year. The pair of un-attached young women had been invited by the Delmers so that they might be company for the dashing Fleming and the evening's eighth dinner guest—Prince Bernhard of the Netherlands.

Fleming knew a good deal about the twenty-nine-year-old Bern-hard, the German-born husband of the heir to the Dutch throne. He knew that in 1936, at the Winter Olympic Games at Garmisch-Partenkirchen in Bavaria, Bernhard had met Juliana, only child of Queen Wilhelmina of the Netherlands. Both Princess Juliana and Queen Wilhelmina had taken an instant liking to Bernhard, and the queen saw him as a poten-tial consort for her daughter—Bernhard was a Protestant, as was the Dutch royal family, and he was already a prince from a royal house. Their engagement had been comparatively brief, and Juliana and Bern-hard married at the beginning of 1937; their daughter Beatrix was born a year later. Fleming also knew that, after Bernhard had sent his wife and their two young daughters, Beatrix and Irene, to safety in Canada in June, he himself had stayed in England with his mother-in-law, the queen—whom he called "Mother"—declaring that he wished to join the war effort against Germany.

Fleming had made a point of getting to know Bernhard since the prince's arrival in England. He had in fact ingratiated himself with the political and military leaders of numerous European refugee groups that had made England their home since German occupation of their homelands, such as the Free French and exiled Poles. So his friendship with the Dutch prince was a surprise to no one. Outwardly, Fleming was hobnobbing with the European social elite, which suited his rakish lifestyle handsomely. But with his spy's hat on he was also using his high-level contacts to keep tabs on these Europeans and on what they were doing.

Tall, solidly built, with a round face and round spectacles, Bernhard was considered to be the most flamboyant, charming and amusing member of the Dutch royal family. But as Fleming knew all too well from experience in the intelligence game, you can't judge a book by its glossy cover. Bernhard presented an interesting case for Fleming. The prince was, after all, a German by birth. And his younger brother, Aschwin, also a prince, was serving in the German army, fighting against the British. Yet, ever since his marriage to Princess Juliana in 1937, Bernhard had renounced his German citizenship and professed himself wholly Dutch; he had become very popular with the people of the Netherlands. This past June, three days after the fall of France, Bernhard had gone on BBC's overseas radio service to publicly label Adolf Hitler a tyrant and to express his belief that Germany would be defeated in this war.

Shortly after arriving in England, Bernhard had asked the British government to permit him to join its intelligence services. With his German background, this request had immediately raised suspicions at Whitehall, and the advice given by the security chiefs to Prime Minister Winston Churchill was that such a move was, at best, premature. It had been suggested that the prince instead learn to fly a Spitfire fighter aircraft and join the Royal Air Force's 322 Squadron, a fighter unit made up entirely of Dutch pilots. In the meantime, Fleming would befriend Bernhard and catch up with him frequently, giving his superiors reports on the prince and his trustworthiness. Most recently, just two weeks before the Delmer dinner party, the pair had lunched at the Carlton Hotel's posh Carlton Grill. Over lunch, Bernhard had enjoyed his favorite cocktail, a vodka martini—shaken, not stirred—which would famously become James Bond's preferred tipple.

Even though Bernhard was considerably older than the average rookie fighter pilot, he had always been interested in flying and eagerly embraced the idea of training to fly the Spitfire. No doubt, this October evening, he brought Fleming up to date on his latest flying exploits. He'd been allocated his own personal RAF trainer—Flight Lieutenant Murray Paine. Bernhard wasn't exactly Paine's star pupil, having wrecked two aircraft on landing, but he would eventually qualify as a fighter pilot, racking up 1,000 hours in the "Spit."

As the party sat down to dinner, Fleming was his usual charming yet circumspect self. When Delmer asked him what he'd been up to lately, he passed off the question with a casual reference to a trip to the port city of Dover in Kent the previous week, where he'd had a close shave during a German air raid—a building had been demolished around him by a bomb, yet he'd walked away unscathed. He failed to reveal that the purpose of this Dover trip was to coordinate a potentially vital intelligence operation that he had devised, Operation Ruthless.

Fleming's Operation Ruthless plan was like the plot for an adventure novel. A British crew would crash-land a captured German Heinkel 111 bomber in the North Sea near the coast of German-occupied Denmark; when a launch of the Seenotdienst, the German air-sea rescue service, arrived to pluck them from "the drink," the British airmen would kill the crew and then speed the launch to an English port—complete with its top-secret naval radio code book. For, while Britain had already cracked Germany's army and air force codes, which came to be code-named "Ultra" by the British, the naval code was still a mystery. Operation Ruthless would be postponed and later abandoned when it was realized that the Seenotdienst was an arm of the Luftwaffe and that its launches would be using the air force code, not the navy code. But Fleming would plot plenty of other daring schemes during the war. As for Germany's naval code, that would eventually be cracked after code material was snatched from sinking U-boats in 1941 and 1942.

Dinner was proceeding splendidly in the Delmer flat when the sound of wailing air raid sirens met the diners' ears. The Blitz, the now nighttime bombing of British cities by Germany's Luftwaffe, was little more than a month old by this stage, and the brave and the bold had yet to take it entirely seriously. The air raids had forced Ian Fleming to move out of his own top-floor flat in Ebury Street because its large skylights couldn't be effectively blacked out, and he was currently residing at several gentlemen's clubs of which he was a member, the Lansdowne and the St. James's.

There was a confident, impregnable air about the master spy that would stay with him throughout his life. Ignoring the sirens, he calmly lit another cigarette and resumed his conversation. "He had a very dominating personality," observed Lady Ann O'Neill, who was having an adulterous affair with Fleming during this period and much later became his first wife.[2] Taking Fleming's lead, Prince Bernhard and the other guests stayed put, and the dinner continued, with no one bothering to retreat to the air raid shelter below. But, as Sefton Delmer himself would relate, a small and select bomb now dropped on his small and select dinner party.[3] For the second time in a week, a building was shattered around Ian Fleming by a German bomb.

Yet, no one at the dinner table was hurt. Shaken, but not stirred, Prince Bernhard was the first to overcome the shock of the blast and rise to his feet. He led the way out the flat door to the landing outside, only to find that the bomb had detonated at the bottom of the building's stairwell. The entry foyer had been demolished, as had a twenty-foot length of the ornate staircase. Undaunted, Bernhard lowered himself from the end of the severed staircase, then dropped athletically to the rubble-strewn floor below.

Looking up at the faces of his seven fellow dinner guests staring anxiously down at him from the landing, Prince Bernhard smiled and said, "Thank you for a most enjoyable evening." Then he turned and departed.[4]

Ian Fleming, not to be outdone by the foreigner, followed the prince's example and reached the ground in the same manner. He, too, thanked his hosts as they looked down from above, then walked out into the evening air, leaving the others waiting for the emergency services to arrive and rescue them with their ladders. As searchlight beams crisscrossed the sky, antiaircraft guns "crumped" nearby, and German bombers droned overhead, Fleming walked to his parked car, finding it covered with dust from the bombed building.

As Fleming drove back to the club where he was currently staying, he had no idea that, just several years before, Prince Bernhard had been a member of the Nazi Party and, quite probably, an active German spy while working for IG Farben. Or that, within another four years, Fleming would be called upon by Prime Minister Churchill to give the prince a security clearance—a clearance that would pave the way for Bernhard to set up a hugely unlikely and daring operation, an operation that would go down in the annals of the US Army Air Force as its most risky, most rewarding yet most unsung of the Second World War.

4

THE BRIDGE TOO FAR

THE FAILURE TO
LIBERATE HOLLAND

Prince Bernhard completed his flying training in 1941, graduating as a pilot under Murray Paine's patient guidance. Britain's Royal Air Force (RAF) gave Bernhard the honorary rank of wing commander, the equivalent of a lieutenant colonel in the US Army Air Force, and under the cover name of Wing Commander Gibbs, he became an operational pilot with the RAF. Over the next three years, he flew B-25 Mitchell bombers on missions ranging from raids on Pisa in Italy to maritime patrols against U-boats. In the first half of 1944, he flew a B-24 Liberator against V-1 rocket launch sites in France.

Following the D-Day landings in Normandy in June 1944, and with the Allied invasion of Belgium and the Netherlands believed to be imminent as US, British and Canadian forces swiftly advanced through France, Queen Wilhelmina recalled Bernhard to London in late August, informing the Allied governments that she planned to give him the rank of lieutenant general and appoint him commander in chief of all Dutch armed forces. Futhermore, she had created the new role of inspector general of the army for Bernhard. If anyone in the Dutch military thought that Bernhard's post of commander in chief was to be a purely ceremonial one, there would be no mistaking his power to pry into military affairs in his capacity as inspector general. The forces that would come under Bernhard's command did not amount to much—a scattered navy, a few exiled airmen and soldiers and Dutchmen who had, like him, escaped to Britain and put on the uniform of their country.

Most importantly, Bernhard's command would extend to the newly created Binnenlandse Strijdkrachten (the BS), the Dutch Forces of the Interior, as the disparate resistance groups in the Netherlands were now to be collectively called. Having read in the press that the Allies had recently accorded the underground fighters of the French Resistance the official status of combatants, which required that they be treated as prisoners of war if captured by the enemy, the queen had successfully lobbied the Allied governments for similar status for the Dutch Resistance. At first, Supreme Allied Commander Eisenhower resisted recognition of the BS and the appointment of Bernhard as its commander. Eisenhower feared that the Resistance fighters would not only resist the Germans but would resist control from abroad and act prematurely and without coordination if involved in Allied operations.

Meanwhile, Prime Minister Churchill was uncomfortable with the German-born prince sitting as a member of the highest Allied war councils and receiving top-secret intelligence. The fact that President Franklin Roosevelt was godfather to Bernhard's youngest child, Princess Margriet, who had been born in Canada in 1943, didn't sway Churchill one iota. Up to this point, Bernhard had not held any position of responsibility and had not been privy to the sort of intelligence information that Churchill received every day. Prepared to offend Queen Wilhelmina, if need be, by refusing Bernhard access to the war's most senior commanders and the Allies' most prized secrets, Churchill called in a senior security officer, one he could trust, and asked him to vet Bernhard and present him with his security recommendation.

The man chosen by the British prime minister to give the Dutch prince a security clearance was none other than Ian Fleming. Over the past five years Fleming had become a good friend of the man he was called on to vet. Completely unaware of Bernhard's Nazi background, about which he lied, and the likelihood that he had routinely spied for the Nazis while with IG Farben in Paris before the war, Fleming gave the prince a clean bill of health—according to Fleming, Prince Bernhard was a fine fellow who could be trusted implicitly. Churchill accepted Fleming's recommendation.

In the interim, Bernhard had spoken with General Eisenhower and strove to convince him that the Dutch Resistance groups had the discipline to follow his orders, and that he had the ability to oversee the implementation of those orders. Queen Wilhelmina was able to phone Bernhard on the evening of August 31, 1944, her sixty-fourth birthday, with the tidings that the BS was now official, as was Bernhard's appointment as their country's commander in chief—Churchill and Eisenhower had agreed to both initiatives. The prince was, the queen recorded, at first surprised by the news but quickly became enthusiastic. "Bernhard," Wilhelmina was to say, "had at last found a task that was suited to his status and capacities, a fine and honorable assignment."[1]

Bernhard had rank and position and, crucially, a seat at the Allied war councils alongside the representatives of the other Allied powers. Doors previously closed to Bernhard now opened to him as if by magic. The most senior Allied commanders were now under orders to keep the royal commander of Dutch forces fully apprised of their plans and operations. Bernhard could make a difference, for good or ill. With a crisis soon to emerge in Holland, the opportunity to make that difference was not far off.

ON FRIDAY, SEPTEMBER 1, 1944, with Allied forces pushing into Belgium and southern Holland next on their agenda, Dr. Arthur Seyss-Inquart, Nazi Reichskommissar, or governor, of German-occupied Holland, ordered all German civilians in Holland to evacuate to the east of the country, to be closer to Germany. He himself left his offices in The Hague and transferred to a bunker complex he'd had built for his use underground at Apeldoorn, in Holland's southeast, fifteen miles from the Rhine-straddling city of Arnhem. Two days later, with the news that the British had captured Brussels, the Belgian capital, and were poised to take the important Belgian port city of Antwerp, just miles from the Dutch border, Seyss-Inquart dispatched his wife, Gertrud, from the country altogether, sending her to the safety of the alpine town of Salzburg in his native Austria. She traveled with five packed suitcases.

That evening, the official Dutch government radio station in London, Radio Oranje, broadcast the news of Prince Bernhard's appointment as Dutch commander in chief and head of the new BS. Bernhard himself then gave a speech in which he urged all Dutch Resistance fighters to refrain from premature action and not to start a general uprising in occupied Holland. Bernhard's address was then followed by a speech from General Eisenhower, who said that the hour of liberation of Holland was near. Dr. Pieter S. Gerbrandy, the fifty-nine-year-old London-based prime minister in the exiled Dutch government, spoke next and excitedly announced that Allied troops had crossed the Belgian-Dutch border near Breda. Gerbrandy's private secretary, in drafting his boss's speech for broadcast, had written that Allied troops were "approaching" the border, but Gerbrandy, in his enthusiasm, stated that they had actually crossed it. Many Dutch listeners in southern Holland fully expected to awaken next morning to the sight of Allied troops in their towns and cities, and they flooded into the streets in anticipation of their liberation. They were to be bitterly disappointed.

The Germans heard all this, too, and the next day Dr. Seyss-Inquart declared a state of emergency in Holland. For days, tens of thousands of exhausted German troops, retreating from the inexorable Allied advance through northern France and Belgium since the June 6 landings in Normandy, had clogged the roads of southern Holland. This had only added to the belief in all quarters that the liberation of Holland was imminent. That evening of September 4, in the city of Utrecht in southeast Holland, Anton Mussert, leader of the Nationaal-Socialistische Beweging (NSB), the Dutch Nazi Party, convened a meeting of his frantic party leaders. Henk Feldmeijer, commander of the Dutch SS, also attended this meeting, and he brought an offer from the German authorities of twenty-five trains to evacuate the wives and children of NSB members to Germany. In return, male party members were required to enlist in the Landwacht, the Dutch Home Guard, to fight the advancing Allies alongside German troops.

The offer of the trains was accepted, and the next day, September 5, saw thousands of Dutch Nazis at railroad stations with their families. But most of the men ignored the requirement to stay and join the Landwacht, instead departing with their women and children, as abandoned furniture and personal belongings that couldn't fit on the trains piled up at the stations. Almost every Dutch Nazi official from across Holland, including many German-appointed town mayors and administrators, fled in this wave of departures, which was to last for several days. The women and children would be cared for by a German charity in displaced persons camps in Germany. Their menfolk would soon be sent back to Holland by the German authorities. The Dutch came to call Tuesday, September 5, 1944, this first day of the local Nazi exodus from their country, Dolle Dinsdag, or "Mad Tuesday."

In London on the morning of September 5, Prince Bernhard came away from a meeting with Queen Wilhelmina at her headquarters at 77 Chester Square and drove to his own new Mayfair headquarters at

Stratton House, home to the Dutch government-in-exile, on the corner of Stratton Street and Piccadilly. After hearing the reports of the rapid Allied drive through Belgium, with Antwerp falling to the Allies on September 4, and of the panicked Nazi evacuation of Holland, the queen was convinced that the liberation of her country was at hand. She instructed Bernhard to telephone Princess Juliana in Canada and tell her to make arrangements to fly to England at once in readiness for the royal family's return home to the Netherlands as soon as the Germans had been evicted from their country.

Bernhard put through the call to his wife at the Rockcliffe Park estate in Ottawa, where she and their children had lived for the past four years. But he was not as enthusiastic as his mother-in-law. While he passed on the queen's instructions to Juliana, who was delighted by the news, he was not convinced that Wilhelmina was right. Over the past three days, reports had been arriving on his desk from his underground sources in the Netherlands telling him that the Germans and their Dutch Nazi lackeys had certainly been in a state of panic and disorder in Holland, but the latest news suggested that this was already abating, like a storm that was blowing itself out. And despite the exodus of Dutch Nazis, German troops continued to garrison Holland. Just the same, said Bernhard's Resistance sources, the time was still right for an armored thrust into the heart of Holland, one that would overwhelm the Germans and free the country while it was in chaos.

Bernhard also placed a call to Dutch prime minster–in-exile Gerbrandy, who admitted with considerable embarrassment that the exuberant radio broadcast he'd made two days earlier, telling the people of occupied Holland to prepare to welcome the Allied troops under British Field Marshal Sir Bernard Montgomery as liberators, had been a little premature. It was now almost certain, he said, that Allied troops had not yet crossed the border into the Netherlands as Gerbrandy had claimed on air. Prince Bernhard wondered aloud why the British advance had apparently stalled. Gerbrandy was as mystified as he was.

Bernhard was in regular contact with Major General Walter Bedell Smith, General Eisenhower's chief of staff at SHAEF (Supreme Headquarters Allied Expeditionary Force) and was always put straight through when he telephoned. Now, when Bernhard called Ike's subordinate and queried the state of the Allied advance into Holland, Bedell Smith urged him to be patient. Even though Montgomery had been extremely rude to Bedell Smith in the recent past, the American general now stood up for the British field marshal, telling Prince Bernhard that the advance in Montgomery's sector was very fluid and was changing hour by hour.[2]

After Bernhard hung up, he told his staff that he was still ill at ease. He had been paid lip service by the American general, and he knew it. He was passing on all the intelligence he was receiving from his Resistance sources in Holland to Montgomery's HQ. As a result, he reasoned out loud, Montgomery should be fully aware that Holland was his for the taking, if he acted quickly while the Nazis there were in chaos. Bernhard wondered if Montgomery was taking the information coming out of Holland seriously. Could it be that, because this intelligence was not coming from British sources, Montgomery and his staff were giving it little or no credence? Did Montgomery perhaps have suspicions about the trustworthiness of any information that passed through the German-born prince's hands? Or had something drastic gone wrong with the advance, something that no one was prepared to admit to him?

What Bernhard didn't know, but what General Bedell Smith and Field Marshal Montgomery did know, was that Allied priorities were changing. It was no longer the Allies' intention to liberate all of Holland before advancing into Germany. For weeks, Montgomery had been lobbying General Eisenhower for approval of an operation that he had conceived. Called Operation Market Garden, it was designed to bypass western Holland and put Montgomery's forces across the Rhine at Arnhem and into western Germany's Ruhr Valley. From here, he would drive to Berlin and terminate the war in Europe before the end of the year. That at least was the plan, a plan that was being kept from the new Dutch commander in chief. On September 10, Eisenhower would give Montgomery approval to proceed with Market Garden.

Determined to find out just what the situation was, Bernhard instructed his staff to contact SHAEF and obtain permission for him to fly himself to Montgomery's HQ in Brussels, where he would see the field marshal in person and learn what was going on. Permission was promptly received, and Bernhard drove at once to Hendon airfield in north London. There, he took the controls of *PB1,* his own handsome five-seat Beechcraft D17S Staggerwing biplane, which he'd purchased new from the American manufacturers in October 1941. He proceeded to pilot himself across the North Sea to Belgium. For company, he took along his little white Sealyham terrier, Martin, who frequently accompanied him on his travels.

Montgomery's temporary field headquarters in Belgium filled an array of tents occupying the Royal Palace Gardens at Laeken, several miles beyond downtown Brussels, and here Bernhard arrived for his meeting with Montgomery. Monty, as he was known, saw him under sufferance. He didn't like the thirty-three-year-old prince, considering him flippant, and certainly no soldier despite his lieutenant general's rank. But as Bernhard's visit had been authorized by Eisenhower's office, Montgomery was forced to give him several minutes of his time. When the Dutch Bernhard asked what was the holdup with the advance into Holland, the British Bernard curtly informed him that he had no supplies and that it was too risky to push ahead in the present circumstances. Not only did Montgomery lie to Bernhard's face, he told him nothing about his plans for Operation Market Garden, which would be launched in twelve days' time. Despite the fact that Bernhard had received clearance at the highest level, Montgomery did not trust the German-born prince—or anyone else outside his inner circle of British officers.

The prince produced copies of the intelligence reports he'd received from the Dutch Resistance, which described chaos in Holland. He assured the field marshal that the German troops there were totally demoralized and urged him to continue the drive and liberate Holland in one fell swoop, estimating that Monty's forces would be able to clean up Holland in a couple of days. With an abrupt sweep of the hand Montgomery dismissed these Resistance reports. Secretly, he was not interested in freeing the bulk of Holland. It was apparent to Bernhard that Montgomery trusted neither the Resistance reports nor this foreign prince. And then the meeting was over. Dejected, Bernhard departed.

ON SEPTEMBER 11, Allied troops did fight their way across the Belgian-Dutch border, at Visé in the province of Liège. Three days later, they occupied the city of Maastricht, capital of the province of Limburg, as German troops withdrew into western Holland. A correspondent for Radio Oranje, the Dutch radio station operating out of London, reported from the city that Maastricht was a sea of orange as the celebrating residents of the city displayed their national sporting color for the first time in almost five years.

Without waiting for permission from anyone, Prince Bernhard jumped into his little Beechcraft aircraft and flew across the North Sea to Maastricht, where he was welcomed by tearful Dutch who treated him as a conquering hero. But Bernhard found the Allied troops at Maastricht settling in for a long stay. There appeared to be no plans to advance any farther into Holland. After flying himself back to England, Bernhard ramped up his efforts to have the Allied armies push all the way into Holland and liberate the country as a whole. But at that moment, Field Marshal Montgomery's eyes were looking across the Rhine, as far as

Berlin. Monty was determined to beat the armies led by his Allied rivals to the German capital. The competitive and vain English field marshal especially wanted to beat the charismatic American general George S. Patton to Berlin. Patton's US 3rd Army was driving through northern France with the objective of entering Germany via the Ardennes region, south of Montgomery's forces. With Eisenhower's blessing, Monty was about to launch an operation designed to get him to Berlin first.

Montgomery had planned Market Garden as two operations in one. Operation Market would be the first phase; 40,000 paratroopers would be dropped by parachute and glider on three cities in southeast Holland—Eindhoven, Nijmegen and Arnhem—and would secure and hold them to permit Operation Garden to succeed. This would involve a British 2nd Army armored column pushing up the highway from Belgium, through Eindhoven and Nijmegen and crossing the Rhine into Germany via the bridges at Arnhem. The task of taking Eindhoven had been assigned to the American 101st Airborne Division. Taking Nijmegen and its two bridges over the River Waal, a major tributary to the Rhine, was the assignment of the US 82nd Airborne Division. Arnhem was to be taken by the British 1st Airborne Division, supported by the 1st Polish Airborne Brigade. Prince Bernhard was left in total ignorance of all this.

ON SATURDAY, SEPTEMBER 16, at his quarters at Horham in Suffolk, Lieutenant Colonel Bill Lindley of the USAAF's 95th Bombardment Group received instructions to report at once to 3rd Air Division headquarters at Elveden Hall in Suffolk. He was given no indication of what awaited him there. As Lindley was driven by jeep the short distance from Horham airfield to the grand rural mansion, the property of Lord Iveagh, a member of the Guinness brewing family, a range of possibilities for this summons flashed through his mind, from a transfer to HQ to being shot at dawn for some horrendous screwup of which he was unaware.[3]

At Elveden, Lindley was conducted to the operations office, where he was briefed on a special single-bomber mission the next day. He was informed that a massive drop of paratroops was to take place over Holland on September 17, involving both the US 82nd and 101st Airborne Divisions of XVIII Airborne Corps. The commander of the XVIII Airborne Corps, Lieutenant General Matthew Ridgway, wanted to be as close to his boys as possible during the drop without actually being on the ground, and he'd asked for a B-17 to fly him over the drop zones next morning so that he could obtain an accurate picture of what was going down on the ground. Lindley was tasked with flying Ridgway in and back again at 20,000 feet for this unique bird's-eye view of the operation.

Ridgway knew that Operation Market Garden, conceived by Field Marshal Montgomery, would involve American, British and Polish paratroops being dropped at Eindhoven, Nijmegen and Arnhem in Holland to secure the highway and key bridges for an armored division and a supporting infantry division that would push up the road and cross the Rhine at Arnhem and drive into Germany on the opposite side of the great river. This mass drop of Allied paratroopers would be the largest airborne operation in history, being twice the size of the previous largest, the German airborne invasion of Crete in 1941.

Lindley hurried back to Horham and called in veteran navigator Bill Steele and pilot Robert Hastie. Briefing them for the mission, on which Lindley would fly as pilot with Hastie as his copilot, he instructed them to get a B-17 and a top crew together pronto. Hastie's regular "Fort" was loaded with supplies for a parachute drop to Polish resistance fighters trapped in Warsaw by the German army, so another B-17, called *Screaming Eagle,* was allocated to the mission. This name seemed particularly appropriate because the men of the 101st Airborne were known as the Screaming Eagles.

First thing next day, Sunday, Lindley, Hastie and their crew took off from Horham in *Screaming Eagle* for the short hop to an airfield near

Newberry, eighty miles west of London. There, the men of the 101st
Airborne were sealed off behind barbed wire, waiting impatiently for
the order to board their transport aircraft. At Newberry, General Ridgway and an aide, a junior officer, met the crew who would be taking
them over the battlefield. Ridgway, a gruff and tough fifty-year-old Vir-
ginian from a distinguished military family, was known as "Old Iron
Tits" by his men. On D-Day, June 6, 1944, he had commanded the 82nd
Airborne when it dropped behind the Normandy beaches, landing in
a glider. But now that Ridgway was a corps commander, orders from
above prevented him from actually landing with his troops this time.
The planned exploit in the B-17 was his creative way of showing support
for his men and being on the scene at the time of their landings.

Both Ridgway and his aide were experienced parachutists, but neither said a word as Lindley and copilot Hastie strapped the pair into the
B-17's two spare parachutes and told them how to use them if the need
arose. Ridgway informed Lindley that he wanted to be over the drop
zones when the air fleet carrying his paratroopers arrived and would tell
the pilot when he was ready to go home again. When Ridgway learned
that he would be flying over the battlefield at 20,000 feet, he scowled
and asked how much he could see of the parachute drops from up there.

"Not a hell of a lot," Lindley confessed.

"What height do you recommend?" Ridgway asked.

Lindley replied that it would make sense if they went in at the same
height as the troop-carrying C-47 "Gooney Birds" and gliders. He con-
fidently declared that he could dodge heavy German flak, and as there
would be so many airplanes in the air for the Germans to shoot at, the
B-17's chances of coming out without a scratch were as good as anyone
else's. Ridgway liked that. In Lindley's words, the general bought the
whole package.[4]

So they all took their places aboard *Screaming Eagle* and took off for
Holland without a bomb load but with all guns loaded and with their

valuable passenger aboard. As they took to the air, so too did the 3,500 transports, towing aircraft and gliders involved in the first day of Operation Market air drops.

A little west of Maidenhead in Berkshire, the residents of Stubbings House came out into the garden and looked to the sky, summoned by the roar of aircraft engines passing overhead. This rambling eighteenth-century red-brick mansion was the seat of a large rural estate and had been provided to Queen Wilhelmina as her country residence while she was living in exile in England. The queen had come to the estate from London for the weekend and was joined by Crown Princess Juliana, who had flown across the Atlantic to England from Canada only days before after being summoned by her husband. Now mother and daughter witnessed the heartwarming sight of American aircraft filling the sky overhead.

The headquarters of the 8th Air Force was nearby at High Wycombe, and the queen had become accustomed to seeing American aircraft flying overhead to and from the airfields in the area. One of those airfields was located right next door to the Stubbings House estate. Like Prince Bernhard, the queen had not been forewarned by the British government about Operation Market Garden or its objective, but the number of aircraft and the sight of the gliders alerted Wilhelmina and Juliana to the fact that something big was underway. Only later, along with the rest of the civil population in Britain, would the queen learn the significance of this sight on September 17. She would write, "A large American air fleet, part of which had taken off from the airfield near my house, was on its way to our Fatherland with its supplies and paratroops."[5]

Out over the North Sea flew the aerial armada bound for Holland. It would arrive like a giant cloud over the sunny skies of western Europe. The armada followed two routes. The squadrons that took off from airfields north of London flew the northern route and crossed the sea making a beeline for southern Holland. Flying due east, they would cross the Dutch coast south of Rotterdam. Following this route were the aircraft carrying the US 82nd Airborne and the British 1st Airborne Divisions. From airfields west of London came the squadrons carrying the US 101st Airborne Division, flying the southern route, which would take them over Belgium south of Antwerp, after which they would turn north toward Eindhoven in southeastern Holland. Beneath each route, flotillas of Allied ships patrolled the sea between England and the Continent to rescue men aboard any aircraft that went down in the drink as a result of enemy action or mechanical failure.

Speeding along between the two routes was a lone B-17 bomber, *Screaming Eagle,* with Bill Lindley and his precious cargo aboard. To obtain the best view possible of his paratroopers landing, General Ridgway and his aide occupied the bomber's nose compartment, usually the domain of the bombardier and navigator. Lindley took the B-17 over the North Sea at 5,000 feet and then overflew the Dutch coast where he knew the flak was least heavily concentrated. Soon, ahead and below in the clear sky, ranging between 2,000 and 3,000 feet and stretching as far as the eye could see from horizon to horizon, was the first stage of the Market Garden armada—hundreds of C-46s and C-47s and gliders in long, precise lines.

Lindley dropped down and joined the front rank of the armada's southern echelon. Because the transport aircraft were so slow moving, Lindley had to drop fifteen degrees of flap to slow down the faster bomber and do an occasional S-turn to keep from flying ahead of the crawling transport fleet. Below, Dutch civilians were visible in the streets of towns and villages they overflew, gazing up and marveling at the sight of the mass of aircraft passing overhead. In front of the armada, as it approached the first US Army drop zone at Eindhoven, orange smoke rose up to mark the existing Allied front line several miles to the south of the town. American P-47 Thunderbolt fighters could be seen dipping and diving with their eight machine guns blazing as they shot up farmhouses, roads, even haystacks in the landing areas in case there were German troops lying in wait down there, leaving buildings and haystacks ablaze and sending smoke billowing into the still morning air.

Eindhoven was an industrial city and home to the headquarters and factory of the Dutch electrical giant Philips, which had been taken over by the Germans. As the day dawned, the population of the city had begun what they expected would be a typical Sunday. It was soon to become far from typical, with hundreds and possibly thousands of Dutch civilians dying in the battle that would soon be raging here— there would be no record kept of the precise number of civilians killed and subsequently incinerated in burning buildings or hurriedly buried in mass graves. They had been given no warning by the Allies of the impending assault, who reasoned that a warning to the civilians would also have been a warning to the German defenders. Four miles to the west lay an airfield that had been, until recently, a major operational base of the Luftwaffe. The airfield, as well as the city and its bridges over the small Dommel and Gender Rivers, comprised the objectives of American airborne troops. Just to the north of Eindhoven, the southernmost Operation Market airdrop began. First, supply canisters went out the open doors of the transports, floating down to earth beneath brightly colored parachutes that denoted what they were carrying—a different color for weapons, ammunition, rations, medical supplies, and so forth. And then men of the 101st Airborne began jumping.

Lindley and his passengers and crew could see the paratroops come to aircraft doors, briefly look up, then jump feet first into the void in rapid succession. Soon their olive-drab chutes were filling the sky beneath the airborne fleet. As those aboard *Screaming Eagle* watched, the troops hit the ground after a drop of less than two minutes, then quickly collected their equipment, assembled and dashed to the nearest hedgerows to go into action as German defenders began to offer resistance. This was what Old Iron Tits had come to see.

So engrossed were they in what was happening down below that copilot Hastie only now noticed German 20 mm and 40 mm tracer fire arcing up toward them from the ground and saw light flak shells bursting blackly among the transport fleet. Lindley circled the drop zone for a time as Ridgway watched paratroops in action and as gliders landed and disgorged more men of the 101st. The general then asked to be taken to the next American drop zone, farther north at Nijmegen on the Rhine. On they flew.

Nijmegen had begun life as a first-century BC military camp during the time of Julius Caesar, becoming Noviomagus, base of the Roman 10th Gemina Legion in the following century. From the hills surrounding this city not far from the German border it was possible to see the Rhine valley and Germany itself. Capture of its two bridges across the broad River Waal—a railroad bridge and a large road bridge—during Operation Market was critical to the success of the subsequent Operation Garden. *Screaming Eagle* arrived over the city just as the Nijmegen drop of the 82nd Airborne was taking place, right on schedule.

But as Lindley's B-17 reached the scene, those aboard saw a number of C-47s hit by ground fire and bursting into flames not long after their passengers had hit the silk, then dropping onto one wing, plummeting from the sky and crashing in exploding balls of fire. It was a gut-wrenching sight for those aboard *Screaming Eagle*. Heavy loss of transport aircraft to ground fire had caused Adolf Hitler to ban the Luftwaffe from large-scale paratrooper drops following the Battle of Crete in 1941. The Germans had won that battle, but their elite airborne troops had been mostly confined to ground operations thereafter to preserve the Luftwaffe's transport fleet.

Angered by the losses being inflicted on the C-47s by German flak gunners, General Ridgway decided to intervene personally. From the nose of *Screaming Eagle*, his aide spoke to pilot Lindley on the intercom and asked if he and the general could use the two .50 caliber machine guns on either side of the navigator's compartment and the pair of chin turret guns. Lindley told them to go right ahead. So as Lindley flew them around the Nijmegen landing area, Ridgway and his aide opened up on everything and everyone they spotted in field gray down below. When they'd both exhausted their ammunition, a fresh supply was taken forward to them from the upper turret. Meanwhile, as the flight stretched into the afternoon, both the B-17's tail gunner and the gunner occupying the ball turret beneath the fuselage also got into the act and emptied their guns into German ground targets. While this was going on, a second drop of 82nd Airborne troops took place.

Once Ridgway had seen all he wanted to see here, he asked to be shown the most northerly drop zone, at Arnhem, where the British 1st Airborne Division had gone in. When they arrived on the scene over Arnhem, those in the B-17 could see plenty of crashed gliders and burning Allied transport aircraft littering the fields down below and fierce fighting between the British paratroopers and German ground forces. At Ridgway's request, the B-17 returned to the Nijmegen and Eindhoven DZs, and after circling each for a time watching the fighting going on just a few hundred feet below, Ridgway declared that he had seen enough. Lindley took *Screaming Eagle* back up to 5,000 feet and set a course for England.

Once they had landed back in England, Ridgway went to each and every member of the crew of the B-17 and shook him by the hand, thanking him. When Lindley asked Ridgway if the B-17 flight had met his expectations, the general produced a grim smile and said, "Best command post ever."[6]

AMONG THE AMERICAN GLIDERS that General Ridgeway saw land outside Eindhoven was one carrying twenty-eight-year-old war correspondent Walter Cronkite, who would go on to gain fame as the anchor of *CBS Evening News* on television for nineteen years. As a reporter with

United Press in 1944, Cronkite was attached to the 101st Airborne for this operation.[7]

As Cronkite's glider skidded along the ground, the wheels came ramming up through the floor. The impact of the landing was so great that the helmets being worn by Cronkite and the score of paratroops with him flew off.

Once his careering glider came to a halt, Cronkite grabbed the first helmet he saw, put it on, took a firm grip on the bag containing his Olivetti portable typewriter, then went out the door. Once outside, he hit the ground and began crawling toward the canal that was the rendezvous point for the men he was with. As he crawled, Cronkite looked back and saw that half a dozen men were following him expectantly. Checking the helmet he'd appropriated, he found that it had two vertical stripes on the back—it was the helmet of a lieutenant.[8]

IN THE CELLAR OF A VILLA in the village of Velp just three miles northeast of Arnhem, as Allied and German shells and bombs pounded Arnhem and its surrounds, Baroness Ella van Heemstra and her fifteen-year-old daughter cringed in fear. That daughter was the future Hollywood star Audrey Hepburn. She had been born on May 4, 1929, in Ixelles, a municipality of Brussels, and christened Audrey Kathleen Ruston. Her father, Joseph Ruston, was an Anglo-Austrian banker. Later, he would change his name to Hepburn-Ruston to incorporate the Hepburn branch of his family into his name, and Audrey would follow suit. Audrey's mother, Ella, was a member of an aristocratic Dutch family. In 1935, when Audrey was six, her father walked out. According to family legend, the hair of the deserted thirty-five-year-old Baroness van Heemstra turned white overnight as a result. Audrey, for her part, never got over the loss of her father. In later years she would tell US television interviewer Phil Donahue that her father's desertion of the family left her with a sense of insecurity that pervaded all her future relationships.[9]

Audrey, her mother and her half-brothers, Ian [10] and Alex,[11] struggled to survive in Kent, England, for the next four years. When war clouds formed over Europe in 1939, the baroness decided that she and her children would be safer in Ella's native Holland. During World War One, Holland had declared itself neutral, and the Germans had respected that neutrality. The dethroned German kaiser, Wilhelm II, had even gone into exile in Holland in 1918 following Germany's defeat. Wilhelm had lived there in a large country house at Doorn until his death in June 1941. The leading dignitary at his funeral was the newly appointed Nazi governor of occupied Holland, Dr. Arthur Seyss-Inquart.

Baroness van Heemstra, expecting that, should war break out, Holland would again remain neutral and that Adolf Hitler would respect that neutrality as the kaiser had done, had taken Audrey and her brothers to Holland; she and the children moved into an Arnhem townhouse at 8a Jansbinnensingel owned by Aarnoud van Heemstra, Audrey's grandfather. Mayor of Arnhem between 1910 and 1920, Van Heemstra had been appointed by Queen Wilhelmina to be governor general of the then Dutch territory of Suriname in South America. He had served in that role for eight years before retiring in 1928, the year before Audrey's birth.

Having settled in apparent safety at Arnhem, Audrey and her mother received a rude shock when the Germans invaded and occupied Holland in May 1940. The invaders confiscated much of Aarnoud van Heemstra's property and wealth and later executed his son-in-law, the husband of Audrey's Aunt Miesje, during reprisals for Resistance sabotage. The Nazis also executed one of Audrey's cousins. Worried that Audrey's English birth name might attract the attention of the Germans, the baroness had instructed her to use the name Edda van Heemstra from then on. Similarly, Audrey was under orders never to speak English outside the house—for fear that she would catch the ear of the Germans and be arrested and interned as an enemy alien.

Like most other residents of Holland, mother and children had lived a difficult existence under the occupiers since 1940, obeying the nightly curfew and the regulations that banned the Dutch flag, the national anthem, free press, elections and freedom of religion, and that allowed the Gestapo, the German Sicherheitsdienst (SD) and Dutch police to arrest anyone without a warrant or due process, and to interrogate, imprison and execute with impunity. The Germans also introduced a forced-labor program, sending Dutch males aged seventeen and above to work on war production in German factories. This was supposed to be voluntary, but Audrey's brother Ian was no volunteer when he was caught in the German recruitment net in 1942 and sent to work in a munitions factory in Berlin.

As a result, Audrey's mother had moved her family to her father's villa at out-of-the-way Velp, with Audrey's other brother Alexander going into hiding on his grandfather's property to avoid also being sent away as a forced laborer. Audrey had continued to go to school at the Arnhem Conservatory, bicycling in from Velp each day. There, under dance mistress Winja Marova, she had discovered a natural talent for dance. Audrey possessed the slim, long-legged figure of a ballerina—she reputedly had the exact same looks and physique as her father's mother.

All through more than four years of Nazi occupation, Audrey and her mother had dreamed that Allied forces would come to Holland and liberate them. Now Allied troops had indeed come to Arnhem. But instead of liberation, they brought a maelstrom of fire and death raining down on the city and its residents. Worse, Audrey and her mother and grandfather were surrounded by German soldiers—the 10th SS Panzer Division had relocated its headquarters to Velp as soon as the first British airborne troops landed in the Arnhem area. Audrey would remember her mother weeping with fear.[12]

From passersby Audrey was to learn that the Battle of Arnhem had not gone well for the Allies. As the first British paratroops arrived, the

Germans destroyed the railroad bridge and a pontoon bridge that crossed the Lower Rhine at the city. The British had subsequently seized Arnhem's massive road bridge intact. With raised approaches that extended for more than half a mile on either side of the Rhine, the bridge was elevated to permit shipping to pass underneath. On the third day of the battle, British paratroops occupying central Arnhem and the vital bridge across the Rhine had been overrun by SS troops after desperate fighting. Others were holding out in the affluent Oosterbeek area on the western side of Arnhem. And then, after a week of fighting, the shelling and the shooting all stopped. The Dutch learned that some Allied survivors had withdrawn south while others surrendered. Relieved residents of Arnhem and surrounding villages such as Velp, who emerged from their cellars, fully expecting to welcome Allied liberators, were shocked to find the Germans still in charge of their now shattered and burning city. The unthinkable had happened. The Allies had lost the battle for Arnhem.

The once scenic city beside the Lower Rhine was in ruins, and hundreds of residents had died in the battle for it. German commanders now instructed all residents of Arnhem to evacuate within twenty-four hours. They were permitted to take with them only what they could carry. Under Hitler's express orders, all clothing and textiles in the city were to be gathered up by the Wehrmacht and sent to German families in the Ruhr who had suffered in Allied air raids. The German governor of Holland, Reichskommissar Dr. Seyss-Inquart, extended this order to cover all intact furniture in Arnhem, which was also sent to bombing victims in the devastated Ruhr. As soon as the city was emptied, German military engineers moved in to demolish wrecked and intact buildings alike and build new defenses.

As the city was turned into a German military strongpoint, streams of Dutch refugees clogged the roads north and west of Arnhem looking for somewhere to relocate. At Velp, Audrey did what she could to help when old Baron Van Heemstra took in forty of these refugees. The baron gave these people of Arnhem shelter, but he had no food to give them; there was barely enough for his family.

Now, too, Audrey's brother Alexander briefly emerged from hiding. Considering the villa at Velp too close to the enlarged German garrison, he bade farewell to his family and went looking for a new hiding place. With the Arnhem Conservatory now closed, Audrey set up her own ballet school in her grandfather's villa. Having dance bars installed around the walls of the spacious house's large, tall-ceilinged entrance foyer, she would set about teaching the youngsters of Velp to be dancers. It took young minds off their empty bellies.

OPERATION MARKET GARDEN, Field Marshal Montgomery's intended daring dash through southeast Holland and into Nazi Germany as a prelude to a drive to Berlin and an early end to the war, failed to achieve its key objective, the seizure of Arnhem and the crossing of the Rhine at the city's crucial road bridge. To the south, American paratroopers and the British tanks supporting them took their objectives at Eindhoven and Nijmegen after intense fighting. The 101st Airborne had secured Eindhoven within twenty-four hours. By the evening of September 20, the 82nd Airborne had secured Nijmegen and both bridges across the Waal after making a daring and bloody crossing of the river in small boats and attacking the German defenders at both ends of the bridges. But the British 1st Airborne Division became trapped at Arnhem when armored reinforcements were stopped in their tracks by German forces just to the north of Nijmegen and were unable to fight their way through to the 1st Airborne and the bridge across the Rhine at Arnhem. That bridge at Arnhem famously became "a bridge too far."[13]

Some surviving men of the 1st Airborne were successfully evacuated, but on September 25, after eight days of fighting, the few British troops still holding out on Arnhem's western outskirts surrendered to German forces. Of 10,000 British paratroops dropped in to take

Arnhem, almost 8,000 were killed or taken prisoner. Overall, Allied casualties during Market Garden numbered some 17,000 men. These losses exceeded those of the D-Day landings the previous June. In addition, close to 90 British tanks and 150 British and American aircraft were lost during the operation. US casualties were in the region of 4,000, with the 101st Airborne suffering the highest losses—2,118 killed and wounded. Field Marshal Walter Model, who commanded the German counterattack at Arnhem, put total German casualties there at 3,300 killed and wounded, while author Cornelius Ryan would estimate, from interviews he conducted with German commanders involved in the fighting, that overall German casualties in all the Market Garden battles could have been as high as 7,500 to 10,000 killed, wounded and captured—still something like half the Allied losses. There are no reliable figures for the number of Dutch men, women and children killed at Arnhem, Eindhoven and Nijmegen and villages in between as a result of Allied and German air attacks, shelling and street-to-street fighting. Neither the Allies nor the Germans kept a record of this "collateral damage." The minimum figure is put at 500, although some Dutch estimates suggest that the civilian death toll extended into the thousands.[14]

Following the failure of Operation Market Garden, the largest airborne operation ever undertaken, Arnhem and its Rhine crossing would remain in German hands until a Canadian push the following March. Field Marshal Montgomery would come in for significant criticism for Market Garden's failure—not least for ignoring intelligence from Dutch Resistance groups that had warned of a major German troop and tank presence in the Arnhem area. Prince Bernhard had received the same intelligence and had attempted to stress to Montgomery's HQ his belief in the genuineness of that intelligence. But Montgomery and his staff had dismissed that information as unreliable. Similarly, they had failed to involve Prince Bernhard or any of the experienced Dutch military officers on his staff in their planning of drop zones or the route that Allied tanks would follow to get to Arnhem. The route chosen by Montgomery required the tanks to use a single narrow road that ran along the tops of dikes, a road that could be, and was, easily shelled and blocked by the enemy.

Despite being rebuffed by Montgomery earlier in the month, Bernhard established a small headquarters for himself in Brussels, near to Montgomery's 21st Army HQ, and tried to keep abreast of the battle as it unfolded from September 17. Five days later, on Friday, September 22, Bernhard learned that British tanks being funneled up the single highway from Eindhoven to Nijmegen en route to link up with the British troops holding out in Arnhem had been stopped in their tracks at Elst, between Nijmegen and Arnhem, by fierce German counterattacks. He also learned that the Polish airborne brigade sent to reinforce the 1st Airborne at Arnhem had been dropped at Driel, three miles southwest of Arnhem, instead of close to the Arnhem bridge where they were needed to eject German Panzer Grenadier troops holding the river crossing and keeping the British paratroops trapped in the town. With three miles of German-held territory and a broad river crossing between them and the trapped British, the Poles were never going to make it, never going to relieve the surrounded 1st Airborne.

Prince Bernhard, at his headquarters in Brussels, had exploded with uncharacteristic rage. "Why? Why couldn't the British listen to us?" he said to his then chief of staff Colonel K. "Pete" Doorman. "Why?"[15]

The answer was simple. Montgomery didn't trust Bernhard, and he had no respect for the local knowledge of the Dutch officers under him, men who had been serving in the Dutch army at the time of the German invasion in 1940. In fact, Colonel Doorman had conducted a Dutch Staff College exercise just prior to the war on how to launch an armored attack on Arnhem from Nijmegen. Back then, officers who had followed the same route employed by Montgomery had failed the exercise, just as

Montgomery's tanks failed to break through to relieve the surrounded troops at Arnhem.

Montgomery and his staff had also believed that German forces in Holland were few in number, exhausted and poorly equipped, and would not put up much of a fight. As it happened, the reports from the Resistance were accurate, and the British and Polish airborne troops who tried to support them came up against two resting SS Panzer divisions equipped with Tiger tanks, the most formidable German heavy tanks then in service. Prince Bernhard would not learn until much later that Montgomery had been personally warned of the presence of the two German tank divisions, the 9th and 10th SS Panzer, by none other than General Eisenhower's chief of staff, Major General Walter Bedell Smith.

Bedell Smith had been alerted to the two SS Panzer divisions by SHAEF's chief of intelligence and, with the blessing of General Eisenhower, had flown urgently to Brussels from SHAEF HQ to warn Montgomery and urge him to either change the operational plan for Market Garden or allocate a second parachute division to the Arnhem drop to deal with the German armored units. But the British field marshal, who didn't much like the American, had dismissed his concerns. And as Eisenhower had already given him the green light for Market Garden, Montgomery plowed on regardless. At the same time, when the British intelligence officer for the 1st Airborne Division came across aerial reconnaissance photographs of German tanks outside Arnhem and showed them to the division's commander, Lieutenant General Frederick Browning, he was told not to worry about it and was then promptly sent on sick leave.

Unaccountably, too, the Allied air forces, which dominated the skies over western Europe, had failed to provide continuous air cover throughout the week of the battle. Once the fighter-bombers that General Ridgway had seen attacking the drop zones had gone home, the

paratroop transports had been on their own. Scores of transports carrying the Polish airborne reinforcements had been pounced on by twenty-
five Messerschmitt fighters, which had cut a swath through them. And
German fighters made unopposed low-level strafing runs with guns and
bombs against Allied positions for days, even shooting up their own
troops in error on one occasion. Only in the last days of the battle did
USAAF Thunderbolts reappear over the battlefield and engage German
aircraft; by then the damage on the ground had been done.

Various excuses were offered for this failure to provide adequate
air support. The weather had been foul and far from ideal for flying. Yet
the Luftwaffe had still managed to get its aircraft aloft daily. Within
days of the assault on Eindhoven, British Typhoons were based at the
former Luftwaffe airfield there, just forty miles from Arnhem, but they
were never called on to support the struggling troops that were losing
the battle at Arnhem. Montgomery and his staff would also be blamed
for this lack of air support. Wing Commander J. E. "Johnnie" Johnson,
an RAF Spitfire pilot who operated from Eindhoven during the battle,
was frustrated as he watched Typhoons sent to bomb and shoot up roads
and railroad lines in other sectors while the airborne troops struggled at
Arnhem. He was to say, "We of Second TAF [the RAF's Second Tactical Air Force] were banned from the Arnhem area because the planners
feared a clash between British and American fighters, despite the fact
that we had been fighting alongside each other for almost two years!"[16]

In the end, it was the outnumbered 6,000 troops of the two under-
strength SS Panzer divisions, which Montgomery had dismissed when
warned about them by Bedell Smith, that had made the difference. They
had succeeded in stopping the Allied advance north of Nijmegen and
in overwhelming the British at Arnhem and sealing the fate of the operations as thousands of German reinforcements poured in—while the
Allies could only get hundreds of Polish reinforcements to the battle
zone. Montgomery would also come in for criticism for failing to involve

Prince Bernhard's BS Resistance fighters, who could have disrupted German lines of supply and reinforcement had they been brought into the overall operational plans. Instead, they were ignored. Still, until his dying day Montgomery himself would persist with the view that, because Eindhoven and Nijmegen had been taken, Operation Market Garden, which had been his "baby," had been 90 percent successful.

Prince Bernhard did not share that view. He was to say, of Market Garden and Montgomery's perspective on it, that "My country can never again afford the luxury of another Montgomery success."[17]

In late September 1944, in the wake of the failure of the Allies at Arnhem, the Germans consolidated their hold on western Holland, which included The Hague, Rotterdam and Amsterdam. Three and a half million Dutch civilians were still under the German yoke, watched over by 120,000 German troops, and German propaganda now spoke of occupied Holland as "Fortress Holland." Queen Wilhelmina now dreaded what she expected to be "the terrible reprisals the Germans would exact from our people" in the wake of the failed Arnhem offensive.[18]

And so it was to prove. First, Heinrich Himmler, head of the SS, ordered the immediate removal of all Dutch Jews then in the Westerbork Transit Camp in Holland to the Theresienstadt camp in Czechoslovakia, a transit center on the way to the Nazi extermination camps.[19] And the occupation government set in motion a range of punitive measures against the general population of Holland.

5

THE GERMANS GO ON
THE OFFENSIVE

At the commencement of Operation Market Garden on September 17, 1944, 30,000 Dutch railroad workers in occupied Holland had answered the call from General Eisenhower, broadcast by radio from London, to go on strike to paralyze the German transport system in Holland. The railroad workers had overnight halted the rail services in the west of the country on which the German occupiers relied for the transport of troops, forced laborers, equipment, ammunition, fuel and vital supplies including foodstuffs. Leaders of the strike had been imprisoned, but now that the Allied push to the Rhine had failed at Arnhem, the other strikers decided not to return to work. With many of these workers in hiding, the strike could continue indefinitely. While this was to prove a massive inconvenience to the Germans, the strikers' action was about to rebound on millions of their fellow Dutch citizens.

The German occupation government now implemented a series of measures to punish the population. On November 10 and 11, 50,000 Dutch men were arrested in Rotterdam and sent to Germany to become forced laborers. On December 4, the bread ration for the Dutch under

German rule was cut to two pounds per person per week. Two days later, the Germans began removing all Dutch electric trains and their overhead wiring, sending them to Germany to replace the electric train system in German cities that had been destroyed by Allied bombing. Eight days later, a total prohibition on civilian use of electricity in the occupied provinces of North Holland and South Holland was introduced. It was going to be a cold, dark, hungry Christmas for the Dutch. In fact, the winter of 1944–45 in Holland was to become known as the Hunger Winter.

Meanwhile, Adolf Hitler had one last military surprise for the Allies. On December 16, he launched a massive counteroffensive through the thickly forested Ardennes region covering parts of Belgium, France and Luxembourg. The objective was to push through to Antwerp on the coast and split the Allied armies in two, stranding those forces that were in Holland and forcing them to surrender. Three German armies were involved, and hundreds of tanks, including Tigers and the massive new King Tigers. Some German troops in the attack were armed with the new MP44 Sturmgewehr, the world's first assault rifle, upon which the Russians would later model the AK-47.

The well-planned attack also featured English-speaking German special forces dressed in US Army uniforms confiscated from American prisoners. Their job was to cause mayhem behind American lines. Plus, for only the second time since the expensive Battle of Crete in 1941, German airborne forces were parachuted into action, with a thousand paratroopers dropped at night to secure vital crossroads. The offensive took the Allies entirely by surprise, and the German attackers initially overran US positions. The bulge on the map showing the changing front line in the Ardennes, with the Germans advancing west, would give rise to the popular name for this battle that would eventually involve more than 600,000 Americans—the Battle of the Bulge.

ON DECEMBER 24, Christmas Eve, as the Battle of the Bulge raged in ice and snow just to the southeast, from his bunker at Apeldoorn, Holland's

Nazi governor, Dr. Arthur Seyss-Inquart, delivered another hammer blow to the Dutch people under German occupation—every Dutch male aged sixteen to sixty must report to the German authorities for forced labor in Germany. By war's end, more than half a million Dutch men and boys would have been sent to German factories as forced laborers.

At Velp outside Arnhem, Audrey Hepburn, now using the name Edda van Heemstra to avoid Gestapo or SD attention, was suffering along with the rest of the population as the food supplies dried up. Some days, Audrey and her mother had no food at all, and the baroness became more and more incapacitated. Audrey drank gallons of water to make herself feel full, and went to bed in the afternoon to conserve her waning strength. When there was food, she would deprive herself of much of her ration so that her ailing mother could eat.[1]

At times like these, Audrey would will herself into ignoring the gnawing pangs of hunger, convincing herself she wasn't hungry. In later life, during her career as a chorus-line dancer and then as an actress, she would use the same mind-control technique to go without food in times of stress and to deliberately keep her weight down and her figure svelte. While many Dutch were resorting to sugar beet, dandelions and nettles to eat, Audrey's mother had become a dab hand at turning tulip bulbs into fine flour that could be used to bake cakes and cookies. The only problem was that it took a king's ransom to get hold of the eggs and butter that had to be added to the tulip flour to make those cakes and cookies. As a grim Christmas passed, Audrey wondered what the new year would bring.

ON NEW YEAR'S DAY, 1945, the Luftwaffe made its major contribution to the Battle of the Bulge—or Operation Watch on the Rhine, as the Germans called the ground offensive. For months, the depleted Luftwaffe had been secretly putting together ten elite Jagdgeschwader, or fighter wings, for a surprise air attack. Never before had the Luftwaffe

been able to assemble 1,000 aircraft for a single raid, but this first morning of 1945 an air fleet of 1,100 single-seat propeller-driven fighters and
a couple of squadrons of Messerschmitt 262 jet fighters took to the air
from German airfields to attack Allied ground positions on the Western
Front. Led by three Junkers Ju-88 bombers serving as pathfinders, the
German fighters flitted low across the snowbound winter landscape in
four waves and headed west for Allied airfields in Holland, Belgium and
France.[2]

To ensure that the participating pilots were fresh for the mission, the
German air force's high command (the Oberkommando der Luftwaffe,
or OKL) had banned them from taking part in New Year's celebrations
the night before. This massive German air raid, code-named Operation
Bodenplatte, or Operation Baseplate, by the OKL, took Allied defenders
completely by surprise. In half an hour, hundreds of Allied aircraft were
destroyed. Most were sitting ducks, eliminated on the ground at their
airfields—Eindhoven airfield was particularly badly shot up. Some were
destroyed as they attempted to take off, some in dogfights with attackers
over the airfields.

Since the failure of Operation Market Garden, Wing Commander
Johnnie Johnson and his four squadrons of Mark XVI Spitfires of Number 127 (Canadian) Wing had been withdrawn to a new base at the Allied airfield at Evere on the outskirts of Brussels. A little after 9:00 that
frosty morning of January 1, Johnson heard the sound of numerous approaching airplanes. He thought they must be American fighters, which
frequently flew over the base. Then Johnson heard explosions. Dashing
outside, he saw sixty German fighters—screaming low over the airfield
in ones and twos with cannon belching flame.

Apart from sixty Spitfires, the airfield was home to another forty
aircraft—B-17s, a C-47, Auster and Anson communications aircraft, and
Prince Bernhard's personal Beechcraft Staggerwing biplane. The German attackers here, thirty-five Fw-190s and twenty-five Me-109s from

the Luftwaffe's Jagdgeschwader 26, achieved complete surprise, and there were only light antiaircraft guns stationed around the base. What was more, the German fighters caught a dozen Spitfires taxiing for take-off. They succeeded in shooting down the first Spitfire in line—which managed to take off and shoot down a Messerschmitt before its fate was sealed. They also went on to destroy another ten Spits on the ground and damage a further twelve after their pilots abandoned them and ran for their lives or sheltered beneath them. Several of the transport aircraft were also destroyed, including the C-47 and *PB1*—Prince Bernhard's pretty little Beechcraft. When two patrolling sections of Spitfires arrived back over the field, they took on the Germans, shooting down six in dogfights before, out of ammunition, they fled and left the burning base behind.

"The enemy completely dominated the scene," said Johnnie Johnson later, "and there was little we could do except shout with rage as our Spitfires burst into flames before our eyes." Just the same, Johnson was to marvel at what poor shots the Germans were. "We had escaped lightly. Not one Spitfire should have remained undamaged at Evere."[3] And because few of the damaged and destroyed aircraft contained aircrew, human casualties were surprisingly low. At Evere, just a single Canadian airman was killed and nine wounded.

The story was repeated at airfield after airfield, some of which were barely touched by the often inexperienced German attackers. Some 500 Allied aircraft of varying types were destroyed or seriously damaged. The majority were British and Canadian Spitfires, British Typhoons, and American Thunderbolts. But, as at Evere, very few of their aircrew were killed. Meanwhile, the Luftwaffe lost around 250 of its attacking Messerschmitt and Focke-Wulf aircraft in the short, sharp raid, and it lost almost all the pilots of those fighters, who were either killed in their cockpits or captured after crash-landing or bailing out in Allied territory. It was the single worst day of the war for Luftwaffe pilot losses. Most of

the German aircraft destroyed were knocked down by antiaircraft artillery (AAA) fire, including from masses of AAA deployed to defend
against V-1 flying bombs being sent over to England. Some German airplanes were shot down by Allied fighters. A number were brought down
by friendly fire—German flak gunners had not been forewarned of the
operation and opened up as soon as they saw low-flying fighters. One
Me-109 was downed by a partridge flying into its ventilator.

For days afterward, the Allies nervously awaited a return of the
Luftwaffe fighter armada, but it had been a one-day wonder. As a consequence of Operation Baseplate, for seven days the skies over the Western
Front were empty of Allied aircraft, and German ground troops in the
Ardennes could fight without fear of air attack. But that reprieve only
lasted a solitary week. Fresh American and British aircraft and fresh
aircrew were flown in from England, and the numbers quickly made
up. The Luftwaffe did not have the same luxury, did not have the same
reserves to draw upon. Aircraft replacement was not a significant problem for the Luftwaffe—in March and April 1945 more new German
fighter aircraft would be produced in underground factories throughout
the Reich than at any other time during the war.[4] It was the trained man-
power that Germany could not continue to pump out.

"At this time the average German fighter pilot was not sufficiently
well trained to fight on equal terms against either his British or American
opponent," said Johnnie Johnson.[5] To make things worse for the German
planners of Operation Baseplate, they had put a number of bomber pilots into fighters and expected them to become experts at ground strafing overnight, with predictable results. In addition, a large percentage of
the Luftwaffe's most senior, most experienced fighter pilots were killed
or captured during Baseplate.

These pilots could not be replaced in a week the way that American
losses in particular could be replaced by a never-ending stream of fresh
aircrew arriving from the States. Early in the war, the Luftwaffe had

spent thirteen months training each of its fighter pilots, who arrived at his unit with up to 200 flying hours under his belt. By early 1944, that was down to 160 hours, less than half the number of hours put in by a trainee USAAF or RAF fighter pilot. Germany no longer had the time or the young men to recruit—already, fresh-faced boys of the Hitler Youth were being thrown into the ground war.

In February, the last Luftwaffe pilot training schools would be closed and their instructors sent to frontline squadrons in an attempt to fill the gap in the number of experienced pilots.[6] This desperate step would signal the beginning of the end for Hitler's air force, and for Nazi Germany. Operation Baseplate, that grand and wasteful gesture, an 1,100-fighter raid, had only hastened the Luftwaffe's end. And it had only a marginal effect on the Battle of the Bulge. The greatest enemy, for both sides, was the bitterest winter in living memory, with rain, ice and snow making many forest roads impassable.

Stubborn defense by American troops cut off in and around the Belgian town of Bastogne typified the military hurdles encountered by the advancing Germans. All seven roads through the forests of the Ardennes converged at Bastogne, and it was to this vital crossroads that the 101st Airborne was rushed to hold back the German advance, having been resting and reequipping at Reims in France after the battle for Nijmegen in September's Operation Market Garden. By December 21, the 101st Airborne and other American units were completely surrounded at Bastogne. German commander General Heinrich von Lüttwitz sent them a note calling for their surrender. To which Brigadier General Anthony "Tony" McAuliffe famously gave a one-word answer: "NUTS." When the German officers bearing the surrender demand failed to understand this answer, it was explained to them that it meant "Go to hell!"

American armor from General George Patton's 3rd Army was able to break through to the troops holding Bastogne on December 26, after which the 101st Airborne went on the attack, driving the German troops facing them back to the positions they had held at the commencement of the offensive. American newsreel footage would show a professionally painted sign nailed to a building in the crossroads town: "Welcome to Bastogne, Headquarters of the Battered Bastards of the 101st Airborne."

On January 25, the Battle of the Bulge officially came to an end. The German advance had run out of time and fuel. Fuel had become Nazi Germany's Achilles heel. Its synthetic fuel plants could not keep up with war demand. As a consequence, as part of their orders for the Ardennes offensive, German field commanders were told to seize fuel supplies from American forces as they overran them. Without that American fuel, the attack would literally stall. German forces had raced to try to seize vital bridges before American engineers blew them up, and they raced to secure American fuel storage dumps behind the lines. In the first hours and days of the battle, this had been achieved via the element of surprise. But as the days passed and German tanks struggled against appalling weather and stiffening American resistance, bridges were blown up in their faces, and the fuel dumps had been increasingly emptied by the Americans before the thirsty German tanks reached them. As German armored vehicles ran out of fuel, their crews were forced to abandon them and walk back to Germany. The operation, the Battle of the Bulge, was the last major German counteroffensive of the war.

But still the people of western Holland were fated to remain under the German yoke and to face starvation through the freezing winter as civilian food supplies began to run out.

6

SURVIVING THE HUNGER WINTER

In Rotterdam, the family of fifteen-year-old Arie de Keyzer was becoming desperate for food as January 1945 stretched into a succession of bitterly cold days. By this time the daily ration allowed the population of occupied Holland had been reduced by the Germans to 600 calories, a third of what it had been in 1941—which itself had been way under the 3,000 calories of the contents of the three daily K-ration packs used by the troops of the US Army.[1]

The enterprising De Keyzer family had come through the early days of winter with relatively full bellies. They lived near the Waal harbor, where the Waal River entered the sea at the end of its fifty-mile passage from the Rhine. Here Arie and his two younger brothers daily caught fish for the family table. The boys had plenty of time for fishing because schools had been closed. The previous August, they had gone out to farms and walked behind the mowing machines harvesting wheat and rapeseed. On the orders of the occupation government, the harvest was sent to Germany, but the De Keyzer boys were able to collect sufficient wheat lying on the ground behind the harvesting machines to enable their mother to bake bread through the early part of the winter.[2]

The brothers also collected a little rapeseed from which their father produced cooking oil using a homemade press. In addition, the De Keyzer boys also had a way of snaring sugar beet. Trains carrying the Dutch sugar beet harvest to Germany passed close by where the family lived, and at night the boys speared beets from passing railroad wagons, using a long stick with a spike on the end. They'd take their catch home for their mother to boil the sugar beet down to create a sweet syrup. She used the pulp to make cookies.

An uncle of Arie's had a bakery in the city, and one of the few delicacies that he was able to continue to produce through the Hunger Winter was little "meringues," made using water, sweetener, coloring and baking powder. Not only did they taste good, they helped fill empty stomachs. When Arie eyed a tray of meringues one day, his uncle offered him the job of cranking the old cream-whipping machine that turned them out. Arie's reward, said his uncle, would be something to fill his stomach. Envisaging a plateful of meringues, Arie cranked for four hours straight until he couldn't lift his aching arms to crank any more. To his disappointment, his reward was half a loaf of unleavened bread. The loaf was as dense as a block of wood and tasted much the same. Still, it was food, and it was welcome.

But by the new year, with ice covering Waal harbor, the fish were no more. The wheat and rapeseed oil had been used up, and the beet trains were no longer running. All around the De Keyzer family, thousands of Dutch were dying from starvation. Arie de Keyzer decided that it was time to go on a foraging expedition inland. He and a school friend rode into the countryside on bicycles with solid tires. For three weeks they worked on a farm in the province of Drenthe in the northeast of the country, returning home to Rotterdam with saddlebags stuffed with food. Two weeks later, they made a similar expedition, this time east to the Achterhoek region. Again they came back with fresh food. But this time, on his return Arie found that his pet dog was missing. He never saw it again and was convinced that someone had stolen it—to eat.[3]

It wasn't only food that had become scarce. With no functioning railroads to transport them, coal and wood supplies dried up that winter, too. Ignoring the German regulation that banned the cutting down of trees in the cities, the residents would nightly sneak out to quietly lop branches and then cut down entire trees for their cooking fires and heating. Once-beautiful tree-lined avenues were quickly denuded and left stark and characterless. After that, the city dwellers turned indoors in search of fuel for their fires. One Amsterdam resident, teenager Bep Haagedoorn, watched her father progressively strip their household of its woodwork, starting with cupboard doors. By cannibalizing the family home in this way, Bep's father was able to keep a solitary fire burning through the winter.

By February 1945 the Haagedoorn family, like so many others, was embarking on desperate treks to the countryside in quest of food, especially potatoes. Many Dutch farmers would not take the currency circulated by the Germans in occupied Holland so, to get food, Bep's mother and father began by bartering their gold rings, watches and jewelry. Then they exchanged their best bedding and linens. When that was gone, Bep and her sister Ans slipped out of the house one night after curfew, taking along their mother's finest embroidered lace tablecloth, which had yellow roses around the border. Using Ans's bicycle, which had rope for tires, and with Bep riding pillion, they headed out into the country in the pitch dark.

At the nearest farm they woke the occupants and offered them the tablecloth in exchange for food. They came away with a small bag of potatoes. On their way back to Amsterdam, they rode into a massive hole that had been dug in the road, perhaps by the Resistance. Bep never let go of the bag of potatoes even though she and her sister were catapulted through the air like rag dolls. Battered and bruised but otherwise unhurt, the pair managed to find their way home without further incident. The next evening, the Haagedoorn family had the luxury of potatoes for dinner.[4]

Jantita Smittenaar was another Dutch girl with vivid memories of bartering for food. Her parents had bartered away all of the portable valuables in their house when they had the opportunity to get their hands on five pounds of split peas. The price was Jantita's favorite doll, complete with all its clothes and an antique doll carriage. As a result, Jantita and her family members had some greens in their diet for a week, but Jantita never forgot that doll. She emigrated to North America following the war but frequently returned to Holland to visit friends, family and familiar places. And every time she saw a rummage sale in Dutch cities and towns, she went looking for a doll just like the one she had surrendered for five pounds of split peas in the spring of 1945.[5]

It was now impossible for the millions of city dwellers in occupied Holland to buy "luxuries" such as eggs and butter in their local stores. Sometimes they were able to beg, buy or barter eggs and butter from farmers far out in the countryside and then smuggle them back to their families. But first it was necessary to have a bicycle for the long journey—there were no buses or private cars on the roads, and the trains were no longer running. Then they had to pass through numerous German checkpoints to get to and from the farms. Next, a generous farmer was required. And finally the foodstuffs had to be smuggled back into the city—if German troops found the contraband, they would confiscate it and likely arrest the smugglers.

The Dutch soon found that their children made the best food smugglers. German troops at checkpoints let children pass through with little scrutiny. And farmers could be expected to be more generous to children than to adults. Many Dutch teenagers excitedly volunteered for smuggling missions; not only would it be an adventure, but it would mean that they and their family would be able to eat relatively well for a few days.

Sixteen-year-old Audrey Hoeflok of The Hague joined the ranks of the bold young food smugglers. Her father was employed as night watchman in an office building in The Hague where German troops worked during the day. These Germans kept their own food stocks in the building's basement and because he had keys to the entire building, Audrey Hoeflok's father and an associate frequently "liberated" small amounts of food from this stockpile—small enough for the thefts not to be noticed. But by the beginning of March 1945, the German troops in Holland were also conserving food. Now almost cut off from Germany by land, they were watching their stores carefully. The German military commander in Holland, Generaloberst (Colonel General) Johannes Blaskowitz, knew that, at best, his troops had enough food to last them until September. But the local population's food situation was much more critical. Many city dwellers didn't know where their next meal would come from.

In The Hague, the food situation had become so grave for the Hoeflok family that Audrey volunteered to bicycle to the home of a distant relative who owned a farm in the country to try to get hold of a little fresh food for the family. Because the Germans had commandeered 50,000 intact Dutch bicycles for their troops and had taken the tires from others, Audrey's mode of transport for her exploit was an old bicycle with homemade tires like those used by Arie de Keyzer and many other Dutch—her father screwed thin pieces of wood onto the wheel rims; onto these he nailed strips of rubber from an old car tire. Audrey's ride was bumpy and exhausting, but it was better than walking all the way.

Setting off from the city early one March morning, Audrey reached the home of the country relative after a four-hour journey. She handed over a letter from her father and some cash and was welcomed warmly by the farmer and his family. They gave her a hot bacon sandwich, washed down with milk. Audrey had not tasted either in years. They filled the leather saddlebag straddling the rear of her bike with potatoes, onions, carrots, a cabbage, a small bag of flour, a sliver of bacon, three eggs and a small bottle of cooking oil.

Well fed, and carrying her treasure with her, Audrey rode all the way back to The Hague without encountering any problems. But as she entered the city, she ran headlong into a German military checkpoint blocking the street. As it was too late to turn back, she dismounted and walked up to the sentries, trying to act as casual as possible, pushing her bike and her luck.

"Papers," said a fresh-faced German soldier who looked to Audrey to be not much older than she was. Typically, many of the soldiers garrisoning Holland were the quite young and the comparatively old. The former were hastily drafted youths without military experience. The latter were frequently veterans carrying physical and mental wounds from battles fought on the Eastern Front, in Italy, in Normandy and elsewhere.

Teenaged Audrey handed over her identification papers. The soldier inspected the papers, then instructed her to open her saddlebags. With a heavy heart and fearing the worst, Audrey unfastened the latches on the bags. The soldier poked around in the bags. He held up one of the three precious eggs.

"Please let me keep them," Audrey pleaded. "For my sick mother."

The young German smiled. "If I do, will you go out with me?" he asked.

Audrey quickly overcame her surprise. To keep her treasures, Audrey would say just about anything. She agreed to a date with the German and also set a time and meeting place in the city center the next day. The soldier replaced the egg and closed the saddlebags, telling Audrey to proceed. She held out her hand to reclaim her papers.

But the soldier only smiled. "Tomorrow," he said.

So, minus her vital papers—she could be shot for being without them—Audrey went home. The family ate well that night, thanks to her. The next morning, Audrey hurried out on an urgent mission—not to keep the date with the German soldier, but to the local police station. There she reported that her papers were missing. The Dutch police gave her temporary papers and instructed her to report back in a week's time to see if her original papers had been handed in. Seven days later, Audrey returned to the police station. But there was no sign of her original ID.

Audrey Hoeflok had all but forgotten about the incident when, three weeks later, she was summoned to the police station. With trepidation, she returned and was handed her original papers by the police. The young German soldier had finally turned them in. He never informed his superiors that he had found Audrey carrying contraband.[6]

7

AN OFFER FROM NAZI
GOVERNOR SEYSS-INQUART

It was Sunday, April 1. April Fool's Day. This year it was also Easter Sunday. Dr. Arthur Seyss-Inquart, German Reichskommissar of occupied Holland, had made a dangerous 350-mile road journey north to Germany. His destination was Oldenburg in Lower Saxony, a German state bordering the north of Holland. Seyss-Inquart had come to visit Albert Speer, Hitler's minister for armament and production since 1943.

Once Hitler's personal architect, the charismatic Speer was one of the youngest members of the Nazi hierarchy—he had turned forty just two weeks prior to this. He was also one of the most powerful and effective government ministers. Under Speer, the production of tanks, aircraft, U-boats and V-weapons had multiplied enormously. By January 1945, even though Germany was losing the war on all fronts and was being bombed relentlessly day and night by the USAAF and RAF, production was at its highest level of the war. In underground factories out of the reach of Allied bombs, and using forced labor from throughout occupied Europe, Speer's lieutenants had worked industrial miracles. The output of single-seat fighter aircraft alone had risen to more than 10,000 in 1944. In 1940, that figure had been just 500.[1]

But in March, Speer had received a chilling order from Hitler—to implement a "scorched earth" policy that destroyed the infrastructure of the Reich. Every factory, power station, bridge, road and rail line was to be wrecked. Under this order, as the Allies advanced farther and farther into the Fatherland and Nazi-occupied territories, they would find nothing but a wasteland. Seyss-Inquart, as governor of German-occupied Holland, had received the same order from the fuehrer— Hitler expected him to utterly destroy the Netherlands. Considering Speer the least fanatical and most cultured member of the Nazi hierarchy, Seyss-Inquart wondered if Speer would press him to implement that order; that was why he had come to Oldenburg.

As the Russians closed in on Berlin from the East, Speer had relocated his headquarters to Oldenburg. He had chosen well. Even though the nearby port city of Bremen had been pulverized by Allied bombing, Oldenburg, with its ornate medieval castle, had been virtually untouched. When the urbane munitions minister and the anxious governor sat down in Speer's headquarters to discuss the current war situation, both men were aware that on the previous day, a message had been broadcast by Allied Supreme Commander General Dwight D. Eisenhower on Allied radio, calling on all German soldiers in all German armies to surrender. Further resistance was futile, Eisenhower had declared. There had been no reply from the German side. Adolf Hitler had called on his armies to fight to the last man and had called on his flunkies to lay waste to Germany and the occupied lands. Would the fuehrer's orders be obeyed?

Arthur Seyss-Inquart explained to Speer that, after receiving the fuehrer's scorched-earth order from his powerful secretary Martin Bormann, he had had a study carried out to see how western Holland could be most easily and effectively destroyed. For strategic reasons, a number of polders—reclaimed land—had been deliberately flooded across Holland by the German military. Seyss-Inquart had recently received a report that detonations at dikes in fourteen to sixteen locations would result in the entire country being completely inundated by the North Sea within three to four weeks. Holland would cease to exist. Yet, Seyss-Inquart went on, he could see no military necessity for destroying the Netherlands. According to Seyss-Inquart himself, he added that he did not wish to impose any more damage on Holland.[2]

Speer was pleasantly surprised by this and admitted that he was personally "frustrating" implementation of the scorched-earth order in the Reich. Then he gave Seyss-Inquart what was, for him, a startling piece of information. "The war, for Germany, will end in a relatively short period of time. Armament production simply cannot be kept up."

"How long?" Seyss-Inquart asked.

"Two to three months." Even that prediction would prove optimistic.[3]

As he would later admit, up to this time Seyss-Inquart had not wanted to believe that the end of the Third Reich was near. Like many Germans, he had had a premonition that Germany was losing the war after the 1943 defeat of German forces at Stalingrad, only to convince himself that all would be well. But Speer was not a man to exaggerate. And if anyone should know the true situation, it was he. As Seyss-Inquart departed from this sobering meeting with Speer, he became consumed with thoughts of saving his own hide once the war ended. Before he left Oldenburg to hurry back to Holland, he put in a telephone call to The Hague. He called a subordinate, Dr. Ernst A. Schwebel, the German Reichsrichter, or administrator, of the Dutch province of South Holland, which included two of the country's largest cities, The Hague and Rotterdam. Schwebel was a man Seyss-Inquart trusted. And he was, in the words of Dutch historian Henri van der Zee, "one of few decent Nazis in The Hague."[4]

Over the telephone, Seyss-Inquart told Schwebel in confidence that he had decided to disobey the fuehrer's standing instruction to all his political and military chiefs not to negotiate with the enemy. Seyss-Inquart had seen an opportunity for self-aggrandizement. He was fully aware that the millions of Dutch civilians under his control were running out of food. What if he proposed to the Allies that he permit them to ship food into Holland at once? That, he figured, should stand him in good stead when the war eventually ended with an Allied victory. He informed Schwebel that he was prepared to allow the Allies to feed the Dutch on condition that they guaranteed not to advance any farther into Holland. He instructed Schwebel to arrange a discreet meeting for him with the most senior Dutch official in charge of food distribution in the German occupation government of Holland to see if such a plan was workable.

At 8:00 p.m. the following day, April 2, that Dutch official, Dr. H. M. "Max" Hirschfeld, secretary general for trade and agriculture in the German puppet government of Holland, arrived at Schwebel's comfortable residence on the Sophialaan in The Hague. For forty-five minutes Hirschfeld waited in Schwebel's sitting room, and then in walked Dr. Seyss-Inquart, having arrived back from Germany a short while before.[5] The fifty-two-year-old Seyss-Inquart, an Austrian by birth and a lawyer by training and briefly, in 1938, chancellor of Austria before handing his country over to Hitler, had received a serious leg wound while serving in the Austrian army during the First World War. It had left him with a crippled leg and a slight limp. The Dutch had soon come up with a nickname for Seyss-Inquart after Hitler appointed him to govern occupied Holland in 1940. That nickname, "Zes-en-een-kwart," was coined because it sounded like Seyss-Inquart. It meant, literally, six-and-a-quarter. The Dutch, who hated Seyss-Inquart, said that the quarter referred to his crippled leg.

Schwebel also joined the meeting, and as the trio sat in conversation Hirschfeld found the Reichskommissar composed and clear headed despite having been on the road for hours on the return from Oldenburg, under threat of Allied air attack all the way. Seyss-Inquart informed the Dutchman of the decision he had made at Oldenburg—to get the Allies to feed the Dutch. He said that he had just come from a meeting with General Blaskowitz, the German military commander in chief in Holland, who had declared that he must follow the fuehrer's order to defend the Dutch coast from Allied attack to the bitter end. But Blaskowitz had told the governor that he was prepared to avoid unnecessary destruction in Holland if that was possible.

When Hirschfeld replied that the war must be ended at once because the Dutch were starving to death, Seyss-Inquart responded that there could be no question of German capitulation in Holland. Not yet, anyway. The governor reminded Hirschfeld of the fate of a German general who had agreed to surrender terms with the Allies—Hitler had him executed. Seyss-Inquart was clearly thinking of his own fate and that of members of his family, including his wife, Gertrud. Even though Gertrud Seyss-Inquart was now living in relative safety at Salzburg in Austria, one command by radio from the fuehrer's bunker in Berlin could bring about her arrest by the SS. Hirschfeld gained the impression that Seyss-Inquart might have been planning to use his position to open negotiations that would result in a broad German surrender in Europe, starting with Holland. Above all, the three men at this meeting knew that word of what Seyss-Inquart was embarking upon must not reach the ears of Hitler in Berlin. If it did, the results would be fatal for all three of them.

Yet, said Seyss-Inquart, if the military situation changed and occupied Holland was cut off from Germany, he was prepared to reconsider his position. In those circumstances, a separate peace might well be negotiated. "Then we will be our own king," he said.[6]

Seyss-Inquart then startled Hirschfeld by informing him that the German intelligence service knew all about the existence in The Hague of the Vertrouwensmannen, or Confidential Councilors, since August 1944—the secret agents in Holland of the exiled Dutch government. The seven members of the group had been personally chosen from London by Queen Wilhelmina and Prime Minister Gerbrandy. Instead of having them arrested, the cunning Seyss-Inquart had kept the Confidential Councilors under observation by his counterspies. In fact, the German effort to combat enemy agents in Holland had proved the most efficient of that in all the occupied countries of Europe. Since early in the occupation, Section IIIF of the Abwehr (German military intelligence) in Holland, led by Major Hermann Giskes, had captured every agent sent to the Netherlands by Britain's spy agency, the Special Operations Executive (SOE). Giskes had for years either turned these spies into double agents or had his own operators take over their identities and radio call signs and send London fake messages full of misinformation.

Every agent parachuted into Holland by SOE had been met by the Abwehr and given a simple choice—work for the Germans or be shot. Some had chosen to become traitors. Some fifty British spies had fallen into Major Giskes's net. Giskes's long-running and very successful counterespionage program became known as Operation North Pole. The German intelligence officers in Holland so enjoyed fooling London that they gave the operation the unofficial name of "the England Game." SOE's Dutch section only discovered in April 1944 that its work in Holland been manipulated by the Germans for years, but even then the Dutch Resistance groups were not made aware that London had worked out that the underground in Holland had been compromised.

Major Giskes's operatives had been so effective that Reichskommissar Seyss-Inquart now revealed that he had even been able to read a copy of the Confidential Councilors' Liberation Manifesto. "Very dignified," Seyss-Inquart said to Hirschfeld, before adding with a smile, "I may give it back to them one day."[7]

As Hirschfeld digested this information and realized, with a chill running down his spine, that Seyss-Inquart was fully aware that he was in touch with the Confidential Councilors, the governor suggested that he pass on to them what he had just told Hirschfeld about the German leadership in Holland being prepared to talk with the Allies, without naming Seyss-Inquart as the source of that information. What was more, he said, that leadership was prepared to disobey Hitler's orders to flood all of Holland—if the Allies guaranteed to halt their advance into the Netherlands and hold at their present positions. If such an agreement could be reached, said Seyss-Inquart, he was open to discussing food relief for the Dutch. The door to negotiations, and to ending the plight of the starving Dutch, had been opened.[8]

The next morning, Max Hirschfeld convened a meeting with four Dutchmen he considered reliable, all of whom, like himself, had connections with the Dutch underground. One of these men was A. M. Snouck Hurgronje, formerly head of the Dutch Foreign Office. All agreed that it was essential that they act swiftly to capitalize on Seyss-Inquart's initiative. Hirschfeld and Snouck Hurgronje jointly composed a message to be sent to London outlining the position of "the highest German authorities" in Holland, without naming Seyss-Inquart. Snouck Hurgronje hurried away to pass the message on to the Confidential Councilors for transmission to London by their "secret" radio.[9]

When there was no response from London by Saturday, April 7, one of the Confidential Councilors decided to pursue the matter of food relief personally with the German administration. Confidential Councilor M. A. van der Vlugt, while Dutch, was the Finnish Consul General in Holland—Finland had been an ally of Nazi Germany until 1944. He was also a leader of a major church relief organization. Under these guises Van der Vlugt paid Seyss-Inquart's deputy, Dr. Schwebel, a casual home visit.

As the pair chatted amiably, Van der Vlugt informed Schwebel that he had heard from a reliable source that since Seyss-Inquart had returned from his meeting with Speer at Oldenburg, he had considered returning to Germany to join the fuehrer in a last stand against Germany's enemies, only to change his mind and decide to remain in Holland and work toward a separate peace with the Allies. Schwebel made no comment about this, but, to the Dutchman's surprise, was positive about the possibility of a separate peace for Holland, suggesting that one condition for possible capitulation would be the "correct" treatment by the conquerors of German military and civil officers in the country.[10]

That same weekend, Reichskommissar Seyss-Inquart met with General Blaskowitz, the German military commander in Holland, to size up his reaction to the idea of negotiating directly with the Allies— separately from any potential negotiations initiated by their superiors in Berlin.

ON THE MONDAY, Van der Vlugt convened a secret meeting with his fellow Confidential Councilors. In light of the growing numbers of deaths from starvation among the young and the old in western Holland— the German administration's own figures put the number in excess of 20,000, and the country's hospitals were crowded with malnutrition cases—they agreed that talks with the Germans should be initiated without delay. But the Confidential Councilors stipulated that any such talks should be predicated on unconditional surrender of German forces in Holland. A message would be sent to London to inform Prince Bernhard, his new military deputy Colonel Henri Koot and the Dutch government-in-exile that the Confidential Councilors were pressing forward with negotiations with the German authorities.

At 9:00 a.m. the next day, Tuesday, April 10, Van der Vlugt was at Schwebel's office. But, to Van der Vlugt's dismay, Schwebel had pulled back from the positive position he'd held on Saturday and asked him to consider that meeting informal and unofficial. It turned out that on Monday, Seyss-Inquart had informed Schwebel that Blaskowitz had confirmed during their weekend meeting that he would not proceed with the mass destruction of western Holland. But the general was still determined to follow orders to defend Fortress Holland to the last man and the last bullet. Any suggestion of a separate German surrender in Holland was now off the table.

At best, Seyss-Inquart had informed Schwebel, they could talk about some form of neutralization of parts of Holland. But even for that to happen, the Allies would have to agree not to make any further attacks on Dutch soil, and the Dutch Resistance would have to remain inactive. In return, the Germans would not proceed with the ordered mass destruction, would execute no more civilian prisoners, would cease raiding homes in search of wanted men and would encourage the Red Cross to set up a relief center in Holland.[11]

As Van der Vlugt went away to consult with the Confidential Councilors, Schwebel rang Seyss-Inquart at the bunker he'd had built for himself at Apeldoorn as a secret field headquarters. Seyss-Inquart instructed Schwebel to continue talking to the Dutch, but in those discussions he was not to use the words "peace" or "neutralization." If necessary, said the Reichskommissar, he would become personally involved in the talks. At 4:00 p.m., Van der Vlugt came to Schwebel's office and heard of Seyss-Inquart's reaction with satisfaction. He agreed to arrange for a Confidential Councilor to join him in further negotiations with Schwebel in coming days.[12]

When Van der Vlugt arrived home, he found a telephone message from Schwebel, who asked that he come either to his office at 6:30 that evening or to his house at 7:30. The Dutchman arrived at Schwebel's residence at 7:42, to be informed that Seyss-Inquart wished to meet with him in person the next day at his Apeldoorn field headquarters, and

that the Reichskommissar had no objection to the Dutch government-
in-exile and the Allied commanders being informed of the fact.

At 10:00 next morning, April 11, the Confidential Councilors again
met. There was some resistance among them to sitting at the same table
as the Nazi leader in the meeting now proposed, and some wanted to
dictate terms to Seyss-Inquart. But Van der Vlugt was able to convince
them that the Nazis were too fanatical, and the situation of the civilian population in western Holland too critical, to be putting stumbling
blocks in the way of negotiations. It was agreed that the Germans be told
that the Dutch negotiators had no authority to agree to anything. They
could only take whatever Seyss-Inquart offered and pass it on to the
Dutch government-in-exile, and more importantly, to Prince Bernhard,
who would take it to General Eisenhower. In the end the Confidential
Councilors imposed just one condition on the meeting—that it be held
in private, not at the Reichskommissar's office.

This was quickly transmitted to Schwebel, who agreed to a meeting
the next evening at his house. That night, the Confidential Councilors
sent a message to Dutch Prime Minister Gerbrandy in London. Rather
than spell out details of the next day's meeting—in case the famously
cautious Gerbrandy forbade it—the message simply urged him to be
ready for a very important announcement in the near future that could
well require Gerbrandy's presence on the Continent. The Councilors
envisaged the prime minister taking part in the final stages of the talks
with Seyss-Inquart, one civil leader to another.

At 7:00 on the evening of Thursday, April 12, Van der Vlugt and
another representative of the Confidential Councilors, P. J. Six, were
admitted to Schwebel's house on the Sophialaan to find Seyss-Inquart
waiting for them with a confident smile. In a surreal atmosphere, the
Resistance leaders were served cups of tea. Van der Vlugt had never
met Seyss-Inquart before and immediately took a dislike to him, finding him slippery and vain. There was certainly no air of defeat about

the Reichskommissar. Seyss-Inquart came immediately to the point, informing the two Dutch delegates, as if they didn't know it already, that an exceedingly difficult situation existed regarding the supply of food to western Holland. He then declared that he was prepared to give full support to any relief work.[13]

Seyss-Inquart added a proviso to this: That support for relief work would come "military situation permitting."[14] He then went on to spell out how the food shortage could be alleviated. Five thousand tons of food a week could be shipped to Rotterdam, he said. With the Dutch also freezing through the cold spring that had followed the bitter winter, a thousand tons of coal could be brought in by rail from the Ruhr Valley in Germany.

This was all very well and good, said Van der Vlugt and Six, but obstacles such as the continued execution of Dutch political prisoners by the Germans, and the continued destruction of dikes to inundate more of low-lying Holland must be resolved before any agreement could be reached. Seyss-Inquart did not interrupt as the pair lectured him. The war was over for Germany, and for Germans, they declared. They even quoted Hitler, who had said in *Mein Kampf* that disobedience of orders was permissible if it meant the saving of a nation.

Seyss-Inquart then calmly assured the pair that all orders for destruction of Dutch infrastructure had been withdrawn, and that the only part of Holland that would be defended by the German armed forces would be the coastal region. If the Allies agreed to halt their advance at the Grebbe Line, the current German front line in Holland—which in effect split the country in two from north to south—and committed no further acts of war in the Netherlands, the German military command was prepared to hold back from inundating further parts of the country and to guarantee not to destroy infrastructure of any kind. Seyss-Inquart promised to ensure that Dutch political prisoners were transferred from prisons to less harsh detention camps, and that house raids and executions by the German Sicherheitsdienst (SD) security police ceased. Further, if German personnel were attacked, instead of facing summary execution, the Reichskommissar promised that the culprits, when caught, would be brought before a legitimate court of law.

Seyss-Inquart imposed just one condition—that the truce that would inevitably stem from the agreement he was proposing should be as inconspicuous as possible. Clearly, he didn't want word of it to reach Berlin. And as the Dutchmen were coming to their feet in preparation for leaving, Seyss-Inquart had one more surprise for them. He promised safe conduct through German lines for all Dutchmen conducting these proposals to the other side.[15]

Van der Vlugt and Six went directly from Schwebel's house to a meeting with the other Confidential Councilors, and it was agreed that they would send Dr. Louis Neher to the Allies with Seyss-Inquart's proposals, guided by Jacob van der Gaag, leader of one of the largest Dutch Resistance groups. Forty-year-old Van der Gaag, a native of Utrecht, had made a covert crossing of German lines to Canadian lines in January, successfully returning a short while later.

The stunning news the next day, Friday the thirteenth, beamed around the world from America, that President Franklin D. Roosevelt had died in the United States the previous day, did not affect the momentum of the negotiations that Seyss-Inquart had initiated. Resistance leader Van der Gaag arrived at Seyss-Inquart's office in The Hague and was shown right in to see the Reichskommissar. Seyss-Inquart told the surprised Van der Gaag that he was granting him immunity. "Immunity for what you have done in the past," he added, "but not for anything you may still do against us." The Reichskommissar then surprised the Dutchman even further by expressing the hope that Van der Gaag would do his utmost to save the poor Dutch people from starvation and urging him to hurry to Allied lines.

"Which route should I take?" Van der Gaag asked.

Seyss-Inquart smiled faintly as he replied. "You should go exactly the same way as you did in January."[16]

The Resistance leader was stunned by this. Obviously, Seyss-Inquart's intelligence people were fully aware of Van der Gaag's supposedly secret role in the fight against the occupiers of his country and had been monitoring his movements for months if not for years, yet he had not been arrested. Van der Gaag countered with bravado, declaring that he wanted to cross the lines wearing a uniform and pistol sent to him by the Allies.[17] At least that way he couldn't be shot as a spy if caught by German troops who were not in on Seyss-Inquart's scheme. To this point, no military commander had taken part in the negotiations; the Confidential Councilors had only Seyss-Inquart's word that he, the civil commander in occupied Holland, also spoke for the German military in all this.

The Confidential Councilors' courier Dr. Neher then arrived to join Van der Gaag, and Schwebel took the pair of them in his own chauffeured car to the town of Gorinchem on the River Merwede. Canadian troops occupied the far bank of the river. The mayor of Gorinchem, a Nazi supporter, welcomed the pair warmly and proceeded to regale them with his knowledge of the Resistance movement in the area, including their hiding places. Schwebel meanwhile made arrangements for the two men to cross the river. The mayor had unnerved Dr. Neher, who now developed cold feet and told Van der Gaag to cross the river first to test the German promise of safe conduct.

At 1:00 Saturday morning, two German Wehrmacht officers took Van der Gaag by road to an army headquarters downriver, stopping en route for the Dutchman to collect a local guide. At the German HQ, thirteen officers who had been drinking all night offered Van der Gaag a drink and insisted on watching the Dutchman change into his khaki Allied uniform, which he'd brought along in a suitcase. At 3:00 a.m., Van der Gaag was bid farewell by the merry Wehrmacht officers, who had apparently taken to heart the motto that had become common among many in the middle ranks of the German military over the past two years—"Enjoy the war, peace will be hell."[18]

At the riverbank, Van der Gaag climbed into a small boat, and the Dutch guide he'd collected earlier rowed him across to the far side of the Merwede. From there, Canadian troops drove him to the headquarters that Prince Bernhard had established at Breda. Just after daybreak on April 14, Van der Gaag met with the prince, passing on complicated instructions from Schwebel for a river crossing by Dr. Neher during the day. In accordance with those instructions, at noon, a forty-five-minute truce came into effect on both sides of the river, and a rubber dinghy containing Neher and a German officer was rowed across the river by a pair of German soldiers. At the southern bank a Canadian officer exchanged salutes with the German officer and took over Neher's escort before the German soldiers quickly rowed the dinghy back to where it had come from.

When Neher reached the town of Breda, he found Van der Gaag in conference with Prince Bernhard and the Dutch Minister for War, Professor Jan de Quay, who had flown over from London with Prime Minister Gerbrandy following the tantalizing message from the Confidential Councilors days before. Gerbrandy was now at Nijmegen, and a message was sent to him to come to Breda at once to hear from Neher and Van der Gaag.

Despite a cautious reaction by War Minister De Quay to the proposals that Van der Gaag had brought from Seyss-Inquart, Prince Bernhard was impatient to move forward on them. Without waiting for Gerbrandy to return, Bernhard told Van der Gaag to fly to London with Gerbrandy to brief Queen Wilhelmina and the rest of the Dutch cabinet. Bernhard said that he would meanwhile fly himself to SHAEF HQ in Reims, where he would personally brief General Eisenhower and hoped to receive his go-ahead for the Allies to enter into negotiations with Seyss-Inquart.

Neher was told to wait at Breda for the prince's return—he was then to also fly to London, carrying General Eisenhower's response to Bernhard's approach.

8

PRESIDENT "DUTCH" ROOSEVELT'S PROMISE

How Eisenhower would receive Prince Bernhard's approach would be dictated by two things—Eisenhower's own attitude to the problem of the starving Dutch and his instructions from Washington in the matter. Those instructions would be framed by a promise that President Franklin Roosevelt had made to Queen Wilhelmina.

Six months earlier, on Friday, October 13, 1944, President Roosevelt had received the Dutch minister for overseas territories, Dr. H. J. van Mook, at the White House. It did not prove an unlucky Friday the thirteenth for Van Mook, or for the Dutch people as a whole, although the fruits of this meeting would take time to materialize. With the failure of Operation Market Garden, the continuing railroad strike in Holland and the German crackdown on the distribution of food to the civilian population in the west of the Netherlands, Van Mook had come to the White House bearing a message from Queen Wilhelmina begging the president's aid for her people.

The queen had briefed Van Mook to expect a warm welcome from America's leader. Queen and president were of a similar age; Wilhelmina was just two years older than Roosevelt. Even though they had only met a few times—during a 1943 visit to the United States by Wilhelmina—they had corresponded regularly through the 1930s and 1940s with great mutual respect and affection. Wilhelmina also believed that she had an ace up her sleeve—Roosevelt's Dutch blood. The last time she had seen Roosevelt—in the summer of 1943, when he had personally driven her to the railroad station at Hyde Park in New York State after she had visited the Roosevelts at the president's family home there—FDR had told Wilhelmina that the Netherlands held a special place in his heart. She had good reasons to believe him.

Franklin Delano Roosevelt was indeed proud of his Dutch heritage, which stretched back to his paternal great-great-great grandfather Claes Maartenszen Rosenfelt, a Dutch immigrant from Tholen Island at the mouth of the Rhine. Sometime between 1638 and 1649 he landed in Nieuw Amsterdam, today's New York City, then capital of the Dutch colony in North America. Over several hundred years, and initially via the poor literacy of family members and of clerks filling out official re-cords, the family name changed as many as fourteen times, first to Van Rosevelt, and finally to Roosevelt.[1]

When Franklin Roosevelt was a nineteen-year-old student at Har-vard University, he wrote a sixty-page paper, "The Roosevelt Family in New Amsterdam before the Revolution," for his American History course, doing extensive genealogical research on his family background. His interest in his Dutch roots aroused, he would become active in nu-merous Dutch organizations in the United States including the Hol-land Society and the St. Nicholas Society of the City of New York. An amateur architect, he developed a passion for the Dutch Colonial style of architecture. In 1926, while planning the redevelopment of the Warm Springs health spa resort in Georgia where he had received treatment for polio, which took away the use of his legs, he instructed the architect to include as many Dutch design features as possible.

When the architect came back with preliminary designs for the Warm Springs project, Roosevelt declared that the window arches were not Dutch. The architect countered that they were of Pennsylvania Dutch design, which generated a laugh from FDR—he knew what the architect apparently did not, that the so-called Pennsylvania Dutch design was in fact German in origin. When the Roosevelt Warm Springs Institute for Rehabilitation opened in 1927—it continues to operate to this day—its cottages were indeed of Dutch Colonial design. The Little White House that Roosevelt built at Warm Springs as a presidential retreat five years later was, however, of a more generally colonial design.

The lack of knowledge in the architectural profession about Dutch Colonial design inspired Roosevelt to commission author Helen W. Reynolds to put together an authoritative book on the subject. FDR wrote, tongue in cheek, to Reynolds on June 10, 1926: "It is just a tiny bit amusing to think of your name and mine going before the public as experts on old Dutch houses. Think of the demand for future architectural works that will be made on us."[2] The book, *Dutch Houses in the Hudson Valley before 1776,* would be published in 1929. It was in fact Roosevelt's ambition to revive the Dutch Colonial style in America, and in 1937, when he personally drew the first architectural sketches for the Roosevelt Library at Springwood Estate, his Hyde Park, New York family home, his design had many Dutch Colonial influences that were incorporated into the final structure. In 1937, too, Roosevelt personally designed Top Cottage, a retreat he had built at Springwood Estate, in the Dutch Colonial style.

In 1940, because of his strong affection for Queen Wilhelmina, even though he had not met her by that stage, and as a German invasion of Holland seemed imminent, Roosevelt had urged her to relocate the royal family to the United States. After Wilhelmina chose to remain in England, and Princess Juliana took her daughters and herself to Canada, Roosevelt had invited the princess to visit Mrs. Roosevelt and himself in the United States. Juliana took him up on this offer each summer over the next several years.

In 1943, Juliana rented a house at Hyde Park for three months, to be close to the Roosevelts when they stayed at Springwood Estate over the summer. This proved an idyllic period for all concerned. Roosevelt adored the young princesses, Beatrix, or "Trixie" as she was known in the family, and Irene. One of very few photographs of Roosevelt sitting in the wheelchair that he usually occupied shows him with young Trixie. He was especially fond of the latest member of the Dutch royal family, a third daughter, Margriet, born to Juliana and Bernhard that year, and agreed to be her godfather. FDR wrote to Prince Bernhard in England that summer, telling him that every morning at Hyde Park, baby Margriet was brought to him as he breakfasted, and she played contentedly with a spoon while he ate.

If any further evidence of Roosevelt's love of Holland and the Dutch was needed, Wilhelmina had been told by Juliana that, in May 1944, Roosevelt had written to her in Canada offering her the use of his two adjoining summer houses on Campobello Island in New Brunswick, Canada, which he and Eleanor would not be using that year. In the letter, Roosevelt described the summer houses to Juliana, adding, "They are yours to occupy, and, because we are both Dutch, the terms would be extremely simple—no rent."[3]

Five months after Roosevelt penned that letter, and just days after Wilhelmina's sixty-sixth birthday, Minister Van Mook came to the president on behalf of Wilhelmina and her Dutch government-in-exile to beg the president to put his support where his heart was. Roosevelt had given Van Mook forty minutes to put his case, and he listened intently. As the pair parted, the president assured the Dutch envoy that he would do what he could to help Holland. When, by January 14, 1945, no help for the starving Dutch had materialized, Queen Wilhelmina wrote a near-desperate letter to both the British king, George VI, and

President Roosevelt. She wrote that, if immediate military aid to Holland was not possible, "then immediate aid in the shape of massive evacuation or in the shape of food supplies, clothing, fuel and medicine is necessary."[4] There was no formal reply from Roosevelt.

That March, Princess Juliana came down from Canada and paid her annual visit to the Roosevelts. She would write to her mother the queen that she was shocked by what she saw when she met the president again. The previous year, Roosevelt had been diagnosed with serious heart disease, although he and his doctor kept this from all but the members of his inner circle. The Franklin Roosevelt that Juliana now saw, for the last time as it turned out, was thin, pale and weak. He was clearly a dying man. But still Juliana pursued the case for relief for the Dutch.

On March 21, Roosevelt finally dictated a reply to Queen Wilhelmina's January letter. "You can be very certain that I shall not forget the country of my origin," he said before going on to inform her that he had instructed General Eisenhower to "channel as much food as possible to Amsterdam."[5]

Planning to deliver a major speech at the upcoming United Nations Conference on International Organization in San Francisco, on March 29 the ailing Roosevelt arrived at the Little White House at Warm Springs in Georgia for a rest. Two weeks later, on the afternoon of April 12, still at Warm Springs and while sitting for a portrait painter in the Little White House, Roosevelt suffered a massive stroke. He was dead within minutes.

But what of the supposed presidential directive to Eisenhower to channel as much food as possible to Holland? That Eisenhower had the power to alleviate the plight of the Dutch was not in doubt. Nazi Germany's Lieutenant General Bodo Zimmermann, commander of the Wehrmacht's Army Group D, was to later lament, "Eisenhower, the servant of the great democracies, was given full powers of command over an armed force consisting of all three services [land, sea and air].

With us, living under a dictatorship where unity of command might have been taken for granted, each of the services fought its own battles."[6] Eisenhower could order the Allied armies, air forces and navies to go to the aid of the Dutch in a coordinated operation, and he would be obeyed. What was more, at SHAEF, Eisenhower had the men and the skills to organize such a major mercy mission.

Wilhelmina, in London, grieving the loss of a president and a friend, had received Roosevelt's March 21 letter, but neither she nor Prince Bernhard had received any indication since then that the Allies were making preparations to send massive food aid to occupied Holland. What Queen Wilhelmina didn't know was that on April 10, Winston Churchill had also acted, quite independently, in response to her January letter, which King George had passed on to him. Two days before Roosevelt died, Churchill had cabled the president about occupied Holland: "I fear we may soon be in the presence of a tragedy." He proposed a diplomatic initiative, suggesting that Britain and the United States could make approaches to the Germans via Switzerland, urging them to allow aid to be sent to the Dutch from Sweden. He also thought that the Germans in Holland might be prepared to accept aid for Dutch civilians from areas controlled by the Allies. "We must avert this tragedy if we can," Churchill said. "But if we cannot, we must at least make it clear to the world on whose shoulders the responsibility lies."[7]

Roosevelt, in seeming contradiction of his March 21 assurance to Queen Wilhelmina that he had already instructed Eisenhower to arrange for the Dutch in western Holland to receive food to relieve their desperate situation, cabled back in one of his last communications to the British prime minster that he proposed to give the German government notice that it was responsible for feeding the civilian population in those parts of Holland it continued to control.

On the evening of April 14, as Prince Bernhard flew himself to Reims from Breda, which had been liberated the previous October, he had to wonder whether an order had truly been sent from FDR to Eisenhower to feed the Dutch, as the late president had assured Queen Wilhelmina in his last letter. And if it had been sent, would Eisenhower act on that order now that a new president, Harry S. Truman, occupied the White House? He was soon to find out.

AT REIMS, capital of France's Champagne district, ninety miles northeast of Paris, a jeep drew to a halt at the curb on a street that would be renamed Rue Franklin Roosevelt. Prince Bernhard, wearing his Dutch army uniform and beret, stepped from the jeep outside the unimpressive building that housed one of the most important military command centers in the world—SHAEF, Supreme Headquarters Allied Expeditionary Force. It was from here, a three-story, red-brick former technical college fronting the street, that General Eisenhower had run the war in Europe for the Allies since February, after previously being based at Versailles, and, prior to D-Day, in England. Receiving salutes from the pair of American military police at the front door and returning them, the tall, bespectacled prince strode into the building. Having been given only short notice that the Dutch prince was on his way to him, the Supreme Allied Commander Europe nonetheless saw Bernhard at once, and alone.

Eisenhower, or "Ike" as he had been known to those close to him since childhood, was a five-star general, the equivalent of a field marshal in European armies, and a career soldier. Yet he had never been in combat in his life. A West Point graduate in 1915 along with a class from which fifty-nine members, including Omar Bradley, would rise to become generals, Eisenhower trained during World War One as a tank officer. But a week before his unit was due to ship out to Europe to join the conflict in 1918, the Armistice had been signed, bringing the war to an end. Through the 1920s and 1930s, Eisenhower had spent sixteen years as a major, serving as an aide to General Douglas

MacArthur before falling out with him, and holding down increasingly responsible desk jobs.

Men such as Britain's Field Marshal Montgomery, who had fought in the World War One trenches, were privately disdainful of Eisenhower for his lack of combat experience. But it had been Eisenhower's other talents that had won him promotion and, in 1942, the post of the most powerful Allied commander in the European theater, based in London. Eisenhower was an exceptional organizer and a fine judge of character. He was also a master diplomat. He had to be when dealing with the sometimes incompetent and frequently opinionated generals and political leaders of the member nations of the Allied coalition, from Free French leader General Charles de Gaulle to Winston Churchill. To many at SHAEF and at Field Marshal Montgomery's headquarters, Prince Bernhard of Holland, a general with no military experience of note, fit that category of the incompetent and the opinionated. But ever the diplomat, Eisenhower treated Bernhard with characteristic courtesy and patience.

Fifty-five years old, trim, with assessing eyes and a quiet delivery, Eisenhower gave Bernhard half an hour of his time. He sat and listened to what the prince had to say about the offer from the Nazi governor of Holland as if he had all the time in the world. Born in Texas and raised in Kansas, Eisenhower had a Pennsylvania Dutch background. But, as President Roosevelt had pointed out to his architect in 1926, the Pennsylvania Dutch were in fact German. Eisenhower's ancestors were German, having migrated to North America from southwest Germany in the eighteenth century.

When Bernhard detailed the proposals that Dr. Neher had brought from Seyss-Inquart at The Hague, the Supreme Commander was nonplussed. "It is a question for the governments," Ike declared, indicating that, as far as he was concerned, there was no role for the Allied military here.

This suggested to Bernhard that Eisenhower had not received any instructions from the late President Roosevelt to feed the Dutch in occupied Holland, contrary to what he and the queen had been led to believe. Diplomatically, in light of Roosevelt's recent passing, Bernhard chose not to ask Eisenhower if he had received such an order, in case the answer put the president in a poor light.

"But I think it is a good proposal," Eisenhower added.[8]

Disappointed, the prince flew back to Breda.

Early on Sunday, April 15, Dr. Neher flew to London, where he informed Gerbrandy of what Eisenhower had said to the prince. Gerbrandy put in a call to Winston Churchill, who, not feeling well, had gone to his country house, Chequers in Buckinghamshire, for the weekend. Churchill was nonetheless entertaining a few guests, including the prime minister of South Africa, Jan Smuts, and he invited the Dutch prime minister out to Chequers as well. Gerbrandy wasted no time in driving there. But when he relayed to Churchill the detail of Seyss-Inquart's proposals, a grumpy Churchill was cool to the idea of dealing with the Nazis.

"We have them in our grasp," he growled. His preference was to liberate Holland militarily, with an unconditional surrender by the Germans in the country.[9]

But Gerbrandy, supported by South Africa's Smuts, pointed out that tens of thousands of Dutch civilians could starve to death before any military solution could be imposed on the Germans in Holland. And there was the threat of total inundation of the country should the Germans choose to destroy the North Sea dikes in the face of further Allied advances.

This made Churchill a little more responsive. He told Gerbrandy that he would take up Seyss-Inquart's initiative with the Americans. As the dejected Dutch prime minister was leaving, Churchill shook him by the hand warmly and said of the idea of dealing with Seyss-Inquart: "Please don't believe that I'm rejecting it completely."[10]

After driving back to London, Gerbrandy met with the members of his cabinet, the Dutch Council of Ministers. The two men who had brought the proposals from Seyss-Inquart, Dr. Neher and Jacob van der Gaag, were also invited to the meeting, but they found themselves treated with suspicion by many of the Dutch government's ministers, one of whom wondered in front of them if the pair had not been infected by the Nazis. Gerbrandy spoke up for them, declaring them honest men who had risked their necks to come to London on an important mission.

The ministers also learned that the pair had Queen Wilhelmina's support. As soon as she'd been informed of their mission, she and Princess Juliana had hurried back to London from Stubbings House and extended an invitation for Dr. Neher to meet with her. This Neher did, at Chester Square, on the morning of the next day, Monday, April 16. The queen, impressed with Neher and excited by the possibilities of Seyss-Inquart's proposals, invited the doctor and the Resistance leader Jacob van der Gaag to stay with her. That morning, too, the queen telephoned Winston Churchill at 10 Downing Street and urged him to give the Seyss-Inquart proposals serious thought. There was a noncommittal response from Britain's prime minister.

There, as far as the Dutch were concerned, the whole business seemed to stall.

9

"BEETLE" BEDELL SMITH'S PLAN

On Tuesday, April 17, at SHAEF HQ in Reims, a British air force officer, the slight, mustachioed, balding Air Commodore Andrew Geddes, stepped from a staff car and, stiff from the journey from his own headquarters in Brussels, straightened, then headed toward the front door. Ike's chief of staff and fellow American, Major General Walter Bedell Smith, had summoned the senior British air force officer to be briefed on an urgent, top-secret mission. As the forty-eight-year-old Geddes exchanged salutes with the American MPs on duty outside the front door and strode into the complex, he had no idea why he was here.

For the past two years, Geddes had been in charge of the Operations and Plans Department of Britain's Second Tactical Air Force (STAF). It was to Geddes that all plans for major air operations against the Germans were submitted. It was his job to turn those sometimes cockeyed plans into operations that worked. From Operation Overlord (the D-Day landings) to Operation Market Garden, it had been Geddes who had crafted commands from SHAEF into reality, often with mixed feelings, sometimes with mixed results, but always striving to find a way to maximize enemy casualties while minimizing Allied casualties. Now, with the war nearing an end, Geddes was close to exhausted and ready to cease the business of dealing out death.

General Bedell Smith's longtime secretary, Ruth Briggs, welcomed Geddes and ushered him into the general's office. Sitting at a glass-topped desk covered with papers and telephones, Bedell Smith removed his reading glasses and came to his feet without a smile. A native of Indianapolis with a military career that had begun before World War One, and just a year older than Geddes, Bedell Smith was a handsome man with a dimpled chin and movie-star looks that put some in mind of Hollywood leading man Joseph Cotton. And Bedell Smith knew it; a little vain, he didn't like being photographed wearing his glasses.

It was with a certain level of apprehension that Geddes greeted Bedell Smith, or "Beetle" as he'd been known since childhood—a nickname derived from a play on the Bedell in his name. Geddes had no idea what Ike and Beetle expected of him this time. Besides, Bedell Smith was a formidable, no-nonsense man to deal with. Known as Eisenhower's hatchet man, he had been Ike's chief of staff since September 1942. Bedell Smith moved heaven and earth to meet the supreme commander's demands, and he expected no arguments from those under him and brooked no excuses. Beetle gave you a job to do and expected you to get on with it. Geddes admired Bedell Smith, even considered him a great man. Despite his gruff, tough manner, Geddes had also known Bedell Smith to show great compassion at times.

Today, Geddes found Bedell Smith as stern and serious as ever as he led him to the giant map of northwest Europe on the wall behind his desk. What Bedell Smith now told Geddes came completely from left field as far as the Briton was concerned. It was the last thing he had expected this briefing to be about.

"Geddes, the Dutch are starving," Bedell Smith began, indicating B-2, the section of the map that represented German-occupied Holland. He explained that food was running out for the Dutch and that the Germans could not feed the local population any longer. He said that the Dutch government, the British government and the US government were all pushing Eisenhower to put an end to the situation.[1] He didn't tell Geddes that at this point there was still opposition at the highest levels to a mercy mission to feed the Dutch and that the mission that Bedell Smith was briefing him on had yet to be approved. It seems that Prince Bernhard's impassioned approach on April 14 had convinced Eisenhower to commence planning for the operation on his own initiative, passing the job on to Bedell Smith as usual.

Geddes assumed that Eisenhower had political approval for the operation and had briefed Bedell Smith to make the necessary preparations for a major airborne mercy mission that would occupy virtually every heavy bomber in the Allied air forces. Bedell Smith had certainly been active in the days prior to calling in Geddes. In a short time, he had contacted Air Chief Marshal Arthur "Bomber" Harris, chief of the British Bomber Command, and Lieutenant General Jimmy Doolittle, commander of the US 8th Air Force, and spelled out the resources he required them to provide for the mission. Bedell Smith was aware that the Allied air forces' fleets of transport aircraft were fully committed to flying supplies to the Allied armies. But he reasoned that a bomber's bomb bay could be filled with food instead of bombs.

The general knew that there were well over a thousand heavy bombers now available. On April 6, Bomber Harris had advised that no worthwhile major German targets remained in Europe for the RAF's Lancaster heavy bombers, and the last RAF raid on Berlin would take place on the night of April 21–22. Meanwhile, the 8th Air Force had staged what proved to be its final B-17 heavy bomber raid on Berlin on April 10. With the Russian army now fighting its way street by street into Berlin, the fall of the German capital was imminent. The last major Allied strategic air raids in Europe would come on April 25, with 8th Air Force B-17s hitting the Skoda factory at Pilsen in Czechoslovakia and

B-24s striking Hitler's retreat at Berchtesgaden in Bavaria during the day, and RAF Lancasters attacking Berchtesgaden and a Norwegian oil refinery that night. Bedell Smith knew for a fact that the 8th Air Force's 3rd Air Division had fourteen bombardment groups, made up of fifty-six heavy bomber squadrons, which could be switched over to his Dutch mercy mission at short notice. The British would now have a similar number of heavy bombers that could be similarly employed.

With many hundreds of heavy bombers and their crews sitting idle, Bedell Smith had the means of fulfilling his brief to feed the Dutch rapidly from the air. What he needed was a master planner to come up with an operational plan that would use those bombers, a plan that would work with the precision of a Swiss watch. That was where Geddes came in.

"I want to see you again with a plan to feed three-and-one-half million Dutch by air," Bedell Smith told him. "Drop zones, corridors, the lot."

Geddes looked at his superior in astonishment.

"You have my full support," the general went on. "Bert Harris has been told to give you two bomb groups and sufficient pathfinders. The 8th Air Force has three wings at your disposal."[2]

"Yes, General," Geddes gulped, as he tried to come to grips with the logistical needs of an operation to feed 3,500,000 people from the air.

Such a vast enterprise had never before been tried, by anyone, anywhere. Geddes knew that from late 1942 through early 1943 Germany's Luftwaffe had attempted—and failed—to feed from the air the 285,000-man German 6th Army, which was encircled by Soviet forces at Stalingrad. Set a minimum of 400 tons of supplies to deliver each day, the usually efficient German air force had struggled to even approach its target, and after weeks of trying, the Stalingrad airlift had ended in defeat for the planners at the Oberkommando der Luftwaffe and the surrender of what was left of the trapped German army. How, Geddes pondered, was he supposed to make this much, much larger operation work? And what would the Germans be doing while his bombers were flying food drops over their heads? Would they agree not to oppose it?

Bedell Smith seemed to have read his mind. "We need a prepared agreement for Jerry. No negotiations, just instructions."

"Yes, General."

"Do it, Geddes. Do it quickly! If you need any help, come to me. I'll make sure that Ike backs you all the way. We've cleared an office for you at HQ SHAEF here. Tell me what you need, and who, and I'll get it for you. Thank you."[3]

As Bedell Smith returned to his chair and again took up his reading glasses, Geddes realized that the briefing was over. The general had great faith in Geddes's initiative and great respect for his pluck. In 1940, while the British Expeditionary Force was retreating to Dunkirk ahead of the German Blitzkrieg, Geddes, piloting a dawdling Lysander reconnaissance aircraft, had taken on twenty Ju-87 Stuka dive bombers. He'd shot down one and lived to tell the tale. Later, on the morning of June 6, 1944, Geddes had personally piloted a Mustang flying low over the D-Day beaches in Normandy, bringing back the first reconnaissance photos of the Allied landings for Eisenhower and the Allied chiefs of staff to study.

Now Geddes would have to employ all his initiative and all his pluck as he was sent away to come up with a plan for General Bedell Smith. He would later confess that, as he left Bedell Smith's office on this momentous day, he had no idea where to begin. Shown to a classroom in one of the old technical school buildings, he commenced his new appointment then and there. Given a difficult planning task in the past, Geddes had always come up with the goods, had always conceived a plan that worked. But such an operation as Beetle Bedell Smith demanded was unheard of, and untried. Would this assignment be Andrew Geddes's bridge too far?

AS GEDDES PUT ON his thinking cap to come up with a plan that would meet General Bedell Smith's brief, he had no idea of the political and military wrangling that had been going on behind the scenes, and that would continue for some time, in regard to the plight of the Dutch in occupied Holland. Nor was he aware that, to this point, Eisenhower had received no instructions from above to carry out the relief of the Dutch.

Neither did Geddes know on April 17, as he began planning the operation, that there was every possibility that his plan, like so many operational plans he'd been required to draft during the war, would never get off the drawing board. Eisenhower, it seems, was planning for contingencies and preparing to meet the potential demands of his political masters.

The following day, Wednesday, April 18, the political situation began to change. In London, Winston Churchill summoned Prime Minister Gerbrandy to 10 Downing Street. Churchill wanted a written statement from the Dutch government-in-exile setting out its attitude to Seyss-Inquart's proposals. Gerbrandy hurried back to his own offices at Stratton House. Meetings with the queen and cabinet followed. But a statement that all could agree upon was difficult to come by.

The Dutch cabinet had received reports from the Resistance in Holland that the Germans had executed thirty-four Dutch prisoners and flooded a major polder. They also had a fresh report from the Confidential Councilors' envoy to Seyss-Inquart, Van de Vlugt, who had been summoned to an urgent meeting with Seyss-Inquart's deputy, Ernst Schwebel. Schwebel had apologized for the flooding of the polder. That had been a military necessity, he said, after German military intelligence had learned that the Allies had earmarked that polder for a landing by paratroops. Schwebel assured Van de Vlugt that he and Seyss-Inquart were still keen to open negotiations with the Allies along the lines that the Reichskommissar had already spelled out.[4]

At the same time, Prince Bernhard's deputy, Colonel Koot, was telling the Dutch cabinet that if an immediate Allied airborne landing in western Holland was not possible, then Seyss-Inquart's proposals should be accepted. Otherwise, he feared, the Germans would continue to flood the nation. The cabinet agreed with Koot's view, and Gerbrandy wrote to Churchill the next day, April 19, asking that the Allies undertake to either clear western Holland of German forces by April 30 or enter into negotiations with Seyss-Inquart. The third alternative was a nation overwhelmed by the sea—Gerbrandy, his cabinet and his queen had no doubts that the German leadership in Holland would destroy the country rather than surrender it.[5]

This grave message seemed to do the trick at Downing Street. All of a sudden, British activity became frenetic. Messages flowed back and forth between London and Washington and between London and Reims. British foreign secretary Anthony Eden was in Washington at this time, and on Churchill's instructions he met urgently with General George C. Marshall, chief of staff of the US Army, and placed Seyss-Inquart's specific proposals before him. At the same time, Churchill cabled President Truman, warning that a civilization with a tradition much older than that of the United States was in danger of going under—literally. At the same time, Churchill asked his military chiefs to ascertain Eisenhower's attitude to Seyss-Inquart's proposals. The answer quickly came back that Eisenhower was warm to them, although Eisenhower failed to reveal to his British colleagues that he had already ordered preparations for a food airlift to the Dutch.

Quite independent of all this, on April 18 Eisenhower was contacted by his boss, General Marshall. This was the day after Bedell Smith had set the ball in motion for airborne food drops in the Netherlands by briefing Andrew Geddes on the mission. Marshall asked for Eisenhower's thoughts on possible aid for the civilian population of western Holland. The late President Roosevelt had, as he had assured Queen

Wilhelmina, asked Marshall to discuss food for the Dutch with Eisenhower, and the general was only now acting on that request.

Not that Marshall would have delayed his action for a month through any dislike of or disdain for the Dutch. America's most senior soldier, Marshall was running a war on two fronts; not only was he Eisenhower's overlord in the management of the European war, he was also personally overseeing the war against Japan in the Pacific. In March, the war in Europe had seemed to have some months left to run, and the demands on Allied aircraft and aircrews were then such that there had seemed little capacity to consider any meaningful food aid for western Holland. Now, with Allied bombing operations winding up in Europe, Marshall realized that capacity was about to expand significantly. In their conversation, Eisenhower advocated a mercy mission to feed the Dutch, but it is unclear whether he informed Marshall that his chief of staff had already ordered the creation of an operational plan to facilitate such a mission.

The next day, April 19, following a meeting with Anthony Eden in Washington, General Marshall forwarded Seyss-Inquart's specific proposals to Eisenhower together with Churchill's observations on those proposals. On April 20, Eisenhower told Marshall that he was ready to do something for the Dutch in western Holland even though the size of the mission could mean that it would be at the expense of operations against the enemy. On the plus side, said Ike, if the Allies agreed to Seyss-Inquart's proposals, it meant that they could hold the Grebbe Line in Holland with minimum forces, freeing up troops for other theaters of war. Marshall had told Eisenhower that the Russian delegation to the United Nations conference then taking place in San Francisco was being told about the Seyss-Inquart initiative, and Eisenhower said he hoped that the Russians would endorse American and British efforts to feed the Dutch. Even if they didn't, he added, he was prepared to press forward with the mercy mission because of the advanced state of starvation of the population in the larger cities. But Marshall, not wanting to upset the Russians, ordered Eisenhower to sit tight until a response was received from the Russian delegation.[6]

The following day, April 21, Dutch envoys Dr. Neher and Jacob van der Gaag, who were cooling their heels in London waiting for word of the commencement of food shipments to Holland, lost patience. This was all taking way too long for them, and for the starving millions in Holland. Confronting Prime Minister Gerbrandy, they complained bitterly and demanded to know what the holdup was. Gerbrandy, a compact, balding man with a walrus mustache, could only shrug and say that it was out of his hands. When Eisenhower gave the go-ahead, the operation would begin, he said. But not before. And, on Marshall's orders, Eisenhower was waiting on word of how the Russian delegation in San Francisco viewed Seyss-Inquart's proposals.

On the same day, a new complication arose. In Holland, the numerous groups of Resistance fighters came to hear of the Seyss-Inquart proposals for the first time. The Confidential Councilors had deliberately kept most of the Resistance leaders in the dark about the proposals up to this point, expecting many of them to resist the idea. This was exactly what occurred.

Those Resistance groups, nineteen of them, ranged from socialists of the far left to nationalists of the far right. Wracked by rivalries and arguments over ideology, methods and goals, these groups could rarely agree on anything. The most fanatical among them were opposed to negotiations of any kind with the Nazis. They would accept unconditional surrender by the Germans, or nothing. There was also another factor, as the Confidential Councilors were only now becoming aware— clearly, after what Seyss-Inquart and the mayor of Gorinchem had revealed, the Germans knew a worrying amount about the activities of Resistance leaders in Holland. It was beginning to dawn on some of the Confidential Councilors that there might be double agents in Resistance ranks—double agents who, on German orders, were trying to foil the plan to feed the Dutch in occupied Holland.

Now the nineteen underground groups united to reject out of hand the idea of negotiations with Seyss-Inquart. Some were prompted by their longtime demand for an unconditional German surrender. All expressed the fear that Seyss-Inquart had tricked the Allies and that his suggestion of negotiations was just a ploy to stall the Allied advance into Holland. On this day, under the banner of the Joint Resistance Movements, they sent a message to Queen Wilhelmina, Prince Bernhard, the Dutch government in London and General Eisenhower, declaring that they declined to support any form of negotiation that did not lead to immediate capitulation by the Germans in Holland.

When the frustrated Confidential Councilors heard of this, they sent their own message to the same four recipients, stating that the message from the Joint Resistance Movements was ill-informed and did not have widespread support.

WITHIN A WEEK, Andrew Geddes's room at SHAEF at Reims was filled with people, maps of Holland, paperwork detailing the supply situation in England and the latest intelligence reports from and about Holland, and was the site of feverish activity. Poring over the paperwork with a smoking pipe jutting from the corner of his mouth, Geddes, unaware of the delays and disagreements in the United States, Britain and occupied Holland regarding his project, was getting on with the job given to him by Eisenhower's chief of staff.

As he always did when given a plan to accomplish, Geddes began with an overall outline for his operation. As always, too, he knew that outline had to be simple. The operation was to be laid out just like a bombing raid. Appropriate targets for airdrops were selected, and solutions to several logistical problems were investigated. Geddes soon learned that sufficient food stockpiles existed in Britain for the mission, but the major problem was the method of delivery to the Netherlands. His inquiries established that there were simply not enough spare parachutes in existence to drop thousands upon thousands of food packages over Holland. Yet, landing waves of bombers in enemy-occupied territory to unload food was out of the question—for one thing, prior to this the Allied air forces had gone to great lengths to make all airfields in German-occupied Holland inoperable with intensive bombing of runways and other facilities.

Most importantly, as far as Geddes was concerned, firm rules of operation, for both the Allies and the Germans, had to be laid down. Furthermore, the thousands of aircrew taking part in the operation had to be told what Eisenhower expected them to achieve and how they were to do it. Geddes was very conscious of the fact that the men flying on this operation would not be happy when they received their initial briefings. He expected that none of them would trust the Germans to keep their word not to shoot at them, if indeed the Nazis gave their word not to do so. But he was confident that, if they could get through the first day of mercy flights without major incident, aircrews would become excited and enthusiastic.

When a message came from General Bedell Smith on Monday, April 24, asking when food drops could begin, Geddes was able to respond with confidence that he expected to be able to send the first food-laden bombers to Holland within four or five days. That was all Bedell Smith, and Eisenhower, needed. That evening, at 10:00, the BBC's newsreader announced to the world, and to the Dutch in particular, that Supreme Allied Command had decided to drop food to the starving people in German-occupied Holland from the air.

The brief BBC broadcast said that food supplies would be dropped over Holland from a low level, without parachutes, by day and by night, and that the population should remain indoors when they heard aircraft in the vicinity, as people might be struck and killed by falling food. In fact, Geddes had no plans to drop food at night; all his operations would involve daylight drops—flying at several hundred feet in darkness would be suicidal. But whoever had drafted the SHAEF announcement on Eisenhower's orders was clearly not knowledgeable about air force operations and had assumed that, as both USAAF daylight bombers and RAF night bombers would be used for the operation, drops by day and by night would be involved.

Andrew Geddes never heard this broadcast. He remained ignorant of it when, by late morning of the next day, Tuesday, April 25, his detailed operational plan was complete. All he needed was General Bedell Smith's approval to proceed. Not only had he and his hastily assembled team of clerks and assistants come up with a plan in writing, they had ensured that the dropping of food packages from low-flying bombers, without parachutes and with precision—even though some of the drop zones would be relatively small, certainly compared to the targets for strategic bombing—was practical and possible.

At Geddes's instigation, the RAF had flown trial drops from Lancaster bombers, using full sand bags representing bags of powdered egg. The bombers involved had made their trial drops with undercarriages down and using one quarter flap to slow the aircraft. These trials found that, if dropped from above 500 feet, the bags were likely to burst on impact with the ground. It became apparent that the ideal altitude for dropping the sacks was 400 feet. Meanwhile, that very morning of April 25, the US 8th Air Force had made a trial drop at Horham bomber base in Suffolk, using a B-17 of the 95th Bombardment Group and crates of K-rations. This last USAAF trial was deemed a success.[7]

The operation planned by Geddes would start small but would quickly build over succeeding days as more and more bomber wings were added to the mission. There was no end date for the operation; it would continue for as long as it took to bring the Dutch people back from the brink of starvation. Geddes had given his operational plan a name, inspired by the Old Testament story in the Book of Exodus in which the Israelites received manna from heaven—Operation Manna. When USAAF 8th Air Force commander General Jimmy Doolittle and his senior officers heard this title, they shook their heads. The British could use some obscure biblical reference if they wished, but the Americans would come up with a more American name for their part of the mission. The decision was made by Doolittle that all USAAF sorties during this mercy mission would be flown under the name Operation Chowhound. Meanwhile, unknown to Geddes, the secret behind-the-scenes negotiations with the Germans in Holland were simultaneously continuing, with the objective of setting up a meeting between the Allies and the German commanders on the ground that would formally agree upon the conditions for the operation to which both sides would adhere.

Geddes had to wait until first thing the next morning, April 26, before General Bedell Smith was available to see him. Into Beetle's den he went, bearing his plan and a draft of the document that both Allies and Germans would be required to sign to guarantee the safety of the aircraft flying the mercy missions day after day. Typically, this latest meeting with Bedell Smith did not last long. The general did not question the plan that Geddes had conceived. Ike had given the go-ahead for the operation three days earlier, on April 23, when word had reached him via intelligence channels that Reichskommissar Seyss-Inquart was ready to send representatives to a meeting in Holland, just across the front line, to discuss implementation of relief measures for western Holland.

Bedell Smith gave Geddes's plan his swift approval and ordered the air commodore to travel that same day to the village of Achterveld in the liberated sector of Holland for a meeting with Seyss-Inquart's representatives. There, the document drawn up by Geddes and his team was to be reviewed and signed by both sides, after which the flying operations set out by Geddes were to commence at once—Bedell Smith was painfully aware that every day of delay meant that more Dutch children would die of starvation.

What Geddes and Bedell Smith did not know was that another complication was about to be added to the equation. The same day, a young captain in the Canadian army was embarking on his own secret mission to the German high command in occupied Holland. But his mission was being undertaken without the knowledge or consent of General Bedell Smith—or of anyone else at SHAEF. And it risked jeopardizing the delicate official negotiations being undertaken with the Germans and preventing the delivery of food to the Dutch.

10

FARLEY MOWAT GOES
BEHIND GERMAN LINES

Farley Mowat, who would become one of Canada's most noted and best-selling authors, was in April 1945 a baby-faced, twenty-four-year-old captain in the Canadian army and the survivor of bloody campaigns in the Italian theater of war. The son of a librarian, Mowat had grown up in a series of small Canadian towns in a number of provinces, joining the army in Toronto in 1940. Prior to being transferred to northwestern Europe in the spring of 1945, he had fought in Sicily and Italy through 1943 and 1944, latterly serving as a battalion intelligence officer with the 8th Army. In March 1945, Mowat, now a part of the 1st Canadian Army, had sailed for Belgium and was transferred to a small, specialized intelligence unit operating from the liberated sector of Holland. Mowat was given a new title—technical intelligence officer (material)—and an intriguing new job involving secret weapons.

In the last months and weeks of the war, driven by desperation, German technical ingenuity was showing no bounds as all sorts of new mines, bombs and rockets, or new variations on existing weapons, were produced. The Germans were the first side to put jet aircraft into operational use during the war, while some of the weird, wondrous and wacky German weapons experiments included development of a sonic gun that was supposed to knock aircraft from the sky—it was a failure. There was even a German attempt to produce a rifle that could shoot around corners—another failure. But some of the new German weaponry that Mowat was assigned to look for was much more effective—and deadly.

Captain Farley Mowat was given a half-track truck, a jeep, a Harley-Davidson motorcycle, a team of soldiers and a Dutch liaison officer, and orders to find German secret weapons, assess them and recommend countermeasures. This often meant sneaking behind German lines, or being the first to arrive at depots only recently abandoned by retreating German forces in search of the secret weapons. At one German arms bunker, Mowat had recently discovered a new rocket. Bringing it back to his headquarters at Eindhoven, he had begun to disassemble it only to succeed in setting it off. He, and the men with him, had just managed to get out of the basement room before the rocket exploded. The room was wrecked and the senior officers upstairs alarmed. But the only thing to be hurt was Mowat's pride.

On joining his intelligence unit, Mowat found to his delight that his immediate commanding officer was a close friend, Major Ken Cottam, who, Mowat suspected, had engineered his appointment to his staff. Major Cottam had a wide-ranging intelligence role. Apart from being Mowat's chief, Cottam had an open brief to do pretty much what he pleased—from looking for German war criminals to mounting daring raids behind enemy lines in search of military intelligence. Cottam's superiors let him do whatever he liked now that the 1st Canadian Army was in Holland. Mowat discovered that this had a lot to do with the fact that Cottam was well in with "the palace"—the Dutch royal palace. In reality, this meant that Cottam had the confidence and the ear of Prince Bernhard.

Mowat considered his friend Cottam a latter-day Sir Francis Drake. The full-of-surprises, colorful, unconventional and fearless Cottam never did things by the book. In fact, he threw the book away. And he had a fresh surprise for Mowat. At 4:30 p.m. on April 25, daredevil Cottam walked into Mowat's office in Eindhoven and informed him that the two of them, accompanied by Sergeant "Doc" MacDonald, Mowat's longtime orderly and assistant, would embark the next day on a mission to meet with Generaloberst Johannes Blaskowitz, the German military commander in occupied Holland, to talk truce.

It was a mission entirely of Cottam's conception and had no connection with the complex web of negotiations then going on in Holland involving General Blaskowitz, Reichskommissar Seyss-Inquart, and the Allies. Mowat, as a member of the military intelligence community—and, like Cottam—was aware that Seyss-Inquart was in contact with SHAEF and was discussing highly sensitive issues with them. What he didn't know was that Cottam's little private venture had the potential to derail the plan for the relief of the millions of starving Dutch.

JUST AFTER MIDDAY on April 26, the same day that Andrew Geddes was heading for Achterveld in Holland to meet with Reichskommissar Seyss-Inquart's representatives to finalize SHAEF's food-drop plan, Farley Mowat was sitting in a jeep driven by his friend Cottam as they passed through the frontline positions of the Canadian army's Princess Louise's Dragoon Guards, north of Nijmegen. In Mowat's hand was the transcript of a radio message from the commander of one of the disparate Dutch Resistance groups in Amsterdam. In that message the Resistance man had expressed the view that General Blaskowitz was open to talks about a separate armistice in Holland. Major Cottam had taken this vague message to his superiors at the HQ of the 1st Canadian Army and, on the strength of it, convinced them that he should be permitted to go behind German lines to open a peace dialogue with Blaskowitz face to face.

The radio message from Amsterdam was, to Cottam's mind, as good as a safe conduct through German lines. Farley Mowat wasn't so sure. To him, this whole idea was harebrained. As their jeep sped down the road, leaving the protection of their own forces behind, Mowat hunched down low beside the erect Cottam, expecting a fusillade of German bullets to come their way at any moment. In the back, Doc MacDonald was likewise ducking for cover. From the wire cutter on the jeep's front bumper hung a white flag the size of a bed sheet, but Mowat felt that to be about as useful a form of protection as the piece of paper in his hand.

For long minutes they drove fast across the flat farmland that was the deserted no-man's-land lying between the Canadian front line and the German front line. Ahead, a tree line loomed large. In their path appeared German outposts manned by Luftwaffe paratroopers in camouflage jackets, all with submachine guns and assault rifles leveled and with very wary looks on their faces. The sight of the American-made jeep itself was not enough for the Germans to open fire—jeeps and weapons captured from the British in the Battle of Arnhem were now being used by German servicemen in Holland.

Cottam drew the jeep to a halt and jumped out. A large, imposing man, he spoke perfect German, and he now proceeded to lambast the paratroopers and demand that they let his jeep pass on a mission of highest importance to both sides. Cottam was able to convince the junior German officer in charge to take them to his battalion headquarters, and the paratroop officer climbed into the jeep and joined them for the drive there. Dealing with more senior officers at the headquarters, the Canadian was also able to convince them that his mission was legitimate and of vital importance.

The German battalion commander assigned an escort to guide Cottam and Mowat to the headquarters of General Blaskowitz's 25th Army. A pair of motorcycles, each with two paratroopers on board, took the jeep on the next leg of the journey with one motorcycle in front, the other behind. With Mowat now at the wheel of the jeep, they drove for twenty-five miles along a road that was soon alive with German SS troops on the march, together with Wehrmacht transport lumbering along carrying ammunition and supplies.

That German transport was horse-drawn. Mowat put this down to the German shortage of gasoline. In great part that was true, but, throughout the war, up to half of the Wehrmacht's transport was horse-drawn. To project an image of the Nazi war machine as a mechanical juggernaut, German military cameramen shooting footage for newsreels were forbidden by their superiors to film any horse-drawn vehicles.

When the SS troops blocked their way, Ken Cottam didn't hesitate to stand up in the jeep and bellow orders in guttural German for them to make way—which they did, although grudgingly. Eventually, the jeep and its escort arrived at the 25th Army HQ at Hilversum. The German military headquarters for occupied Holland was spread through a complex of massive concrete bunkers, dug deep into the earth on the outskirts of the town and well camouflaged to hide them from Allied aircraft. The complex was heavily defended, being surrounded by masses of barbed wire, machine-gun emplacements and tanks that had been dug in.

There was a brief delay at the main gate when the German sentry on duty disregarded the so-called safe conduct clutched by Mowat. A tall German captain appeared, and it turned out that he was expecting the Canadians after being forewarned of their mission by the officer commanding the paratroopers at the front line. Instructing Doc to remain with the jeep, but telling Cottam and Mowat to follow him, the captain led the pair of Allied officers down into the bunker complex. In the main bunker, Mowat was separated from Cottam and made to wait while his superior was taken to General Blaskowitz.

Long hours passed for Mowat; come nightfall, he was escorted to the German officers' mess in the underground complex. Numerous polite German officers introduced themselves with salutes, bowing and much clicking of heels. To Mowat's astonishment he was served dinner—German army stew—and was joined for the meal by General Blaskowitz's chief of staff, the tall, thin Lieutenant General Paul Reichelt. The highly decorated German general, a veteran of the Russian Front, apologized to Mowat for the quality of the meat they were eating, which, he said, was mostly horse. Reichelt then proceeded to ply Mowat with Slivovitz, an eastern European plum brandy, of which there seemed to be an endless supply.

To Mowat, this entire situation was unreal, and he was ill at ease as the German officers treated him like an honored guest. He guessed from their attitude that these officers knew all too well that their war would soon be over and that they would become the prisoners of the Allies; they were treating the Canadian captain as they hoped to be treated by his colleagues once hostilities came to an end.

At 11:15 that evening, Ken Cottam reappeared. Bearing what Mowat was to describe as a Cheshire cat smile, Cottam informed his friend that he had succeeded in getting General Blaskowitz to nominally agree to the provision of a truce along the present front line between the 25th Army and the 1st Canadian Army in eastern Holland. Mowat was shocked that Cottam had so blithely inserted himself—and Mowat—into the highly political situation that confronted the Allies over German-occupied Holland. He dreaded to think what problems they might have created for the negotiations between Arthur Seyss-Inquart and SHAEF. And he feared retribution for Cottam and himself for involving themselves in the process once their commanding general got wind of Cottam's lone-wolf venture.

When Mowat expressed his fears to his friend, Cottam was not the slightest bit concerned. He beamed with self-satisfaction at the provisional truce he claimed to have negotiated with General Blaskowitz. "Would have taken those silly SHAEF effers in Paris days to get it all laid on," Cottam declared to Mowat. Cottam was convinced that General

H. D. G. "Harry" Crerar, commander of the 1st Canadian Army, would promote him to colonel for his exploit.

"If he doesn't court martial you . . ." Mowat remarked. "And me too!" he added unhappily.

"Absolute nonsense, chummie. He'll be tickled pink. Now shift your ass! We're off!" Cottam declared.[1]

Cottam's original plan had been to hightail it back to Allied lines with news of his truce, but his success so far convinced him that more adventures lay north, not south, deep inside German-occupied Holland. With Mowat and MacDonald as reluctant passengers, Cottam set off behind the wheel of their jeep, driving at breakneck speed through the night toward Amsterdam. In Amsterdam, Cottam was sure, they could link up with the Dutch Resistance, after which he planned to use the Resistance's radio to send word to SHAEF of Cottam's truce "triumph" with General Blaskowitz.[2]

Sitting beside his manic commander as the jeep sped along, Mowat was left hoping that Cottam's intrusion into the negotiation process had not conflicted with or damaged the official negotiations being carried on elsewhere with Nazi governor Seyss-Inquart. Time would tell.

11

THE ACHTERVELD AGREEMENT

In Reims, the same day—April 26—that Cottam and Mowat were playing their solo hand behind German lines in Holland, Air Commodore Andrew Geddes kicked his heels around the old technical school that housed SHAEF HQ until he was finally presented with special credentials that afternoon. They came fresh with the signature of Major General Sir Francis "Freddie" de Guingand, chief of staff to Field Marshal Montgomery. Those credentials authorized Geddes to go anywhere and get anything he wanted while on this mission.

Geddes was startled but not surprised by the speed with which arrangements were going forward for the implementation of his massive food-drop operation. An hour after receiving his credentials, with his briefcase containing the mission's detailed plans and several copies of the operational agreement for signature by both sides, Geddes was whisked by jeep to Reims airfield, where he boarded a C-47 transport aircraft. As he was flown to the airfield at Gilze-Rijen, near Breda in southern Holland, Geddes laid his head back against the side of the fuselage. He was feeling so, so wearied by the war, but he was determined to finish this last big job for Eisenhower and Bedell Smith. "What a way to end a war!" he thought to himself. His mind turned to the meeting that he would soon be having with senior Nazis. He wondered if the men he was about to meet would be the same as the last Germans he'd come across—arrogant bastards, in his own words. That had been back in 1940 when he'd been evacuating his fighter squadron from Abbeville in France as German tanks rolled up.[1]

At Gilze-Rijen, a tiny, high-wing Auster communications airplane was waiting for Geddes with propeller spinning, and it took off as soon as he was in his seat. The flight was just a short hop to an airstrip outside Nijmegen. This sector was controlled by the Canadian army, and as Geddes jumped down from the Auster, he was met by a Canadian staff car. With two Canadian MP outriders on motorbikes leading the way, Geddes was driven to shattered Arnhem and over the "bridge too far" that had seen the inauspicious end of the previous year's Operation Market Garden. It had been in Canadian hands for the past few weeks.

Continuing northwest through B-1, the Canadian sector of Holland, the little convoy reached the village of Achterveld. Canadian troops had sealed off a perimeter around the village's St. Joseph's Catholic School, where the meeting with the Germans was due to take place, and it was here that Geddes was deposited. The Canadians had set up a field kitchen at the red-brick school, so Geddes was able to enjoy a hot meal with Canadian officers in a room at the school. He was then taken to see fellow Briton Major General De Guingand, who had arrived to act as senior Allied representative at the meeting.

Geddes and Freddie de Guingand were old friends, and that evening they shared a few drinks together and agreed on the procedures they would observe the next morning when the Germans arrived. Geddes was subsequently taken to a room in a village house where a bed had been prepared for him. He slept soundly, but awoke early the next morning. Rising with a mixture of excitement and anticipation, he hurried to the school.

Freddie de Guingand was there ahead of him. "The German delegation has arrived at the railway east of Amersfoort," the general advised.[2]

SNOW HAD FALLEN in the night, and it coated the ground, the trees and every building and vehicle. In the chill of the early morning, four Germans walked toward two Canadian army Packard sedans, their boots crunching on the snow. White flags flew from the mudguard of each car. All the Germans wore long greatcoats, gloves and peaked military caps sporting the eagle and swastika emblem. Canadian troops quickly encircled the quartet and each man's eyes were covered with a blindfold.

A Canadian officer led the delegation to the waiting sedans. "This way, Fritz," he said to the delegation leader, Dr. Ernst Schwebel, taking his arm.[3]

Schwebel's assistant, Dr. Friedrich Plutzar, who spoke excellent English, was incensed at being called "Fritz" and said so. To him, this was an unpardonable lack of courtesy. For the moment, Schwebel himself bit his tongue. Reichskommissar Seyss-Inquart had given him a task to perform and, duty-bound, he would see it through. Besides, this was a mission that Schwebel personally wanted to succeed. He was joined in the back of the first Packard by the unhappy Plutzar. The curtains on the staff car's rear windows had been drawn for the five-mile run to their destination, for the most part to prevent Dutch civilians along their route from seeing and attempting to harm these Germans.

Into the rear of the second Packard climbed the Wehrmacht's Captain Stoeckle, and, representing the Luftwaffe, First Lieutenant Alexander-Ferdinand von Massow of the 6th Parachute Regiment—in the German military, paratroops were part of the air force.[4] Oberleutnant Von Massow's elder brother was Major General Gerd von Massow, a senior Luftwaffe officer and fighter ace. The younger Von Massow had seen the Allied advance stopped in its tracks at Arnhem, had seen thousands of Allied prisoners marched away to POW camps. As far as he was concerned, the war was not lost, he and his fellow German soldiers had a firm hold on Fortress Holland, and he and his superiors were coming to this meeting to negotiate from a position of strength. It would only be with the German military's cooperation that the proposed Allied food drops could go ahead. There was also the nagging worry that the Allies were up to something. Was this so-called mercy mission a subterfuge? A cover for a bombing campaign perhaps? Or, more likely, would the Allied squadrons actually be carrying paratroops to take up where the last drop of airborne troops had failed the previous year to take Fortress Holland from German hands?

The sedans pulled up outside the school at Achterveld, and the Germans stepped out. A long path led to the school door, where several Allied officers and a handful of Canadian soldiers in berets stood nearby, eying them curiously. In the spirit of the agreed truce, none of those soldiers were visibly armed. The Canadian officer in charge of the delegation's escort led the way up the path, and, in single file and with set expressions on their faces, the Germans strode toward the school door.

Standing under a tree to one side, Andrew Geddes had come out to watch the German delegation arrive and to size them up. He then followed them up the path and entered the schoolhouse via another door. Inside, the Germans were instructed to wait in the hall, and Geddes slipped past them to join General De Guingand in a nearby classroom. De Guingand was impatient to get this all over and done with, but he was determined to keep the Germans on edge, so he kept them waiting several minutes before giving instructions for the senior civil official and senior military man in the delegation to be sent into the classroom to present their credentials.

Schwebel and Stoeckle entered, and, to the irritation of the British officers, Stoeckle gave the Hitler salute, with right arm outstretched and a click of the heels. When Schwebel handed over the delegation's credentials, De Guingand merely glanced at the papers and then handed them to Geddes. The remaining German pair was then called in, and the two parties took seats on either side of two large tables that had been drawn together in the middle of the classroom. The atmosphere was tense as the Germans laid their caps upside down on the table, depositing their gloves inside them.

Geddes unbuckled his briefcase and laid it on the table, ready to remove the documents in English and German that it contained, then studied the faces of the Germans opposite. Schwebel looked to him to be a typical Prussian Junker type from another era, with his prominent nose and dueling scars on his cheeks from his student days. Plutzar looked like a gentleman, out of place among the military men around him. Stoeckle's face glowed with contempt, while young Von Massow's eyes took in everything once he had taken pen and paper from his briefcase and prepared to take notes. He would prove to speak perfect English, and Geddes suspected that Von Massow was an intelligence officer, sent to gain an idea of Allied strength in the sector—which Geddes hoped he would do.

"I have full authority to speak on behalf of the Supreme Commander, General Eisenhower," General De Guingand began before quickly adding, "I don't intend spending too much time on details."[5]

Lieutenant Von Massow was busily noting down every word that was said. A Canadian army interpreter at the table translated from English to German, but every now and then Von Massow would interject to correct the translation.

Like Geddes, De Guingand focused on the faces of the men opposite, hardly able to take his eyes off Schwebel's monstrous nose, the end of which he likened to a pair of strawberries. De Guingand went on to say that, as the Dutch were starving and the Germans were incapable of helping them, the Allies would. "The Air Commodore here has a plan." He nodded to Geddes, who slipped several copies of the draft agreement from his briefcase. "If you carry it out to the detail, we can alleviate the plight of the Dutch. Speed is essential, so I suggest we all get to work in a hurry."

Schwebel replied stonily, using Plutzar as his interpreter, that he could not sign the document. "I am not present to make any deals," he said. "The Reichskommissar has sent me to hear what you have to say. All I am to do is to report back to my superiors."

Geddes glanced at De Guingand, whose face betrayed his annoyance. But the British general took a deep breath and continued, suggesting that they all go through Geddes's proposals. This they did, with Plutzar laboriously translating the dialogue back and forth between the two sides as they proceeded. Geddes's plan provided for a trial run by two Allied bombers to drop food at Duindigt Racetrack near the Dutch capital, The Hague. If they completed the drop without incident, a further 240 bombers would take off later the same day to make drops at six specified locations in western Holland. Apart from the racetrack at Duindigt, these would include airfields serving the major cities of Rotterdam, Amsterdam and The Hague.

De Guingand made it clear that the Allies would not negotiate on any of the points in Geddes's plan, and both sides agreed on specified air corridors along which the Allied bombers making the drops must fly and also agreed that the bombers fly no higher than 400 feet over their targets. An aircraft straying from its air corridor or flying higher than 400 feet would be considered by the German commanders to be flying on an offensive mission and to be a legitimate target for their flak gunners.

With these points agreed upon, De Guingand suggested a second meeting as soon as possible, saying that he expected the Germans to provide experts in all the areas covered by the plan to make sure that it was implemented to the letter. "I expect you to return with proper people, chaps I can deal with."

Schwebel agreed to a second meeting, proposing that it take place in German-held territory. De Guingand quickly scotched that idea, saying that at this stage of the war, the Germans were in no position to dictate where meetings would be held. Schwebel gave way on this, and it was agreed that the next meeting would take place back at the school in Achterveld. It was also agreed that a link would be established between the two sides for the exchange of telegrams. As the meeting was winding up, De Guingand raised the subject of a truce covering German troops and Allied troops in Holland. This, he privately hoped, would be the first step toward German surrender in the Netherlands.

Through Plutzar, Schwebel replied. "If there is to be talk about a truce, the Reichskommissar wishes to meet with General Eisenhower himself." This caused De Guingand and Geddes to glance at each other. "If the Reichskommissar is to make a major decision," Schwebel went on, "then he must confer with the highest Allied general."

With a sigh, De Guingand said that he would see what could be arranged. Schwebel responded that it would take several days for arrangements to be completed on the German side—the assembling and briefing of the experts that De Guingand called for—and for Schwebel to discuss with Seyss-Inquart the Reichskommissar's presence at the next meeting. As the Germans were getting up to leave, the British general added, "I should tell you that General Eisenhower has determined that food drops should commence in Holland tomorrow."[6]

It was the Germans' turn to glance at each other. Then, donning hats and saluting, the delegation members hurriedly took their leave. Out on the path, Schwebel and Plutzar strode along together in whispered conversation, with Stoeckle and then Von Massow following behind.

As the Canadian staff cars drove away, taking the Germans back to their lines, Freddie de Guingand put in an urgent call to Walter Bedell Smith at SHAEF HQ in Reims. De Guingand had not been bluffing about commencing air drops as soon as the next day. Over the past ten days, Eisenhower had been under pressure from the Dutch queen via Prince Bernhard, then from the British prime minister and latterly from General Marshall to implement the mercy mission. Come hell or high water, and even without a signed agreement with the Germans in place, Ike was determined that the first food drops would take place on April 28. Even if it meant risking his aircrews' lives to do it.

12

THE FIRST NERVOUS TEST FLIGHT

The weather over England and northwestern Europe on April 28 had been appalling, with rain and storm lashing airfields and fog reducing visibility to next to nothing, grounding Allied aircraft and putting paid to Eisenhower's plan to commence food drops over Holland at once. But overnight the weather cleared, and early on the morning of Sunday, April 29, a day later than planned, two Lancaster heavy bombers of the Royal Air Force's "special duties" 101 Squadron sat on the tarmac at the Ludford Manga bomber airfield, northeast of the city of Lincoln in the East Midlands, with their engines roaring, ready to start the mission.

Andrew Geddes's plan for the Dutch air drops called for two guinea pigs to test the credibility of the stated intention of Seyss-Inquart not to interfere with relief efforts for the civilian population of western Holland. These bombers were those guinea pigs. If the Germans had not been genuine, or if Seyss-Inquart was unable to prevent German troops in Holland from firing on the two low-flying aircraft, this would be a suicide mission for the crews involved.

One of those crews, in the lead aircraft, consisted of five Canadians and two Britons. Their commander was a twenty-one-year-old combat veteran of two years, Royal Canadian Air Force Captain Robert "Bob" Upcott from Windsor, Ontario. His Lancaster was nicknamed *Bad Penny*—stemming from the old saying "A bad penny always returns"—with the crew hoping and praying that their aircraft would always bring them safely back to base. For the airmen of 101 Squadron, returning safely from their missions was particularly difficult, as this top-secret special squadron had the highest aircraft loss rate of any bomber squadron in Britain's air force.

With the USAAF flying daytime bombing raids over Nazi targets in Europe, RAF Bomber Command flew most of its raids at night. Aircraft of 101 Squadron flew with the night bomber stream carrying one more crewman than the ordinary bomber. Sitting in a curtained-off section near the rear of each aircraft was a German-speaking radio operator. He was in charge of the top-secret "Airborne Cigar" radio equipment aboard, and it was his job to locate the wavelength of the Luftwaffe's ground control radio and either jam it or lock onto it and give German night fighter crews false instructions for intercepting the bombers. The problem with Airborne Cigar was that its equipment gave out powerful radio waves on which the radio direction–finding equipment aboard German night fighters could home in. As a result, 101 Squadron aircraft were often the first to be shot down.

For this mission over Holland, the Airborne Cigar equipment had been stripped from the two chosen aircraft so that, should they be shot down, the state-of-the-art equipment would not fall into enemy hands. Today, each Lancaster carried the normal bombing raid crew of seven. Its payload was far from normal—food for the Dutch, bagged in readiness for being spewed from the bomb bay and onto the drop zone. Behind *Bad Penny* on the tarmac sat a Lancaster with a mixed Australian-British crew commanded by Peter Collett from Sydney, Australia. Like Upcott, Collett was just twenty-one, yet a veteran of several years of the air war over Europe. Like Bob Upcott's crew members,

Collett and his crew were nervous about the mission but impatient to get on with it.

Both aircrews' patience had been tested to the limit the previous day by the atrocious weather. Three times the crews of the two Lancasters had walked out to their aircraft when there was a break in the weather and taken their places for takeoff, only to be ordered each time to stand down as the weather closed in again. The two crews had risen the next day after a sleepless night to a better forecast, and, as the sun rose, a break in the clouds began to appear. The mission was on. It was only when the two crews had received their flight briefing that they knew where they were going and why. At the briefing they were told that ground crews had loaded their ships with large bags of food by climbing in through a small opening in the bomb doors and stacking the bags on the top of the doors.

Sitting at the controls of *Bad Penny*, waiting calmly for the signal to take off, Bob Upcott was habitually chewing gum. He knew that his crew was tense, worried about the mission ahead. At least they knew what to expect with a bombing mission. The flight ahead was a flight into the unknown. And nothing is more scary than the unknown. Still, there had been the usual banter as they prepared for the mission, led by the crew's joker, bulky mid-upper gunner Orval "Ozzie" Blower from Lakeville, Ontario. Little did Upcott know that Blower had been putting on a brave face. Blower was convinced he was going to die that day.[1]

A green Very light arced into the sky from the control tower. The flare from the flare gun, invented by American naval officer Edward Very, was literally the green light for the mission to finally proceed. The four Merlin engines of each Lancaster raced, and first *Bad Penny* and then the second Lancaster lumbered down the runway and slowly clawed their way into the air. Once the bombers were airborne, they found themselves in thick clouds and lost sight of each other. *Bad Penny* was still over England when an 8th Air Force B-17 Flying Fortress suddenly appeared out of the murk on the Lancaster's starboard side, on a collision course with it. Bob Upcott instantly took evasive action. He had two choices—dive or climb. If the B-17 pilot made the same choice as he did, both were dead men. Upcott put the Lancaster into a dive. The B-17 climbed. *Bad Penny*'s radio operator, Stan Jones, calculated that the two bombers missed each other by inches. As Upcott leveled out, there was not a sound from his crew members. They were too shaken to speak.

Upcott crossed the North Sea flying only on instruments, following the heading provided by navigator Bill Walton, a heading that kept them in the "safe" corridor specified by Andrew Geddes and the Germans at the Achterveld meeting two days earlier. The clouds parted, revealing the Dutch coast ahead, and in the clear sky Peter Collett's Lancaster eased in beside *Bad Penny*, flying off its port wing and a little behind. Upcott was keen to get in under German radar so as to not be seen coming, and together the two airplanes dropped to less than fifty feet above the choppy waves. They flew so low that at one point Collett's right wing dipped and the propeller on his starboard outer engine clipped the waves. The engine began to shudder. Collett corrected and flew on. He could have aborted the mission at this point and flown back to base with the excuse of a damaged prop, but there was no way he was pulling out. "He continued on with the engine running a little bit rough," Upcott would later say of his Australian colleague, also noting that a prop damaged in this way could shake an engine from its mounting. And this was enough to bring an aircraft down.[2]

Gaining a little height with land looming ahead, the pair crossed the heavily fortified coast of Holland. Upcott could see not only the barrels of the guns of the German coastal flak posts pointing up at them, he could see the faces of their crews. More than once Upcott found himself literally looking down the barrels of 88 mm guns that could have knocked *Bad Penny* and its companion from the sky. Relieved by the fact that the German guns had remained inactive, Upcott and Collett turned north and flew across the flat Netherlands landscape.

Their target, the Duindigt Racetrack, was a little over six miles north of The Hague at the quaint village of Wassenaar, which grew to become one of the most affluent outer suburbs of the Dutch capital. As recently as the previous month, Wassenaar had been receiving visits from Allied bomber aircraft with more lethal payloads than those being carried by the two Lancasters today—until then, the village had been a German V-2 rocket launch site. To reach his target, Upcott was flying on instructions coming from navigator Walton, who, at the flight crews' briefing, had been given specific man-made landmarks to navigate by— instructions now coming over the intercom.

That morning, in the weak but welcome spring sunshine that was bathing western Holland, fifteen-year-old Dutch boy Peter Buttenaar was walking across a field. Peter was on his way to attempt to steal a little food from a nearby German garrison, something he had succeeded in doing previously. Hearing approaching aircraft engines, he turned to see two Lancaster bombers hurtling toward him, seemingly just feet above the ground.[3]

Running for a ditch, the youth dove in. From the ditch, he looked up just in time to see the two bombers pass overhead and Canadian Bill Gray, bombardier, in the nose of lead aircraft *Bad Penny* wave to him. Years later, Peter Buttenaar would emigrate to Canada, where he would one day meet up with members of the crew of *Bad Penny* and tell them of his experience on that day. He told him that, terrified and convinced that the two bombers were about to crash, killing all on board, he ran all the way home to tell his parents and two elder sisters.[4]

Lead pilot Upcott was looking for a major landmark that was re- ported to be right beside his racetrack target—a five-story Dutch hos- pital with a large red cross painted on its roof to identify it to Allied bombers and ward off air attacks. Spotting the hospital up ahead, Bob

Upcott eased *Bad Penny* down to just fifty feet. Beside him, Collett did the same with his bomber. The deserted expanse of the racetrack loomed up on the Canadian more quickly than he'd expected, and he was almost too late in telling Gray to let their payload go, for the bomb bay doors opened slowly. From the bowels of *Bad Penny,* and moments later from the Australian's airplane, spewed burlap bags filled with flour, margarine, tea and chocolate.

The loads missed the clear space of the track where they were supposed to land and rained down instead on the bleachers beside the finish line, crashing into the wooden tiers of seating, bouncing and sometimes bursting open. But they were down, that was the main thing. As Upcott and Collett applied full power and pulled up the noses of their Lancasters to gain height, they banked left, turning for the coast. At this moment Upcott spotted eight Dutch nurses on the flat roof of the hospital below. From somewhere, the nurses had acquired a large British Union Jack flag, and they flew it, waving excitedly at the bombers climbing away toward the sea. Meanwhile, Upcott's bombardier Bill Gray caught sight of a German tank located beside the hospital. The tank's turret was turning, following the bombers, with its cannon trained on one of them.[5] But it did not fire. Now, as the two Lancasters hastily departed the scene, astonished civilians began to appear at the racetrack and set about collecting the manna from heaven.

Upcott ensured that he was flying the safe corridor out of Holland specified by the Germans and, as they crossed the nearby coastline and were over the North Sea and able to climb to several thousand feet, he followed orders received during their briefing that morning and instructed radio operator Jones to break radio silence and send a message back to base. The message was that the mission had been completed successfully, without incident.[6]

As the two bombers returned to base, completing a flight of a little over two hours, Bomber Command reported to SHAEF that the mission had been a complete success, and SHAEF issued a statement to be released by the BBC when it broadcast the usual eleven-minute Dutch segment that lunch hour, and also by US Armed Forces Radio. In occupied Holland, tens of thousands of Dutch civilians listening on covert radios heard the statement, which announced that, as a result of an agreement between Allied authorities and the German occupying forces in the Netherlands, hundreds of Allied aircraft would that afternoon drop food to the starving Dutch people at six specified locations in western Holland. The broadcast also urged the Dutch people to organize the orderly collection and distribution of the food.

Listening via headphones to the BBC announcement on a secret crystal set radio in the basement of his family's house in Rotterdam's Dunantstraat was teenager Henry Ridder. As his younger brother Willem, or "Wim" as he was known in the family, joined him and asked what the latest news was, Henry took the headphones from his ears and excitedly told Wim that General Eisenhower's headquarters was sending hundreds of airplanes to drop food to the Dutch, at Rotterdam and other places, that very afternoon. The airplanes, he said, must already be on their way! The pair ran upstairs to the kitchen, where the rest of the family was huddled around a tiny stove in their winter coats, trying to get warm.

When Henry blurted the news, no one would believe him. The boys' mother was especially disbelieving. She could not imagine how it could be done and was convinced that food dropped from airplanes would fall apart. She shook her head. "They won't do that."[7]

But Henry could not be discouraged or dissuaded. He reported that the BBC had said the airplanes carrying out the food drops would be flying at rooftop height. They would be easy to see, he declared. Between them, the boys were able to convince all the family to go out onto their balcony, which had a wide view of the surroundings. And there they waited, with ears pricked for the sound of aircraft engines and eyes peeled for signs of the air armada promised by the BBC.

The German authorities in Holland had also heard the radio announcements from London. In response, the Luftwaffe and the Wehrmacht rushed antiaircraft guns and troops to four of the six locations in case the drops were a cover for landings by paratroops, and the Sicherheitsdienst (SD) sent men to all the locations with instructions to open food-drop packages at random to make sure they did not contain weapons for Dutch Resistance fighters.

At 2:30 that afternoon, 240 Lancasters laden with food took off from bases throughout southeast England and flew to the six Dutch targets, including Rotterdam, preceded by sixteen twin-engine Mosquito fighter-bombers acting as pathfinders. In Rotterdam, the Ridders had been waiting for some time by mid-afternoon; just as several members of the family were giving up, there was a faint humming in the distance that grew into a mighty throb. It was aircraft, but they were flying very low, as Henry had predicted. And then, to their utter astonishment, a Lancaster bomber flew low past their balcony, seemingly close enough to reach out and touch. As it passed, the bomber waggled its wings, seeming to wave at the Ridder family.

A picture of that airplane would lodge in the memory of young Wim Ridder for the rest of his days. Its markings, with the letters *XY* on one side of the RAF roundel, and *S* on the other side of it, would be permanently imprinted in his mind. Wim burst into tears of joy. And then the sky in front of the family was filled with low-flying bombers, all turning toward the avenue called the Pieter de Hoochweg, which contained buildings housing German headquarters in the port city.

"Come on!" yelled Henry, heading for the stairs, with Wim close on his heels.

The two boys led the family in a rush downstairs and into the street to follow the course of the stream of bombers. As the family ran to the Pieter de Hoochweg, many more Rotterdam residents came out into the streets to join the crowds. Wim Ridder looked at the buildings lining the elegant avenue and saw German clerks and secretaries leaning out windows and actually waving to the aircraft as they passed overhead. Did they think they were German airplanes, or were they welcoming the Allied bombers? In contrast, Wim saw that, outside a university building on Pieter de Hoochweg (today part of the Hogeschool University of Applied Sciences), the two German sentries on duty at the gate dashed to don their gasmasks, thinking it must be an air raid.

As Wim returned his eyes to the sky, the wave of bombers flew on toward the Maas River and the Waalhaven Airport on the south side of the river. And as he watched, bomb bay doors opened and food packages fell like confetti toward the airport. Absolutely elated, and convinced that the war was at an end, the Ridder family returned to their home. Only then did Wim Ridder notice that in his excitement he had run out into the street wearing just socks on his feet.[8]

The aircraft that Wim Ridder had seen right outside his family's balcony, the Lancaster with the markings *XY-S,* was a bomber from the RAF's 186 Squadron code-named *S for Sugar.* It was piloted by Alexander "Alex" Howell, another twenty-one-year-old Aussie, from Geelong in the Australian state of Victoria. Four days earlier, Howell and his 186 Squadron crew had flown their last bombing mission, dropping a blockbuster bomb on Hitler's Eagle's Nest retreat at Berchtesgaden high in the mountains of Bavaria.

That night raid by a number of British, Canadian and Australian bomber squadrons followed on the heels of a daylight raid by the US 8th Air Force on the same target. It wasn't that the mission's planners expected Hitler to be in Berchtesgaden. The bombers had been sent to pulverize the fuehrer's favorite retreat as a symbolic gesture. The aircrews participating in these two raids had no idea that Hermann Goering, number two in the Nazi hierarchy and chief of the Luftwaffe, had been sheltering in a tunnel through the mountains below them as their bombs rained down, with his entire Luftwaffe High Command staff—they had evacuated to Berchtesgaden from Potsdam to escape Allied bombing. Goering had become a prisoner of the SS, who arrested him on the orders of Hitler's secretary Martin Bormann. Goering's crime had been the suggestion that, with Hitler trapped in Berlin, the Reichsmarshall might initiate peace negotiations with the Allied powers.[9]

Now Alex Howell and his 186 Squadron colleagues were in unfamiliar territory in more ways than one. For the past three years, they had been flying night raids. All of a sudden, not only was their bomb bay full of nothing more lethal than cigarettes and chocolate, they were expected to fly in daylight, and at just 400 feet. And with the fear that the Germans might fire at them. Grimly, Howell had taken his Lancaster down to cross the Dutch coast at the prescribed height, leaving behind the rough North Sea. First passing over coastal batteries with silent guns pointing their way, he'd followed the rest of the squadron inland. Guided by the voice of his navigator Denis Down in his ears, Howell had sent their Lancaster flitting over the Dutch countryside toward Rotterdam and their assigned drop zone at Waalhaven Airport.

Flying low over the city center, the bombers of 186 Squadron banked to commence their run to the airport on the south side of the Maas River. It was at this point that the Ridder family had seen them pass and had run into the street to follow their progress. Ahead of the bombers, Alex Howell could see to one side a hospital with a huge red cross painted on its roof. As with the hospital at Wassenaar, the red cross was designed to identify it in the hope of preventing Allied air attacks. There were Dutch nurses on the hospital roof, waving like crazy people at the bombers, using towels and anything else they could lay their hands on.

Then, in the open, there appeared another massive cross, white this time, laid by Luftwaffe personnel using bed sheets. Earlier, four fast Mosquito fighter-bombers had been supposed to drop flares to identify the drop zone, but by the time Howell's bomber arrived, the white cross was the sole marker of the bombers' target. Howell and his crew could see hundreds of civilians surrounding the drop zone—mainly old men and women and children. Just like the nurses at the hospital, these people had heard or been told about the same broadcast that young Henry Ridder had listened to, a broadcast that had named the drop locations. And this had brought the people thronging to the site to collect the goodies, rushing like ants to spilled honey.

As the bombers ahead of *S for Sugar* opened their bomb bays and rained down bags of food, many of those people excitedly ran out to grab them, ignoring the aircraft that still had to let go their consignments. Alex Howell's bomb bay doors opened, and out spewed his load, right on target. Howell's radio operator Peter Weston felt sure that they must have hit some of the people down there with the contents of their drop. In fact, a small number of people would be injured during the food drops in just this manner, hit by falling containers. *S for Sugar* turned for home, and, two hours and forty minutes after takeoff, Alex Howell landed his ship back at base in England, where he and his crew celebrated the completion of the most unusual mission they had ever flown.

Following the corridors set down by the Germans, all the aircraft on the mass run of April 29 made their food drops on the six specified targets—with German flak guns pointing at them and SD secret policemen checking their loads once they hit terra firma. The Lancasters dropped 526 tons of food to the Dutch on this first anxious day of the mission, delivering more than the Luftwaffe had managed to send in a day to Stalingrad at the height of its 1942–43 airlift. And the USAAF had yet to join the operation.

At SHAEF, when news of this success was received, there were smiles all around. Ike and Beetle knew that if the Germans would hold to the cease-fire, the airlift stood a good chance of saving the Dutch. On the ground, under the eyes of German troops and black-uniformed Dutch police, tens of thousands of civilians converged on the drop zones.

Yet, to the amazement of many who expected that, after the deprivations suffered during the Hunger Winter, all public discipline would break down following these food drops, with people greedily taking away all they could carry and fighting among themselves, the Dutch acted with enormous restraint and civility, gathering and piling up the supplies for organized distribution. At the same time, the Germans made no attempt to keep any of the food for themselves.

At Schiphol Airport alone, 4,000 Dutch men, women and children formed into collection teams that carefully collected, stacked and catalogued the food before it was distributed far and wide by Dutch civil officials. The only means of mass transport that remained to the Dutch took the form of the barges that plied the many canals of western Holland, and these were loaded up. In the end, the people of the major cities of Holland were delivered their share of the April 29 bounty by volunteers on bicycles and on foot.

What most Dutch to this day do not know is that Prince Bernhard was behind this organized collection and distribution of the food dropped by the Allied bombers. The creator of the detailed air-drop plan, Air Commodore Andrew Geddes, was aware of this. From the outset he had been concerned that it was not enough just to drop the food over Holland. For the operation to be a success, that food had to be gotten to those who needed it, especially the young and the elderly who were confined to their beds or their homes. Prince Bernhard, Geddes was to say, made that possible.[10]

Geddes also knew from SHAEF intelligence that there were a number of competing Dutch Resistance groups on the ground, with no central control of Resistance activities. Fortunately for the operation, and for the Dutch, nearly all the Resistance groups respected and bowed to the will of Queen Wilhelmina, who had arrived back in Holland from England on April 26. She had set foot on home soil again with the same single suitcase with which she had departed in 1940. Flying back with her daughter Princess Juliana and three staff members, the queen had chosen a deserted castle, Anneville, near Breda, as her temporary home until she could return to The Hague and the sovereign's palace following the liberation of the Dutch capital.

The majority of Resistance leaders also respected the queen's choice of Prince Bernhard as head of the Dutch military. Geddes had contacted Prince Bernhard, who by this time had his headquarters at Spelderholt, near Apeldoorn in the liberated sector of southeastern Holland. Geddes was full of praise for the enthusiasm and sense of urgency that Bernhard had brought to the table when advocating Allied food deliveries to the Dutch months before, when everyone else had been skeptical, even suspicious. Geddes filled the prince in on the air-drop plan and sought his help in organizing the efficient distribution of food once it hit the ground. Bernhard had told Geddes to leave the problem for him to sort out in occupied Holland, using his many contacts there. Which he did.

"Great credit is due His Royal Highness Prince Bernhard of the Netherlands," said Geddes forty years later, "who was the 'linch-pin' of the very complex organization involved in getting the foodstuffs from the airfields to the actual distribution points in occupied territory."[11]

To show how efficient the system organized by the prince proved to be, on May 1, two days after the first food drops of April 29, the family of Peter Buttenaar, the boy spooked in the field by pilots Upcott and Collett on the morning of the trial flight, would receive its ration of food after the distribution of the first drop at Wassenaar. In the same orderly way, food reached families in cities and towns throughout western Holland in the first days of May.

It was only after the pair of trial-run bombers piloted by Upcott and Collett had landed back at Ludford Manga in Lincolnshire that the two aircrews came to comprehend what an important and risky role they had played in launching one of the greatest airlift operations of the war. Back on the ground, Collett, accompanied by a curious Upcott, went to check the propeller on the Australian's starboard outer engine, the one that had clipped the water. Standing beneath the engine, they could see that the ends of the prop blades had been bent back by their brief contact with the waves on the low-flying inbound run across the North Sea. "All three blade tips were bent backward so perfectly they retained a semblance of balance," Upcott was to observe.[12] Without that balance, Collett's Lancaster may have ended up in the sea.

A day later, Bob Upcott received an interesting piece of information about his own aircraft from his ground crew. As they'd been giving *Bad Penny* the usual once-over following its mercy mission, the maintenance men had found a new bullet hole in the fuselage, on the right side of the aircraft, near the tail. *Bad Penny*'s ground crew worked out that the hole had been created by a 9 mm bullet, the kind fired by German pistols.[13] Apparently, a German officer had fired his pistol at the bomber as it flew low overhead on April 29. Upcott had to wonder how many other Germans would likewise lose their cool, disobey orders, and fire at the waves of Allied aircraft that were due to take part in the operation in the coming days. For, as Upcott was aware, the Germans had yet to sign a single document agreeing to authorize the flights and to hold their fire.

THAT SAME SUNDAY, young Canadian captain Farley Mowat was in Amsterdam together with his adventurous superior, Major Ken Cottam. Cottam seemed unconcerned that the truce he had supposedly agreed to with General Blaskowitz had not yet come into effect; Cottam was thinking about his next adventures. While in Amsterdam over the previous two days, Cottam and Mowat had witnessed skirmishes between increasingly bold Dutch Resistance members and Dutch Nazis—briefly joining one such skirmish in the Dam Square. They had heard of collaborators being executed by the Resistance and had seen Dutch women being paraded through the streets with heads shaved and daubed with paint, accused of sharing the beds of German soldiers of the occupying forces.[14]

But Amsterdam was still a city under German military occupation, and Mowat would note that there were a surprising number of civilians in the streets this Sunday, all in a celebratory mood. He didn't have a chance to find out why. In fact, the food drops from the air that day had convinced many Amsterdam residents that the end of the war was as imminent as the next morning and created a false sense of security among many in the population. But the German military, the SS, the SD and the local Nazis still controlled the city, and high hopes for liberation overnight would be dashed.

The truce between Allied troops and German troops in Holland that Ken Cottam would take credit for came into effect this Sunday. The negotiations at Achterveld had finally cemented this truce in place, with Arthur Seyss-Inquart instructing General Blaskowitz to observe it to permit the food-relief operations to go forward. The irrepressible Major Ken Cottam, meanwhile, was spoiling for a new exploit—he wanted to be the first Allied officer to enter Rotterdam, Holland's premier port city. That afternoon, he, Mowat and Mowat's orderly, Doc MacDonald, were on the move again, trying to depart from Amsterdam to drive to Rotterdam.[15]

Inside the city of Amsterdam, the sight of these three Allied soldiers in a jeep brought excited crowds of civilians thronging into the trio's path. Some thought that the sight of a Canadian army jeep in their city meant that liberation day had come. But one jeepload of Canadians did not a liberation make. Puzzled Dutch made way for the lone jeep. Once out of the city and driving on the highway beside Schiphol Airport, the location for Amsterdam's now daily food drops, Cottam had to push through formations of disciplined and heavily armed German troops who were stationed there to watch the drops—their superiors continued to fear that the Allies would make a paratroop landing under cover of the food drops. As wary German troops blocked the jeep's way, Cottam again gave a confident tongue-lashing in German to anyone who dared defy him. The way opened up, and Cottam was able to drive them out into the countryside and head south for Rotterdam.

That night of April 29–30, en route to Rotterdam, Cottam, Mowat and MacDonald would stay in a former German officers' club, drink it dry and trash it—with Cottam driving their jeep in through a front window. Fortified by drink, MacDonald, a slight, normally quiet fellow, surprised Mowat by spraying bullets from his Thompson submachine gun all over the building's ornate plaster ceiling.

Mowat was by this time a grudging participant in Cottam's games; he had grown weary of the manic major's adventures and of the war. Nonetheless, he had no choice but to obey orders and go wherever Cottam dictated. Mowat was to confess that he had in fact become frightened of Cottam, who was increasingly looking less like a genius and more like a madman. Mowat was now praying for the war to end as soon as possible so that he would survive Cottam's antics. He only hoped that their sojourn behind German lines had not screwed up any genuinely important official initiatives.[16] As it happened, one of those initiatives was still to play itself out at Achterveld.

Lieutenant General Walter Bedell Smith. As chief of staff to Supreme Allied Commander General Dwight D. Eisenhower, it was his job to organize Operation Chowhound and conduct face-to-face negotiations with the Nazis to permit the operation to go ahead. Photograph courtesy of the Library of Congress, Prints and Photographs Division, LC-USZ62-93383.

Lieutenant Colonel "Grif"
Mumford, who led the first
American air raid on Berlin,
and then Major General Jimmy
Doolittle, who led the first
American air raid on Tokyo.
Doolittle was in command of
Operation Chowhound, while
Mumford was in charge of
implemention for the 3rd Air
Division of the USAAF's 8th Air
Force. Photograph courtesy
of the 95th Bomb Group
Heritage Association,
Horham, England.

German-born Prince
Bernhard with his
wife, Princess Juliana
of Holland, and their
daughters. Photograph
courtesy of the
Library and Archives
Canada, accession
number 1964-087
NPC, C-038996.

May 3, 1945, the third day of
Operation Chowhound. B-17Gs
of the 412th Squadron, 95th
Bomb Group, drop their loads of
K-rations from low level at an
airfield at Utrecht in German-
occupied Holland. The B-17
in this picture, Umbriago,
was piloted by F. F. Beard. The
bomber partly in picture in the
foreground was piloted by D. D.
Shulz. Photograph courtesy
of the 95th Bomb Group
Heritage Association,
Horham, England.

Norman Coats of the 390th Bomb Group, guarded food stockpiles on May 1, then flew his first Chowhound mission as an air gunner the next day. Photograph courtesy of Eric Heijink, Operation Manna website, Holland.

B-17s skim low over rooftops of The Hague on their way to make a Chowhound drop. Photograph courtesy of Eric Heijink, Operation Manna website, Holland.

Dutch civilians gather food sacks at Terbregge after a Chowbound drop. Photograph courtesy of Eric Heijink, Operation Manna website, Holland.

Claude Hall's crew with their Flying Fortress Hotter 'N Hell, 390th Bomb Group. Photograph courtesy of Eric Heijink, Operation Manna website, Holland.

Taken from Hotter 'N Hell, *B-17s of the 390th Bomb Group fly low over the Dutch coast on their way to make a Chowhound run as German guns below remain silent.* Photograph courtesy of Eric Heijink, Operation Manna website, Holland.

Robert L. Miller and his 493rd Bomb Group crew were among the thousands of B-17 aircrew from ten 8th Air Force bomb groups who took part in Operation Chowhound. Photograph courtesy of Eric Heijink, Operation Manna website, Holland.

At the Acterveld Conference, April 30, 1945, Prince Bernhard (middle), with an unidentified American officer, surveying RK-1, Nazi Reichskommissar Seyss-Inquart's Mercedes limousine, which Bernhard had appropriated. Photograph courtesy of J. M. DeGuire/Canada. Dept. of National Defence/Library and Archives Canada/PA-134409.

May 8, 1945, the day the war in Europe ended, Arthur Seyss-Inquart (2nd from right), Nazi governor of occupied Holland, lands at Hengelo, Holland in the custody of former "Mounty" Lieutenant Colonel George Ball (3rd from left), of the 1st Canadian Army. Photograph courtesy of C. E. Neye/Canada Dept. of National Defence/Library and Archives Canada/ PA-176570.

13

IKE'S HATCHET MAN TELLS THE NAZI GOVERNOR STRAIGHT

Andrew Geddes noticed that Beetle Bedell Smith was in a bad mood when he arrived at Achterveld's St. Joseph's School on the morning of Monday, April 30.[1] Reichskommissar Seyss-Inquart was coming to meet personally with Eisenhower's deputy to put his seal of approval on the food-drop operation and to very visibly associate himself with the mercy mission. Bedell Smith had already signed off on Geddes's operational plan, which would see more than 800 heavy bombers delivering up to 1,800 tons of food to the Dutch every day for as long as needed. He had also approved plans for tons more food to be brought into Rotterdam by sea from neutral Sweden and by road from the Canadian sector in southern Holland. He wasn't asking Seyss-Inquart and his lackeys for permission. He was telling them that this was how it was going to be.

From the latest intelligence out of occupied Holland, Bedell Smith knew, as Dwight Eisenhower knew, that four days earlier the final government distribution of flour had been made to bakeries in Dutch cities. And the Germans had no plans to share their military food stockpiles with the civilian population. Every day that passed meant that more vulnerable young and elderly Dutch would perish. That knowledge was enough to make General Bedell Smith even more irritable. But it was the demanding Arthur Seyss-Inquart who annoyed him most of all. As much as the general wanted this operation to proceed, taking time out from marshaling the Allied war machine in northwest Europe to nail the Nazi governor to the agreement that Andrew Geddes had put together was not something Bedell Smith wanted to waste too much time on.

Even Seyss-Inquart had realized that it was futile to expect the Allied Supreme Commander himself to meet his original demand to turn up for this meeting. Eisenhower was busy running a war while Seyss-Inquart was only running a backwater. Haughty the Austrian may have been, but he was also a pragmatist. A pragmatist with an eye to his own future. And Eisenhower's right-hand man was still someone he felt he could deal with and retain his dignity, while putting on the record at the highest level his willingness to be seen as a man of compassion, not a war criminal. Such a conference with General Bedell Smith was not a meeting that would go unnoticed once the war was over and the Allies were bent on bringing senior Nazis to account; or so Seyss-Inquart hoped.

General Bedell Smith wanted to get this conference over and done with as quickly as possible, but as Ike's representative there were formalities he first had to observe. As a courtesy to the Russians, who were equal partners in the agreements negotiated by Soviet premier Josef Stalin with the other senior Allied partners, Roosevelt for the United States and Churchill for Britain, Bedell Smith had sent a message to Moscow, inviting the Russians to send a military delegation to these talks with the German governor of Holland. To the surprise of many, the Russians had promptly assigned a senior representative to the meeting. Major General Ivan Susloparov, who was based with the Russian delegation to Paris, turned up at Achterveld for this latest meeting.

Susloparov, an artillery general, came with a sizeable entourage, all in uniform, and the Communist officers trooped into the Catholic schoolhouse, crunching over the covering of snow that coated the ground. Indoors, they joined General Bedell Smith and other senior Allied military representatives, including Freddie de Guingand, Lieutenant General John Clark, who was chief SHAEF liaison officer to the Dutch government, Major General George Strong, SHAEF's chief of intelligence, and Major General Alexander Galloway, commander Holland District, who was responsible for stockpiling food for delivery into Holland by road.

Representing the Dutch government, Prince Bernhard had been among the first to arrive at Achterveld that morning, driving himself there from his field headquarters at Spelderholt. Just as he flew himself, Bernhard always drove himself wherever he went, in staff car or jeep. It may have been partly through a desire to display a "common touch," but Bernhard also loved driving. He particularly loved big powerful cars. The car he drove today turned a lot of heads. It was Reichskommissar Seyss-Inquart's big black Mercedes cabriolet limousine, which had been "liberated" by the Dutch Resistance some weeks before and presented to Bernhard.

The powerful Mercedes now had large white stars painted on the front doors, hood and trunk to identify it as an Allied vehicle, but Bernhard had deliberately retained the sedan's Nazi registration plate, emblazoned with RK-1, identifying it as the Reichskommissar's former property. Bernhard, behind the wheel of the Mercedes, and escorted by a jeepload of Canadian troops, parked directly outside the front gate of St. Joseph's School, precisely where the German delegation would be set down.

Red, white and blue Dutch flags hung everywhere, and many Achterveld residents had gathered to watch the day's comings and goings. Kept back by Canadian troops, they cheered Prince Bernhard and called out greetings to him and his family as he alighted from the big Mercedes. Two young Dutch girls, Marietje and Corrie Kok, were permitted to approach the prince with their mother, bearing a bunch of flowers. As the girls presented the flowers to the bareheaded, bespectacled prince, they said, in Dutch, "Happy birthday to Princess Juliana."

Bernhard looked suddenly embarrassed as he accepted the bouquet. Consumed with war matters and working an average of sixteen hours a day, he had entirely forgotten that today, April 30, was his wife's thirty-sixth birthday.[2] The prince turned to his accompanying staff, including chief of staff Colonel Charles van Houten. None of his Dutch assistants had remembered that it was Princess Juliana's birthday either. When Bernhard telephoned his wife later that day with belated birthday wishes, she told him that she found it hard to believe he had forgotten her birthday, but he eventually convinced her and won her forgiveness. For now, Bernhard put his faux pas behind him and waited, leaning on the Nazi governor's former limousine, for the man himself to put in an appearance.

Finally, at precisely 12:30 p.m., the Germans arrived, once again in a convoy of Canadian army staff cars and jeeps with fluttering white flags. It was a much larger German contingent that attended this meeting. Not only had Seyss-Inquart himself come to Achterveld, he had brought experts from the German air force, army and navy with him. This meeting was designed to formalize the air drops of food over occupied Holland and also to agree on food shipments by sea from Sweden and by road via the Canadian zone in Holland. Out of the lead Canadian car stepped Seyss-Inquart, in a long greatcoat and peaked cap.

Dutch onlookers booed him loudly although he seemed not to notice. His attention had been grabbed by the sight of his former limousine, with the new owner, Prince Bernhard, lounging against it. Bernhard saw the Austrian's face drop. Then, composing himself, the Nazi governor quickly walked up the path to the school entrance, with his limp evident. Other members of his party followed briskly in ones and twos, among them Lieutenant General Hermann Plocher, Luftwaffe commander in

Holland. A junior German officer trotted to catch up with his superiors as a Canadian army cinematographer captured the arrivals briefly on celluloid from a building across the road.

A group of seven men in civilian clothes who had arrived in this final convoy hung back from the German party. All were Dutch—civilian officials employed by the German occupation government at The Hague. They were led by Dr. Stephanus L. Louwes, secretary-general for food distribution in occupied Holland. Seyss-Inquart had brought the Dutch officials along so that they could organize the distribution of food aid once it was delivered to occupied Holland by the Allies. Louwes and his staff had always made their antipathy toward their German masters obvious, but Seyss-Inquart had nonetheless retained their services because they were supremely efficient in delivering food to their countrymen. Anxious not to be considered part of the German contingent, and to avoid being accused of being Nazi collaborators once the war was over, Louwes and his fellow Dutch officials asked to be treated as a separate delegation.

Prince Bernhard now came to them and, speaking Dutch, welcomed them warmly, handing out the first real cigarettes they had smoked in years and putting them at ease. Bernhard also made sure that once the seven Dutchmen were led into the school, they were kept apart from Seyss-Inquart and his party, who had been ushered into a classroom and told to wait. Andrew Geddes, standing outside the schoolhouse to watch the various delegations arrive, was touched by the emotion on the faces of the Dutchmen—they were all in tears as they spoke with the prince and members of his staff. As a consequence of Bernhard's cordial reception, Louwes and his officials would work very closely with him in the days and weeks ahead.

All the various delegations had now arrived, including several representatives from neutral Sweden who would act as observers. In one school classroom the men of the Allied delegations were provided with the best refreshments that could be organized. The Germans, waiting in another room, were offered combat rations. As 1:00 p.m. approached, all were ushered into a single classroom and took their seats, with the senior delegates facing each other across a long table.

At one o'clock, proceedings began, with British general Freddie de Guingand, who had chaired the last meeting here at Achterveld, taking up where he'd left off, repeating the proposals that he had sent Reichsrichter Schwebel away with on April 28. General Bedell Smith then took over, with the American declaring, in his inimitable businesslike way, that the objects of the meeting were two-fold. First, the feeding of the Dutch population, prisoners of war, political prisoners and internees in German-occupied Holland. And second, the discussion of the proposed truce in Holland, a truce that would allow the first objective to be achieved. Bedell Smith then asked Seyss-Inquart if he agreed to the implementation of the overall food-delivery plan and, if so, whether a detailed examination by both sides could proceed.

Through the interpreters, Seyss-Inquart agreed that negotiations on individual points in the Allied proposals could now commence. The conference broke up into a series of smaller meetings, all with their own interpreters. The air force men from both sides met with Dutch officials to haggle over the fine points of the air drops. The navy men and Dutch officials discussed the delivery of food by sea from Sweden with the German navy providing an escort and opening the port of Rotterdam to enable the unloading. Army commanders and Dutch officials worked through plans for distribution of food on the ground and the delivery of food by road, rail and canal from the Canadian sector to occupied Holland. This latter activity, involving road convoys as well as train and barge transport, had its own Allied code name, Operation Faust.

Watching the study groups getting down to work, with the room filled with the buzz of numerous voices all talking at once, General De Guingand found it difficult to believe that he wasn't dreaming. He almost had to pinch himself as a reminder that these were senior Nazi officers sitting with the Allied officers in civil, constructive conversation after years of trying to kill each other. He would later say that in many ways it looked like a British army staff-college exercise.[3]

In the air-drop study group—which was chaired by Andrew Geddes and covered the single largest and most important part of the proposed food program—Geddes found his Luftwaffe counterparts determined to drag their feet over the drop zones that he had chosen. As each was raised, General Plocher and his subordinates found reason after reason why they were not suitable. It would turn out that the German military commanders in Fortress Holland were preoccupied with the fear that the Allies would use the food drops as a cover for dropping paratroops on the chosen airfields in order to seize them in advance of a full-scale Allied invasion of western Holland. Geddes had come prepared for such German intransigence, and he countered each argument with a range of facts and figures, winning the point each time.

As the study groups did their work, General Bedell Smith invited Seyss-Inquart, his interpreter, Prince Bernhard, General De Guingand and several others into another room. A bottle of gin was opened and glasses were shared all around. Bedell Smith had decided to use the time being taken by the detailed negotiations to tackle Seyss-Inquart on the subject of a German surrender in Holland—separate from any German surrender elsewhere. The sooner the Germans in Holland could be disarmed, the sooner Bedell Smith could direct troops and resources elsewhere. Bedell Smith was to say later that he'd had one driving imperative for months: "Our task was to end the war swiftly and conclusively."[4]

Seyss-Inquart seemed pleased by the American general's apparent hospitable attitude, but he was no fool and didn't relax his guard. Through the interpreter, the gruff Bedell Smith explained to the Nazi leader that General Eisenhower had been very disturbed by the plight of the Dutch people and was going to hold their German occupiers responsible for any disasters in Holland. He was especially concerned about further flooding of the Dutch countryside, telling Seyss-Inquart, "What has been flooded so far can be justified from the military point of view. If you flood any more now, it is no longer justifiable."[5]

Seyss-Inquart acknowledged this.

Then Bedell Smith said, "It will only be a matter of weeks, or perhaps days, before Germany must admit complete and absolute defeat."

"I entirely agree," Seyss-Inquart replied, surprising Bedell Smith and those with him with his frankness.

"Then why not surrender now?" Bedell Smith suggested.

Seyss-Inquart responded that it was not as simple as that. The previous evening, he had received a telephone call from an anxious General Blaskowitz at his Hilversum headquarters; he had just been contacted by his military superiors in Berlin, who had heard that Seyss-Inquart was up to something and had demanded to know what was going on in Holland. Blaskowitz had panicked, not wishing to be shot as a traitor in the last days of the war, and had pulled rank. Seyss-Inquart now told Bedell-Smith that he had not received any orders from Berlin that would allow him to initiate surrender talks. That, he said, was a matter for the military commander in chief in Holland—General Blaskowitz.

Bedell Smith shrugged. "But, surely, Herr Reichskommissar," he said, "it is the politicians who dictate the policy to the soldiers." He added that, in any event, his information was that no real military high command continued to exist in Germany.

This made a visible impression on Seyss-Inquart as it was translated for him, but he kept up a brave face, asking in return what future generations of Germans would say of him if he ordered a German capitulation in the Netherlands. Seyss-Inquart clearly thought that there would be a place for him in German history, whatever he did.

Bedell Smith now lost patience with the Nazi. "General Eisenhower has instructed me to say that he will hold you directly responsible for any further useless bloodshed," he said gravely. "You have lost the war and you know it. And if through pig-headedness, you cause more loss of life to Allied troops or Dutch civilians, you will have to pay the penalty. And you know what that means—the wall and the firing squad."

This jolted Seyss-Inquart. He seemed to lose his voice for a moment, and Freddie de Guingand, watching him intently, saw his eyes water behind his thick round spectacles. The Reichskommissar then replied, his voice a hoarse whisper, "I am not afraid—I am a German."

Bedell Smith sat back, saying that he wondered if Seyss-Inquart realized that he was giving him his last chance to save his own neck by ordering the surrender of the 120,000 German troops in occupied Holland. Seyss-Inquart answered that he was well aware of that. "You know the feelings of the Dutch people toward you?" Bedell Smith continued. "You know you will probably be shot?"

Seyss-Inquart replied, softly, "That leaves me cold."

"It usually does," said Bedell Smith.[6]

The conversation, and Bedell Smith's snappy final response, would be repeated with many a smile through the corridors of SHAEF and beyond. But Seyss-Inquart would not budge, would not order General Blaskowitz to surrender his army.

Once the study groups had completed their work, the conference broke up. Seyss-Inquart was about to step into a Canadian army Packard for the return to Fortress Holland when Schwebel hurried to join him and tugged at his sleeve. Schwebel had lingered behind as the meeting broke up, entering into urgent conversation with Bedell Smith. Schwebel, who had learned that Bedell Smith's grandfather had served as an officer in the German army in times past, had told the American that while he didn't care about his own future—his wife and sons had been killed in the war—he harbored hopes of securing a negotiated peace and felt that "many lives might be saved by resuming the conversation." Bedell Smith had indicated that he was open to any proposal that brought a swift conclusion to hostilities, and Schwebel now proposed to Seyss-Inquart that he ask Bedell Smith for a safe-conduct to go to Berlin to negotiate a German capitulation across all fronts.[7]

Seyss-Inquart, picturing a role for himself in international politics following the war, warmed to Schwebel's idea and sent his underling back to the American general. But Bedell Smith vetoed the idea on the spot, telling Schwebel that senior German military commanders could approach Allied Supreme Commander Eisenhower following the usual "customs of war" and surrender to him, while Seyss-Inquart was at liberty to surrender Holland at once.[8]

Schwebel returned to Seyss-Inquart with a very different take on Bedell Smith's response to his proposal. He told the Reichskommissar that Bedell Smith was taking the proposition of a safe-conduct to Berlin to General Eisenhower. It is possible that Schwebel misunderstood Bedell Smith. It is equally possible that Schwebel deliberately lied to Seyss-Inquart to give him false hopes about his own future and to ensure that he did not change his mind about cooperating over the delivery of food to the Dutch by the Allies. As a result of this last-minute exchange, Seyss-Inquart left Achterveld in much better spirits than when he'd arrived. Back in German-controlled Holland, he parted from Louwes and his Dutch officials by remarking on what he felt had been a very successful Achterveld conference, describing their "magnificent reception" by the Allies.[9]

General Bedell Smith meanwhile returned to Reims to report in person to General Eisenhower. The Supreme Commander would in turn write the Allied war leaders that while the Achterveld conference had been a total success with respect to the "introduction of food into western Holland," results were otherwise "entirely negative" in terms of a German surrender in Holland.[10]

The Netherlands would continue under German rule. But American food drops to the starving millions there would commence at once.

14

THE US 8TH AIR FORCE
PREPARES FOR CHOWHOUND

From 1943 to 1945, the US 8th Air Force had its English wartime headquarters outside the town of High Wycombe in Buckinghamshire. Surrounded by rolling green fields and trees, Daws Hill Lodge had previously been a posh girls' school and, prior to that, part of the estate of the Marquess of Lincolnshire. The ivy-clad buildings now housed the quarters and offices of Lieutenant General James "Jimmy" Doolittle, commander of the 8th in 1945, and the officers and men who planned and sent the fighter and bomber aircraft of the 8th on their missions each day.

General Doolittle was famous for his daring and his can-do attitude. Prior to the war he had gained fame as an air racer, winning numerous international air race trophies and holding an air speed record at one time. Doolittle had conceived and, in April 1942, led, the first US bomber mission against the Japanese mainland, the famous Doolittle Raid. Doolittle's sixteen Mitchell B-25B medium bombers had struck Tokyo and four other major Japanese cities after launching from an aircraft carrier in the North Pacific, with most landing in China after surprising the Japanese with their audacity. Once Doolittle returned to the United States, President Roosevelt presented him with the Medal of Honor for the raid.

General Doolittle and his 8th Air Force planners had specified that the major American contribution to the Dutch food airlift be known as Operation Chowhound. As far as Doolittle was concerned, if his aircrew was putting their lives on the line for the Dutch, those airmen had to know, from the get-go, what they were doing and why.

It was agreed with SHAEF that Chowhound drops were to take place between 7:00 a.m. and 3:00 p.m. each day. For their first day of drops, the 8th Air Force would use the same four drop zones as the RAF—Valkenburg airfield near Leiden, Duindigt Racetrack, Ypenburg airfield at The Hague, and Terbregge airfield outside Rotterdam— following the path established by the first two days of drops and taking on board the lessons learned during those early sorties. Importantly, by simply upping the number of aircraft flying the now established corridors to the first four drop zones, the Allied air forces were less likely to spook nervous Germans on the ground.

Over successive days, the USAAF would expand its operations to take in half a dozen drop zones. The additional DZs were mostly Dutch airfields. The best known was Schiphol Airport at Amsterdam, which, prior to the war, had been Holland's premier international aeronautical gateway, as it is today. Its wide runways were pitted with bomb craters as a result of Allied air raids over the past five years, which made the airfield nearly useless to the aircraft of both sides. The other new DZs were Vogelenzang airfield at Haarlem on the North Sea coast; IJmuiden airfield, the most northerly of the regular drop zones, eleven miles north of Haarlem, which also served Bergen farther to the north; Hilversum, the most easterly drop zone; and at Utrecht around the Lage Weide on that city's fringe. As decreed by mission planner Andrew Geddes, all locations were flat, clear and easily accessible to the civilians who would collect the food once it was dropped. And with most being established airfields, they offered low-level flight paths to approaching aircraft.

The British bombers flying Operation Manna would also have their own drop zones in the latter days of the operations; they would add to their existing list Gouda, famous for its cheese, and the former Dutch military airfield of Waalhaven outside Rotterdam. According to this plan, with some 900 heavy bombers ultimately in the air each day flying the food-drop missions, there would be little possibility of accidents with bombers from different Allied air forces crossing paths as they flew to the same DZs. Locations for food drops for 8th Air Force aircraft would vary each day of the operation. Too much food dropped at too few locations would cause distribution problems and delays on the ground. By the same token, too many drop zones would also cause distribution problems.

By the end of the operation, American bombers would be dropping at up to seven different designated locations each day. Some B-17s would also be permitted to drop their loads on "targets of opportunity"—smaller locations where food was needed but that had not previously received drops—and decided by pilots on the day subject to weather and other considerations that might preclude individual aircraft from reaching their original designated targets. But first, the B-17 crews had to master the tricky technique of dropping food from a low altitude in tight protective formation. There was no time for trial runs for each crew. They would have to learn as they went, with their superiors hoping that not too much food would be lost or damaged in the process.

Planning for Chowhound depended on supplies being on hand, and thousands of tons of US Army "ten-in-one" ration packs—called K-rations—were trucked to the airfields of the bombardment groups assigned to the operation and stored prior to being loaded aboard the bombers. K-rations had been developed in the United States in the early 1940s, initially for specialist assault troops such as paratroopers operating behind enemy lines. By 1942, K-rations were being produced for all US troops in the line, with the contents changing over the next few years as the government's food experts experimented with various combinations before settling on the contents in use by 1945.

Between 1942 and 1945, Heinz, Patten Food Products and the Cracker Jack Company mass-produced millions of K-ration packs in the United States to strict US government guidelines. There were three different packs—one for breakfast, one for dinner, and one for supper—and between them these three were intended to deliver the American soldier between 2,830 and 3,000 calories a day. By 1945, the breakfast pack consisted of chopped ham and eggs in a circular flat can with a twist key, sixteen crackers in two eight-cracker packs, a dried fruit bar, premixed oatmeal cereal, instant coffee, cubed sugar, Halazone water purification tablets, a pack of four cigarettes plus a box of matches, and a pack of Dentyne or Wrigley chewing gum.

The K-ration dinner pack by the time of Chowhound contained cheese in a can, sixteen crackers in two packs, five caramels, a pack of salt, cubed sugar, a powdered grape beverage to be added to water, four cigarettes and a box of matches, and chewing gum. The supper pack contained beef and pork loaf in a can, the omnipresent sixteen crackers, a two-ounce chocolate bar, a bouillon cube or grape beverage powder, a pack of toilet paper tissues, the cigarette four-pack and matches, and the gum.

K-rations were designed to be used no more than fifteen times consecutively—breakfast, dinner and supper for five days. But in the Far East, particularly in remote parts of Burma, American troops fighting the Japanese often had to exist on K-rations for months at a time. This prolonged use exposed the lack of protein in K-ration pack makeup. Men using K-rations for extended periods lost many pounds in weight, and some US servicemen in these circumstances would refuse to use K-rations after a time. Some were known to vomit at the sight of K-rations when that was all that was available after many months. However, for starving Dutch civilians in Holland's major cities and towns—who had not seen meat or cheese or crackers or salt or sugar in a year or more—K-rations would represent a veritable feast in a cardboard box.

For transport around the world, the manufacturers of the K-ration packs in the United States uniformly packed them into crates made from wood or cardboard, with thirty-two K-ration packs to a crate—a mixture of breakfast, dinner and supper. Each loaded crate weighed between forty-one and forty-three pounds. These crates turned up at the B-17 bases throughout eastern England in the last days of April 1945 in tens of thousands and were stacked ready for loading aboard the Flying Fortresses of the 8th Air Force. It now fell to the ground crews to figure out a way to load as many crates as possible for an efficient drop.

The order from above was to fill each aircraft's bomb bay with K-ration crates and simply open the doors and let the loads fall on the targets. When some pilots became concerned that their drop speed might be too great to make accurate drops, many an ingenious crew chief at one base or another came up with ways of roping the crates in place and releasing them with a tug from a single rope, allowing the bomb bay doors to be opened in advance of the drop zone, creating drag that slowed the B-17's approach speed and permitting, in theory, a more accurate drop. Some aircrew would also worry about hitting civilians with their loads. After all, a forty-three-pound crate, dropped from 400 or 500 feet and hitting someone on the ground on the head, would be sure to seriously injure or kill them. But there was no alternative.

Each bombardment group and squadron was given plenty of latitude regarding how they loaded their aircraft and crewed their flights. But General Doolittle required that all aircrew taking part in Chowhound missions had to be volunteers. Plus, unless they were fired on during a Chowhound flight, aircrew would not receive a mission credit for any Chowhound flight—aircrew received credit for each bombing mission they flew, and their total would determine when they could go home to the States. Despite this restriction, 8th Air Force commanders would be embarrassed by the number of men putting their hand up to take part—including senior officers with HQ desk jobs, men such as former 95th Bombardment Group commander Lieutenant Colonel Grif Mumford, who grabbed the opportunity to fly missions again in these dying days of the war to help make a difference for the Dutch.

Left to their own devices, squadrons made their own arrangements about how they would load the crates of K-rations in their bomb bays. Rules varied from squadron to squadron, too, about who could fly the Chowhound missions.

Lieutenant Henry L. "Hank" Cervantes, a B-17 pilot from Oakley, California, serving with the 100th Bombardment Group based at Thorpe Abbotts in Norfolk, found that the orders from his immediate superiors were that, as neither side was supposed to fire at the other during Chowhound flights, no gunners were to fly on his squadron's B-17s.[1] This instruction meant that only four crewmen would fly the mission—pilot, copilot, radio operator and bombardier. Cervantes was not happy about this and would confess that he felt almost naked without his bomber's air gunners coming along.[2] Gunners in some other squadrons were ordered to point their guns skyward, as a signal to the Germans on the ground that they had no offensive intent. These gunners were told that the German flak gunners would reciprocate by keeping the barrels of their guns depressed.

Hal Province, a bombardier with the 34th Bombardment Group's 319th Squadron, based at Mendlesham in Suffolk, would be equally uneasy when his squadron received orders to leave behind all ammunition for its guns when it took off on its Chowhound missions.[3] Flying with empty guns was not a welcome prospect. The crews of the 390th Bombardment Group's 569th Squadron were also among those told to leave ammunition for their guns behind. Bernie Behrman, top-turret gunner with a 569th Squadron B-17, didn't like this at all. He felt a little more comfortable when his crew decided to wear sidearms for their first Chowhound flight. Bernie and his comrades had heard that the Germans had signed a truce to permit them to make the Chowhound food drops, but they didn't trust the Nazis. A pistol wasn't going to make all that much difference if Jerry opened up on them with 88 mm and 105 mm heavy flak guns, but Bernie and his comrades felt that a little extra insurance, in the form of the pistols on their hips, couldn't hurt.[4]

Ray Powell, another member of the 100th Bombardment Group—which had taken the nickname "the Bloody Hundredth"—was told that there would be no need for the B-17s of his squadron to be armed because a squadron of USAAF P-51 Mustangs would be flying escort off their port side while a squadron of Luftwaffe Messerschmitt Bf-109s would be flying escort to starboard. Needless to say, that wasn't going to happen, but young Powell would rise from his bed on the day of his first Chowhound mission fully believing that he was going to receive an American-German escort, only to realize once he was in the air that his leg was being pulled.[5]

Some squadrons had very strict rules laid down by their commanders about there being no passengers aboard the aircraft taking part in Chowhound. Other squadrons were entirely relaxed about this, and their pilots would invite sightseeing passengers along from among their ground crew. In one case, a B-17 would carry ten such passengers when it took off on the first day of Chowhound.

In the end, more than forty squadrons from ten bombardment groups based between Ipswich and Norwich in East Anglia were tasked with flying the first Chowhound missions. Their bases were located closer to the North Sea and to the Continent than those of their British counterparts, but this actually worked against them in the early stages of the operation because of inclement weather. The American aircraft could potentially have joined the operation a day or two earlier than they did, but fog rolled in from the sea and covered East Anglia, grounding the American bombers, which sat with bomb bays packed with K-rations, ready to go, while British aircraft farther inland were able to take off.

The planners hoped that finally, on May 1, conditions would prove right for Chowhound to proceed. Only later would many aircrew realize that this was May Day, once celebrated as the birthday of the queen of the fairies and more recently invested with importance to organized labor and socialists as International Workers Day. The Germans too observed May Day, but as a Nazi workers day.

15

MAY 1, 1945

B-17s OVER HOLLAND AT 400 FEET

Operation Chowhound got underway shortly after dawn on May 1 with four B-17 Flying Fortress bombers and a single P-51 Mustang fighter of the 8th Air Force taking to the air over East Anglia and heading for Holland. These five aircraft were the weather scouts for the bomber force of 392 B-17s that would soon be lifting off—weather permitting.

The lead weather scout pilot was David A. Mullen from the 3rd Air Division's 3rd Scouting Force. Since September 1944, this specialist unit had been based at Wormingford, six miles northwest of the coastal town of Colchester in Essex, just a little south of the bases of the bombers slated to fly Chowhound. After Mullen checked the weather from high altitude that morning, he dropped his stripped-back airplane down to fly as low as the bomber force was expected to fly to check the visibility on their flight routes. He knew that the bomber pilots would be briefed to make their drops from 400 feet, but to be on the safe side, Mullen went down to a hundred feet. Scudding low over one of the designated drop zones, he found cattle grazing on the abandoned Dutch airfield where crates of K-rations were expected to be landing soon, so Mullen circled the airfield until a farmer appeared on the scene and herded the cattle away from the DZ.[1]

The information from the weather scouts formed part of the briefing that the aircrews were to receive in their dispersal rooms that morning. The weather over England and the North Sea was not good—heavily overcast with thunderstorms on the way. As for the bombers' targets in Holland, they were today in the areas of Rotterdam and The Hague. The weather scouts reported thick cloud above 1,000 feet over The Hague, but below that, visibility was six to ten miles over the targets— ideal for low-level drops. Chowhound was "go."

At ten USAAF bomber bases in East Anglia, yawning crews from forty squadrons were being awakened in the dark by orderlies with flashlights and crawling out of their beds to dress and shave. Aircrew were permitted to grow mustaches, which were relatively popular, following the example of Hollywood stars such as Clark Gable. To some young airmen just out of their teens, a mustache made them look older, more mature. But beards were banned—they didn't permit a snug fit when oxygen masks were donned by aircrew and could cost them their lives.

Dressed and shaved, it was off to a hot breakfast in the combat mess hall before crew members headed for their mission briefings for the day at the group operations building. There, up on stage, each group's intelligence officer pulled a cloth from a display board, and aircrew saw a red line tracing from their base to their squadrons' target for the day in Holland. And they heard about Operation Chowhound for the first time. Aircrew were told, too, that none of them was being ordered to fly on Chowhound; General Doolittle only wanted volunteers for this mission. But once they knew what it was about, although many had reservations about this low-level op, very few chose to opt out. Navigators and pilots received their weather briefing and details of the courses they were to fly in order to stay within the flight corridors agreed on between SHAEF and the Germans—courses designed to get them to their targets and back without being fired upon. And then the crews were taken out to their waiting bombers in jeeps, or they rode out on bicycles to the concrete hardstands where their airplanes stood ready and waiting with fuel tanks full and bomb bays packed with K-ration crates by their ground crews two days earlier.

In the crew briefings that morning, all aircrew were told of the plight of the starving Dutch and the vital nature of the Chowhound flights. At Framlingham in Suffolk, Sergeant Ralph DeSpirito, a twenty-year-old radio operator and waist gunner with *Maiden Prayer*, a B-17 of the 390th Bombardment Group, listened as this information was imparted in typical military fashion without any emotion or elaboration. Still, DeSpirito, a native of Brooklyn, New York, came away from the briefing believing that the mission was important—although he and his fellow crew members seemed blissfully unaware of the dangers ahead, taking their officers' word for it that the Germans would not fire on them.[2] They were in the minority that morning.

At Debach in Suffolk, nineteen-year-old Technical Sergeant Bill Richards, a B-17 radio operator with the 493rd Bombardment Group's 863rd Squadron, listened to the morning's briefing with dismay. Up to this point, Richards had flown twenty-three combat missions over heavily defended German targets; after seeing so many comrades fail to return to Debach, he had secretly come to wonder whether his luck would soon run out and he too would end up dead or a prisoner of the Germans after being shot down. Now he and his fellow crewmen were being told that they were to drop food to the Dutch from a low level with the Germans supposed to hold their fire.

"The Germans would know our route, our arrival time, and pretty well everything else," Richards would later say. "That was pretty scary, and we didn't trust this at all." Worse to Richards and his crewmates was the fact that their squadron was one of those ordered to leave its air gunners behind for their May Day Chowhound mission. Just three other crewmen joined radio operator Richards climbing into their ship at Debach for their Chowhound initiation. "I felt terribly vulnerable without our gunners," Richards would say.[3]

Meanwhile, at Snetterton Heath in Norfolk, under a heavily overcast sky, 96th Bombardment Group pilot Max Krell dismounted from a jeep with three other crew to find his five gunners already at their ship and busy preparing their guns for action. Krell's was another of the squadrons whose commanders had decided to leave their air gunners behind. But as this mission was open to volunteers, Krell's gunners had volunteered to come along anyway, and no one could prevent them. Krell and his comrades weren't unhappy about that. They all felt it wise to take the gunners along. Despite the claim from their superiors that the Germans had agreed not to fire on Chowhound aircraft, Krell and his crewmates felt that no chances could be taken with "the Krauts." Krell looked at the sky. Rain had swept the airfield earlier, and there was still thick cloud cover over the base. At their briefing, 96th BG crews had been assured that the sky over the target was clear, but as Krell clambered up the metal ladder into his B-17, he wondered whether the mission would in fact get off the ground.[4]

At Framlingham in Suffolk, base of the 390th Bombardment Group, not a word was exchanged as pilot Haven P. Damer and his nervous crewmates of the B-17G named *No Credit* climbed aboard their aircraft and took their places well before 7:00 a.m. Their briefing that morning had sent a chill up every spine as they were ordered to fly over Holland at 400 feet and drop food to the Dutch. They had been assured at the briefing that the British had flown their Lancasters over this sector on the previous two days without any problems. But what if the Jerries were waiting for the USAAF to take up the mission? What if Operation

Chowhound proved to be a massive trap, designed to lure hundreds of 8th Air Force B-17s down to 400 feet before they were shot from the sky? This mission seemed insane![5]

One by one, forty 390th BG bombers of the 568th, 569th, 570th and 571st Squadrons took their turns to run down the strip and lift into the sky, and at 7:15 a.m., in the midst of this one-way traffic, *No Credit* took off from Framlingham. Pilot Damer took the bomber up to 1,000 feet and circled the field as his squadron, the 570th, took off and then the group assembled. Looking toward the Continent to the east, Damer and his crew could see that the sky was darkly overcast. The met briefing had been for thunderstorms en route, so once the group had assembled, the formation's lead aircraft took the bombers down to between 500 and 600 feet to cross the North Sea.

The 569th Squadron occupied the group's lowermost position, scudding across the wave-tops—or so it felt to 569th top-turret gunner Bernie Behrman. All the gunners of his ship were aboard, but Behrman was smarting over the fact that his guns, and all the guns aboard his bomber, were empty, as ordered by his squadron commander. Behrman's only comfort was the automatic pistol he'd holstered on his hip that morning as he pulled on his flying gear. In a flash, Behrman's B-17 was flying over an Allied convoy with the ships' astonished deck crews looking up at them and seeming to Behrman to be as close as the distance from one street corner to another.[6]

Higher in the formation, Haven P. Damer's *No Credit* led the 570th Squadron's uppermost element. Through the thinning cloud, Damer and his crew caught glimpses of hundreds of B-17s from other 8th Air Force squadrons; the sky seemed to be filled with them. The crew tensed for the flak bursts that always greeted them as they crossed the Dutch coast, but today not a single shell was fired at them. Down to 400 feet dropped *No Credit*, keeping tight formation with the rest of the squadron. In Damer's ears came the voice of his navigator, giving him landmarks to navigate by. *No Credit* and the 390th BG flew on toward their target, Valkenburg airfield at Utrecht in the center of Holland.[7]

From his base at Knettishall in Suffolk, Frank W. Rone was piloting a B-17 of the 388th Bombardment Group's 562nd Squadron on a Chowhound mission that morning. Rone and his crew were all volunteers for this mission, but none of them trusted the Germans to hold their fire as they flew at just a few hundred feet over Holland. Rone's young crew had such little faith in the agreement that was supposed to underpin Operation Chowhound that they had changed the name of their airplane—to *Sitting Duck*. Rone's B-17 and forty others from the 388th BG had Ypenburg as their target, and Rone tensely flew the route in tight formation with the B-17s around him. Despite his forebodings, apart from his aircrew, Rone had brought along passengers on this flight—ground crew, hard-working men who never got the opportunity to see anything of Europe. Ten of them. If Rone and his crew went down, the "tourists" would go down with them.[8]

A second bombardment group, the 96th, was sharing Ypenburg airfield with the 388th as its target on this first day of Chowhound. The 96th Bombardment Group's senior officers had even less faith in the German promise not to fire on aircraft flying Operation Chowhound than did Frank Rone and his 388th BG crew. They decided that three of the group's B-17s would take off from their base at Snetterton Heath in Norfolk before the remaining thirty-eight 96th Bombardment Group bombers assigned to the day's mission and would make their drops at Ypenburg before the main formation. The plan of 96th Group HQ was that if the three lead aircraft were fired upon by the Jerries, they were to radio the remainder of the group, which would be over the sea by that time, and those aircraft would turn back, aborting the mission, and return to base.

All the 1200-horsepower Wright engines of the 96th's Flying Fortresses burst into life at once, and then the forty-one bombers began the crawling taxi to the head of the runway before they received the green light and, one by one, lumbered down the strip and into the air. The three lead aircraft took off first and, without waiting to assemble with the other B-17s, made a beeline for Holland, line abreast. Meanwhile, the remaining aircraft of the group assembled at 1,500 feet. Max Krell, one of the pilots in the main 96th BG formation that day, was to find that this low-level assembly proved much more difficult than assembling at 10,000 or 12,000 feet, the usual height for putting together formations for a bombing mission.[9]

When the thirty-eight B-17s of the main formation were in their places, like a giant flock of birds they wheeled east and flew out over the sea, bound for southern Holland. As it turned out, fears of being fired upon had been unfounded. The three lead aircraft from the 96th BG made their drops at Ypenburg without meeting any German resistance, and the B-17s of the rest of the group arrived over the target a little later. Lowering wheels and flaps, the group's aircraft made their drops at 130 miles per hour, from 400 feet, also without incident.

Frank Rone and the pilots of the 388th Bombardment Group likewise successfully completed their drops at Ypenburg that day without encountering any form of resistance. Rone took his Fort down to a little above 300 feet for his drop, after which the by then exhilarated pilot continued to fly low, descending to between 200 and 100 feet to let his passengers and crew see the Dutch residents of The Hague who had come out to wave to them. Rone was enjoying the low-level buzz so much that, almost too late, he saw a high stone tower loom up directly ahead. Realizing that he had to rapidly gain at least 80 feet to clear the top of that tower, and that he was only doing 165 miles an hour, Rone pushed the throttles of all four of his engines forward at once and pulled the stick back hard into his stomach. The straining bomber gained height, and missed the top of the tower by inches, narrowly avoiding becoming Chowhound's first casualty. Looking around, Rone saw the white faces of his terrified passengers. Rone would comment, "None of them offered me a drink after the flight."[10]

At Framlingham in Suffolk, the USAAF's Norman Coats was standing sentry duty on May 1. He was guarding the massive stockpile of K-ration crates that had been created at his airfield for Operation Chowhound. A ball-turret gunner with the 390th Bombardment Group, Coats watched as aircraft from his group taxied and took off that morning for their first Chowhound run. Three hours later, he counted the B-17s of the 390th as they touched down at Framlingham again—all forty returned safely to base.

As soon as his duty ended, Coats hurried to his barrack room, where he quizzed the returned aircrew as they came back from their debriefing. Like Coats, the hundreds of men of the 390th who had flown food drops to Holland that day had been nervous about the operation and about the possibility of being shot from the sky as they flew at a few hundred feet. But now they were full of high spirits—the Dutch had come out to wave to them when they made their drops, they said. And the Jerries hadn't fired at them. Coats was due to fly a Chowhound mission the next day. Buoyed by the encouraging stories from his colleagues, he prepared to get a good night's sleep.[11]

The official debriefing reports from the aircrew who had taken part in the first day of Chowhound were generally positive. They had met no resistance from the Germans, although those crews that had been told to point their bombers' guns skyward and to expect to see the Germans with their guns pointing to the ground reported that German guns had not only pointed their way but had sometimes tracked them across the sky as they passed, making the aircrew very nervous. American air gunners would keep their guns at the ready position on future drops, just in case. The close to 400 Chowhound pilots who had flown that day reported dropping their loads from between 800 and 320 feet, and most felt they had landed their food drops on or near their targets.

Photographic intelligence following the drops was not so encouraging. All food crates had landed *near* their targets, but a number had ended up in canals and flooded farmland; some of the 776.1 tons of food dropped by the 8th Air Force on that day were lost. Claude Hall, ground crew with the 390th BG, was filling in as a waist gunner aboard *Hotter 'N Hell*, a B-17 of the 570th Bomb Squadron, when it dropped its load at Valkenburg airfield at Utrecht that day. Hall saw much of the load tumble into water channels beside the drop zone, and saw Dutch civilians dive into the water to try to save it—how successful they had been Hall could only guess.[12]

The word went out from 3rd Air Division HQ—the next day, the B-17s would have to fly much lower, and slower, to ensure that every box from their food drops ended up in the hands of the starving Dutch population. Unknown to all the aircrew flying Chowhound on May 1— who had been assured by their commanders that a truce had been in place to protect them—it would only be on the following day that the food-drop agreement negotiated between the Allies and the Germans officially came into effect. While the documents that Andrew Geddes and his team of planners at SHAEF had consigned to paper and handed to Reichsrichter Schwebel on April 29 had spelled out the air corridors and the drop zones that both sides were supposed to respect, it wasn't until late on May Day that the agreement was actually signed by the Germans, well after close to 400 American bombers had flown their first Chowhound missions and returned to base.

To get the necessary German signatures, Air Commodore Geddes and his SHAEF-appointed deputy, fellow RAF officer Group Captain John H. "Johnnie" Hill, representing General Eisenhower, were driven west into no-man's-land by Canadian troops in a sedan bearing a white flag. The road was long, straight and cobbled and lined with tall trees. On either side of the road stretched flat green fields and untended orchards in late bloom. Geddes's destination was the deserted Dutch village of

Nude beyond the town of Wageningen, between the Allied and German lines. From low hills in the near distance, German troops kept them under observation as, arriving at four o'clock outside a ruined cottage at 118 Wageningen Road, Geddes, Hill and their Canadian escort were met by Oberleutnant Von Massow, who was accompanied by a party of Luftwaffe officers and paratroops. Geddes and Hill handed over four copies of the agreement specifying safe corridors and drop zones—two in English, two in German—and two copies of a map showing the same.

As members of the German party studied the documents and chatted with Hill and the Canadian captain commanding Geddes's escort, Geddes invited Lieutenant Von Massow to take a stroll with him. Out of earshot of the others, Geddes and Von Massow stopped and lit cigarettes—Geddes had given his precious pouch of pipe tobacco to a member of the Dutch party at the Achterveld meeting the previous day. On first meeting Von Massow at Achterveld a few days earlier, Geddes had found him arrogant and full of self-confidence, and he was determined to pull the young German officer down a peg or two. Taking a copy of the US military journal *Stars and Stripes* from his pocket, Geddes showed it to Von Massow, pointing out a map that showed the extent of Allied advances into Germany.

"Propaganda!" Von Massow responded dismissively.

"That may be true," Geddes replied, "but I want you to know that your brother General [Gerd] von Massow is OK and well. We bagged him near Kassel a few days ago."[13]

The lieutenant's mouth dropped open with shock at the news of his elder brother's capture. He then turned and walked back toward his comrades, speaking to them urgently in German. Saying that he would have to take the agreement and map to his superiors, and arranging for a second meeting at 10:00 p.m., Von Massow jumped into his vehicle and was driven away at top speed. Geddes and Hill likewise returned to their own lines.

"What was the matter with that German lieutenant?" asked Group Captain Hill as they drove east toward Wageningen.

"Nothing," Geddes replied with a smile. "I gave him his brother's best wishes."[14]

At 10:00 p.m. that evening the same parties met up again at Nude, and Von Massow handed over the two English copies of the agreement and one of the copies of the map. These had been signed by Seyss-Inquart's deputy, Dr. Schwebel, and General Blaskowitz's deputy, Lieutenant General Paul Reichelt. Geddes and Hill returned to their own lines with the signed documents. At 10:22, using a Canadian army telephone at the war-battered town of Wageningen inside Canadian lines, Geddes called 1st Canadian Corps HQ with the message that the agreement had been signed.

On the north side of Arnhem bridge, Geddes and Hill transferred to their own transport to run down the Rhine the eleven miles to Nijmegen. At the airfield there, a communications airplane was waiting to take Geddes to Reims to report directly to General Bedell Smith.

THAT SAME NIGHT, at 10:30, the last Nazi government radio station still operating in Germany, Radio Hamburg, announced that Adolf Hitler was dead. According to Radio Hamburg, the German fuehrer had died fighting Bolshevism in Berlin on the afternoon of April 30. In fact, Hitler, who had turned fifty-six ten days before his death, had committed suicide in his Reich Chancellery bunker in Berlin after shooting his dog, Blondie. His wife of one day, Eva Braun, had died at his side, taking poison. In his "last testament," Hitler appointed Grand Admiral Karl Doenitz, then head of the German navy, as his successor with the title of Reich president. Among other final appointments, Hitler made Arthur Seyss-Inquart the new German foreign minister, replacing Joachim von Ribbentrop, in whom he had lost faith. Ironically, Hitler, confined to his underground world in Berlin, had been blissfully unaware that the trusted and promoted Seyss-Inquart was ignoring his scorched-earth order and was disobeying his express command that subordinates not negotiate with the Allies.

Many Nazis, senior and junior, would follow their fuehrer's example and take their own lives in the coming days. Seyss-Inquart, for his part, immediately made plans to go to Doenitz at his headquarters in Schleswig-Holstein to discuss the ending of the war in a way that ensured the preservation of his own skin. Many other Nazis would vow to fight to their last drop of blood, and Hitler's death did not mean the immediate cessation of hostilities. The war would drag on, and thousands more would die. Operation Chowhound, with its goal of saving the starving people of Holland, was as vital as ever.

FROM NIJMEGEN, Andrew Geddes was flown to Reims, where he reported to General Bedell Smith that all was now official as far as the food drops were concerned. Two days later Geddes would be back in Brussels, and back in his office at the British 2nd Tactical Air Force HQ, resuming his old post there after two weeks' absence doing General Eisenhower's bidding. Geddes's job was done. The planning was well and truly complete. From this point on, it would be up to the men and women on the ground and in the air to make Chowhound and Manna work as Eisenhower and Bedell Smith had envisaged, and Geddes turned his attention to other matters.

The agreement that had now been signed by both sides stated quite explicitly that the safe air corridors in Holland and across the North Sea were to come into effect the next day, ignoring the fact that the mercy flights had been going on for days. So it was only on May 2 that the Germans in Holland were bound to hold their fire against Allied bombers flying food-drop missions. The nervousness felt by so many American aircrew flying Chowhound on May 1 had had a sound basis in fact. As it turned out, it had been a miracle that no German gunners had fired on low-flying bombers in Holland up to this point. No official agreement had existed at that time, and nothing in the rules of war had prevented the Germans from firing prior to this.

Chowhound flights on May 2, then, should have been a walk in the park for 8th Air Force crews. As it turned out, they would be far from that for some.

16

GERMANS OPEN FIRE ON CHOWHOUND BOMBERS

The drone and rumble of bombers approaching the town of Hilversum in the center of occupied Holland had young Henri van der Zee dashing to the window of his family home. It was May 2, the second day of Operation Chowhound and the first day officially recognized by the Germans in occupied Holland.

Henri van der Zee's gaze fell on the lane outside his house. That lane had been denuded of its once handsome twin rows of old oak trees during the winter—cut down for firewood in the night despite German regulations banning the act. People were emerging from their neglected houses along the lane. They had broad smiles on their faces, and they were pointing to the pale blue sky. Henri rushed out into the lane to see twenty American B-17s of the 385th Bombardment Group fly low over the town, open their bomb bays, and disgorge green-brown bundles of rations that tumbled onto the heath at nearby Crailo. All around Henri, people were shouting or crying. Or both. Henri would recall that he had goose bumps.[1]

What Henri van der Zee failed to see was German flak gunners firing at these B-17s making their drops at Hilversum. The town was the location of General Blaskowitz's well-camouflaged and heavily defended headquarters of the German 25th Army, which Canadians Farley Mowat and Ken Cottam had visited a few days earlier on Cottam's self-inspired truce mission. The antiaircraft gunners were understandably nervous about American bombers making a beeline for their generals' bunkers. That nervousness was compounded by the fact that the site for food drops at Hilversum had not been confirmed at the time the agreement was finally signed on May 1. Hilversum was a last-minute addition to the drop zones, with the Germans required to radio the Canadian army "special set" in Holland that the site was approved and the corridors to and from it safe. It is unclear whether that approval was ever radioed, or, if it was, when.

Oscar Sinibaldi was the bombardier aboard a B-17 of the 385th Bombardment Group's 549th Squadron—one of the Flying Fortresses watched with such delight and wonder from the ground by Henri van der Zee at Hilversum that morning. Sinibaldi's squadron had crossed the Dutch coast without incident and was heading for its assigned DZ outside Hilversum when 20 mm German antiaircraft shells came arcing up toward the bombers from the ground. The aircrews immediately feared that the squadron had strayed from the assigned safe flight corridor, although no one aboard the American bombers had spotted the specified red warning flare that, according to the Achterveld agreement signed the previous day by both sides, was supposed to precede any firing by the Germans.

But this was no time to worry about correct protocols. Sinibaldi's pilot, Lee Marcussen, quickly adjusted course to keep their B-17 well within the "safe" corridor, as did the pilots of the other airplanes of the squadron. The German flak gunners ceased fire as soon as a green flare was fired and burst with a vivid flash—a signal that the bombers were in the corridor.² Back at their base at Great Ashfield in Suffolk an hour and a half later, the crews of the 549th squadron would take a close look at their aircraft and discover that three B-17s had received minor damage from the flak, while a fourth, named *Stork Club*, had been left with a jagged hole in one wing the size of a pair of dinner plates side by side.³ *Stork Club* lived up to the reputation of the B-17 as an aircraft built to withstand severe punishment. Ed Wells, one of the designers of the B-17 and the man responsible for the bomber's award-winning wing design, would go on to work on several generations of iconic aircraft, including the B-29 Superfortress, the B-52 Stratofortress and, after the war, the Boeing 707, 727, 737 and 747 jet airliners.

One of the B-17s to be hit on May 2 had been flying directly behind Oscar Sinibaldi's bomber at the time the German flak gunners opened up. Yet, as luck would have it, none of the damage had endangered the aircraft, which all returned safely to base, and there were no injuries among the squadron's aircrew. *Stork Club* was quickly patched up by its ground crew and would fly three more Chowhound missions without incident.

Just the same, Oscar Sinibaldi was to witness one near fatality on May 2. He made a successful drop at Hilversum, with released K-ration crates bouncing, and in some cases shattering, leaving deep indentations in the ground before they came to rest. But when bombardier Sinibaldi tried to close his airplane's bomb bay doors, he saw the "idiot light" glowing on his control panel. This indicated that the doors had remained open. As pilot Marcussen took their B-17 climbing away from Hilversum and up to several thousand feet for the return to England and their base, Sinibaldi left his post in the nose of the aircraft to investigate the open bomb bay doors. Making his way aft, Sinibaldi came upon a sight that terrified him. The B-17's bomb bay doors were indeed wide open, and the bomber's flight engineer, Gerald D. Shaull, was hanging upside down in the opening, with two other crew members clinging desperately to his legs.

Ground crew had created a jury-rigged system of ropes to release the bomber's food load. This allowed the B-17 to approach the target with its bomb bay doors wide open but with its payload still in place, slowing the bomber down and helping to ensure an on-target delivery. The 549th Squadron had also approached its drop zone with the wheels of each bomber lowered—to create even more drag and further slow the B-17s. It required a crew member such as the flight engineer to pull the release rope to send the load spewing out the open bomb bay. But following the drop by Sinibaldi's aircraft, some of the ropes had become snagged on the open bomb bay doors. The airplane couldn't land with its bomb bay doors open, so flight engineer Shaull was trying to free the snags.

By this time the B-17 had climbed to 5,000 feet, and all Oscar Sinibaldi could see between his flight engineer and Holland was 5,000 feet of air. It was impossible to be heard here for the noise of engines and slipstream, so Sinibaldi used frantic hand signals to convince the men holding Shaull's legs to haul the flight engineer back inside the aircraft. Once Shaull was safe, Sinibaldi was able, with some difficulty, to close the bomb bay doors by hand—they closed with a crunch, he would remember.[4]

After standing guard over food stocks the previous day, ball-turret gunner Norman Coats of the 390th Bombardment Group flew his first Chowhound mission on this day. Coats would never forget that flight. To his amazement, crowds of people came out to watch the bombers of his group drop their loads at Amsterdam's Schiphol Airport. The Dutch gathered in Amsterdam's streets, leaned out windows and massed precariously on rooftops, all smiling, laughing, pointing and waving handkerchiefs at the bomber crews. In his turret beneath the belly of his B-17, Coats had a bird's-eye view of the panorama unfolding beneath him as his bomber made its food-drop run at 400 feet. And as his B-17 released its load, Coats saw German troops below looking up at him and hoped they wouldn't end up getting their hands on half the food the 8th Air Force was dropping over Holland.

Coats's airplane ran into a snowstorm over the North Sea on its return flight to England and was forced to drop down to a hundred feet. As the B-17 scudded across the waves, the bomber was flying so low that Coats felt he could trail his feet in the water. And then they were landing back at Framlingham. Coats was exhilarated by the flight and ready do it all over again.[5]

At the controls of another aircraft of the 390th BG on this run to Schiphol was a young pilot by the name of Joseph R. "Bob" Belgam. This was also Belgam's first Chowhound flight, and he had been totally unaware that the Dutch in occupied Holland were starving until his squadron briefing that morning. That briefing, although technical and unemotional, had pulled Belgam up with a start. The young American had not even been aware that much of Holland was still occupied by the Nazis. Once he knew about the plight of the Dutch, Bob Belgam became very enthusiastic about the mission. After taking off from Framlingham and assembling over East Anglia, Belgam's squadron flew across the sea and found its drop zone with ease. On the run in to Schiphol, Belgam flew low enough to see the expressions of delight on the faces of the Dutch civilians who had gathered in the fields to watch them fly over, to wave and yell at them. Belgam would confess that the sight brought a lump to his throat and to those of his crew.[6]

Schiphol Airport was busy on this day with a total of seven B-17 bombardment groups having Schiphol as their assigned drop zone. The 96th BG was one of them, and pilot Reese Martin, a second lieutenant with the 96th's 338th Squadron, was particularly nervous as he prepared to fly a B-17 to Schiphol on May 2. The previous day he had flown a different B-17 on his first Chowhound mission, but for this second run he was assigned to fly a very famous Fort. It was known as *Five Grand* and was the 5,000th B-17 built by Boeing in the United States. Every employee at the Boeing factory at Seattle had written their name on the bomber, inside and out, and those signatures were still in place, making the bomber look like a graffiti artist's dream. Or, as Reese Martin put it, it looked like a flying page from a notebook.[7]

It was considered a real honor to fly *Five Grand*, which had been on the front pages of newspapers across the United States and featured in the newsreels after it was rolled out the factory door. But heaven help the pilot who lost *Five Grand* while flying her! On May 1, Reese Martin had had difficulty flying his B-17 at low altitude and low speed as he made his run to Schiphol. That bomber had kicked like a mule and had been a real handful to fly straight and level. As Martin climbed up into *Five Grand* on the morning of May 2 at Snetterton Heath, he was more worried about bringing the famous airplane back unscathed than he was about surviving the mission personally.[8]

Bombardier Hal Province of the 34th Bomb Group's 319th Squadron was another Chowhound first-timer on this second day of USAAF involvement in the mercy flights. He and the other members of the crew of his ship, *Purty Chili*, all of them Chowhound novices, were excited when they heard about their mission at the briefing that morning. Since Province had arrived in England that January, he had flown nineteen combat missions, bombing German targets from high altitude. Now Province and his crewmates had the opportunity to make a humanitarian contribution to this war. But, Province was to admit, he and the other members of the crew of *Purty Chili* were also scared. Normally, *Purty Chili* flew over Holland at a height of 15,000 to 20,000 feet on its way to targets farther east; today they were expected to make food drops from several hundred feet. Worse, the squadron had been ordered to fly without any ammunition for its guns. The American flyers were relying totally on the Germans not to fire on them, and Hal Province and his buddies were not comfortable with that at all.[9]

Forty B-17Gs of the 34th BG took off from Mendlesham that morning and assembled over Suffolk, then headed for the Continent, dropping down to scud low over the sea and cross the Dutch coast on a course
for Utrecht. To the relief of Bombardier Province and his comrades,
the German gunners below held their fire. Province saw red, white and
black Nazi swastika flags fluttering from public buildings they overflew.
And he saw the faces of German troops who were standing guard at
railroad bridges across canals and looking up, warily watching the tight
formation of American bombers pass.

Province's squadron was one of those that had lowered flaps and
undercarriages for their drop, and the B-17s eased down to under 400
feet as the lead bombardier lined up for the Utrecht DZ. And then the
first B-17s in the formation were letting go of their cargoes. K-ration
boxes were cascading from bomb bays. Aircraft behind quickly followed
suit. Despite the squadron's low dropping altitude and comparatively
low speed, a number of boxes missed the target; some crashed through
the tiled roofs of apartment houses. Province saw boxes smash through
the glass roof of a greenhouse and watched as others fell into canals bordering the drop zone. And then the bombers were climbing and turning
for home.[10]

Lieutenant Robert L. Miller, a B-17 pilot with the 493rd Bombardment Group, also flew his first Chowhound mission on May 2. Forty
bombers from his group were assigned the Vogelenzang airfield near the
town of Haarlem for their food drops. In close formation, the aircraft
of the group crossed the Dutch coast and eased down to 400 feet for
the run to the drop zone. Below, Miller saw "THANKS BOYS" and "MANY
THANKS" spelled out large in tulip fields via cut flowers and stones, and
Miller would later admit that tears formed in his eyes at the sight.[11]

At their squadron briefing that morning, Miller and his colleagues
had been informed that, over the past year in occupied Holland, no

newborn babies had survived because of malnutrition. That had really brought home the plight of the Dutch to many aircrew flying on Chowhound. Miller's B-17 successfully dropped its load and headed for home. After a flight lasting three hours and forty minutes, Miller landed back at base feeling thrilled with his part in the mission. He would write in his diary how proud he was of having done something worthwhile instead of blowing towns and people to hell as he usually did on his missions. Because of Chowhound, Miller had come to believe that there was still some good left in the world.[12]

May 2 saw 400 B-17s from forty-eight squadrons fly Chowhound missions, dropping close to 800 tons of K-rations between 09:21 and 13:52 hours from altitudes ranging between 300 and 600 feet. Those B-17s flying their missions in the afternoon had to struggle through heavy rain and snow to reach their targets, but they all delivered their loads before turning for home.[13] As for the famous *Five Grand,* flown by Reese Martin, it behaved itself perfectly on the flight to and from its drop zone at Schiphol Airport, and to his great relief, Martin managed to make his drop and bring the celebrated ship home without a scratch. Martin would fly several more Chowhound missions before the operation came to an end. *Five Grand* would survive the war after close to eighty missions, only to be scrapped back in the States in 1946 despite attempts to preserve it as a museum exhibit.[14]

Gerald Shaull's narrow escape from an unpleasant death—falling out the open bomb bay of Oscar Sinibaldi's B-17—didn't figure in 8th Air Force aircrew debriefings that day. After the previous day's experience, pilots from the squadrons involved reported that they had eased down a little lower for their runs on this second day of Chowhound, with more making their drops closer to 300 feet than on the previous day. Still, while several hundred feet had been shaved off the upper limit of the drops for the day, drops from 600 feet were still not the ideal in terms of accuracy and potential damage to food containers.

Pilots would have to fly lower to ensure maximum results. The best way to allow this to happen was to abandon the tight formations that the B-17s had been flying. These formations had been adopted in 1943 as a protection against enemy fighter aircraft, pitting the firepower of all the formation's guns against the few guns of a German Messerschmitt or Focke-Wulf. As there was no fighter threat to Chowhound missions, the need for tight formation flying did not exist. The word went out to each bomb group from HQ at High Wycombe to do away with formation flying for the food drops.

At this point, General Eisenhower had no clear picture of just how effective the food drops were. Was the food getting to the people who desperately needed it? The 8th Air Force aircrews reported on May 2 seeing their loads falling mainly in populated areas, and a number of crews from the last squadrons to drop reported seeing civilians on the ground at the DZs even as the last crates fell to earth, methodically collecting full and broken food packages and stacking crates for transportation of the rations to the places where they were needed. Dutch organization of collection of the K-rations on the ground was precise, with the content of broken crates sent at once to the nearest hospitals and to church organizations that had an established food-relief arm. Intact crates would go to central distribution points, first on handcarts, wheelbarrows and horse-drawn wagons, and then by canal boats drawn by tugboats.

There would be very little pilfering. Previously, the stealing of foodstuffs and wood for fires had been common throughout occupied Holland, both for personal use and for sale on the flourishing black market. "We stole like rats," one resident of The Hague confessed.[15] And if an individual Chowhound bomber's load, or part of it, fell well away from its intended drop zone, the food was quickly gathered up and vanished. But the organization rapidly put into place on the ground at the drop zones ensured that the vast majority of food ended up in the official distribution centers and not in the hands of black marketeers. This was aided by the German military and Dutch police blocking the roads to and from the DZs, and civil officials being appointed to oversee the collection of food containers. Everyone leaving a drop zone after a drop was searched for contraband.

"I thought the system of distribution was very cleverly arranged," said the same Hague resident who had confessed to stealing food.[16] At larger centers, special civil committees were formed to coordinate collection and distribution. At smaller centers, it was the local air raid wardens or even members of the fire brigade who did the organizing. There were some disputes between various groups, with accusations of pilfering, but overall characteristic Dutch efficiency prevailed. Even the Boy Scouts were recruited to help distribute the food. Kees de Haan was one such Boy Scout in Rotterdam. He and other scouts were signed up for a group called Youth Help, and at St. Job's Church they found piles of food that had been brought in from the air drops. The boys worked each day helping deliver the food to shops and the housebound in the city and to surrounding districts using cars and handcarts. Their reward, each afternoon, was pea soup with bacon, an unheard-of luxury for them.[17]

In these early days of the drops there were casualties on the ground as, despite warnings over the radio and in leaflets to stay indoors during drops, members of the public too eager to grab the food put themselves in the way of falling crates and sacks. A story would emerge of an official chasing a food looter at Rotterdam being hit by a food sack falling from a British bomber and suffering a broken leg. At Terbregge, marker flares from British pathfinder aircraft landed off target and started fires that destroyed five homes—fortunately without causing casualties. The British would continue to use pathfinders throughout the missions, but the USAAF never did, relying entirely on the skills of its 8th Air Force navigators and pilots to find their Chowhound targets in all weather. But the people of Terbregge also fared badly when a number were injured by falling food containers. One unconfirmed report had a local woman seriously injured but protected from further injury by a young German soldier who reputedly threw himself over her and was himself killed.[18]

At Rotterdam, a system of rewards was worked out for those civilians who were genuinely helping to collect and distribute the food. Initially, they were given chocolate bars from the day's haul, but later coupons were handed out to be exchanged for meals being cooked at outdoor kitchens set up at the canal quays where the food barges were loaded. All this was arranged and administered by civilians. Later, there would be the occasional unconfirmed report of German troops collecting and taking away food that had been dropped—from the 8th Air Force drop at Vogelenzang on May 1, for example.[19] But the German military and Dutch police increasingly withdrew after May 2, leaving the civil officials to supervise the drops and merely watching over the food stockpiles once they were established to prevent looting.

In addition to the hundreds of B-17s making food drops on May 2, upward of 400 Lancaster bombers made drops across Holland that day. They were flown by crews from Britain, Canada, Australia, New Zealand, South Africa, Rhodesia and Poland. One of those aircraft was *S for Sugar,* Alex Howell's 186 Squadron Lancaster. This was the third food drop flown by Australian Howell and his crew, and this time their target was The Hague. It was to prove a hazardous day for *S for Sugar.* On the final run to the DZ, Howell was forced to take rapid evasive action to avoid another Lancaster that sheared in toward him from the starboard side. This aircraft was itself trying to avoid falling food sacks that had just been dropped by another Lancaster a little ahead and above it. Howell was able to avoid the second ship and right his own aircraft, but in the process he overshot the target.

S for Sugar came around again, doing a wide circuit of the South Holland countryside, with pilot Howell determined to make his drop. The corridor to the DZ was as busy as a rush-hour highway, and Howell had to hang around for a time waiting until he spotted a gap in the bomber formations crowding the sky. Once a gap opened up, he quickly dove in to take his place. *S for Sugar* made a fresh bombing run, and this time its load was on target. But one sling full of food packages became caught up in the bomb bay and wouldn't release. Disappointed that he hadn't been able to deliver a full load, Howell finally turned for home.

Howell kept *S for Sugar* so low as he flew over dikes on the return route that he had to climb to get over the top of them before dropping back down again. And when the Lancaster winged over the top of a village near the coast, it seemed as if every resident had come out to wave to the bomber's crew. Howell decided to give the village a gift. Three more times he flew over the village, on each pass trying to dislodge the last sling of food by diving at the houses below and then pulling up sharply. On the third pass, the sling broke free, and burlap cement sacks full of food rained down on the village.

As Howell and his crew watched, the sacks went crashing through tile roofs. Worried that he might have injured someone, Howell came back for a fifth pass over the village and a look-see. There below were the holes in the roofs that they had just created. And poking up through the holes were villagers, with the biggest smiles on their faces, waving their thanks. Howell and his crew roared with laughter. After a farewell waggle of his Lancaster's wings, the Australian finally put his airplane back on course for base.

But their adventure was not yet over. Still flying very low, Howell was following a road that led to the coast. A girder bridge loomed ahead, crossing a small waterway. Just beyond it, German soldiers were marching along the roadside in a neat line. The sight of the bomber thundering down on them sent most of the troops diving for cover. The exception was a soldier who moved to the middle of the road, put his rifle to his shoulder, and took rapid but very deliberate aim at the Lancaster. *S for Sugar*'s radio operator, Peter Weston, was standing, looking out the bomber's Plexiglas astrodome behind the cockpit. He saw the German raise his weapon, and as the aircraft passed over the man, Weston felt something thud into the metal step beneath his feet.

No apparent damage was caused, and *S for Sugar* flew back to England and landed at base without any problems. But after Howell and his crew climbed out of their ship and gave it an inspection, they spotted a bullet hole in the underside of the fuselage, between the nose and the bomb bay. And when the ground crew did a minute inspection of the interior of the aircraft, they found a bullet lodged in the step where Peter Weston had been standing. Had the bullet continued on, passing through the step, it would have hit Weston and probably killed him.[20]

With Germany's defeat now inevitable and growing closer with each passing day, how many other unhappy Germans would disobey orders and fire on the bombers of the relief armadas, and with something more damaging than a Mauser rifle?

ON MAY 3, close to 400 Flying Fortresses again flew Chowhound missions, this time to seven locations across Holland. Hank Cervantes was copilot of a B-17 of the 100th Bombardment Group's 349th Bomb Squadron that took off from Thorpe Abbotts in Norfolk that morning for Holland. Cervantes was flying his first Chowhound mission.

His bomber left the ground with plenty of strip to spare—the main runway at Thorpe Abbotts had the luxury of being 300 feet longer than most wartime bomber fields. After assembling over Norfolk, the B-17s of the 100th BG winged their way out over the North Sea, bound for Holland. Around Hank Cervantes's bomber, and behind it, flew scores of other bombers from the four squadrons of the Bloody Hundredth, all on the same course.

Like Cervantes, the other members of his crew were tense. The word from group headquarters was that over the past two days German flak in Holland had held its fire on B-17s making Chowhound drops, but Cervantes and his men worried how long that situation would last. None had been made to feel any better when they had been told at the preflight briefing that morning, "Anyone fired upon will receive credit for a combat mission."[21]

To be on the safe side and sneak up on the flak batteries lining the Dutch coast, the formation leader took the group down to wave-top height. As dikes loomed ahead, the bombers rose a little to skim over them. Suddenly, German flak batteries were everywhere ahead of them and beneath them, and Cervantes and his fellow crew members kept a wary eye on the gunners, who, in Cervantes's opinion, squinted at them like duck hunters waiting for the shooting season to open.[22]

And then they were flying over a carpet of color that took Hank Cervantes's breath away—field after field of tulips in bloom. Here and there a bomber would bob up briefly to avoid a telephone pole, but otherwise Cervantes's squadron hurtled along close to the ground, rising a little to pass over farms and villages as they flew toward Amsterdam. Dutch women and children were out in the streets and gardens in the hundreds, joyfully waving at the passing American flyers. Some flew the Dutch tricolor flag. Banned by the German occupiers, these flags had been kept in hiding for five years, to be brought out on an occasion like this.

To Cervantes's amazement, there were US flags flying down there, too. It seemed that Dutch sewing machines had been hard at work over the last few days producing the Stars and Stripes as a way of connecting with the Chowhound crews. As the B-17s flew over open fields, groups of women and children pointed to messages spelled out with stones in large letters. "THANK YOU BOYS," said one. This choked up many a young American airman. And then they were lining up for their drop over the airfield outside Amsterdam. Ahead, the drop zone had been marked precisely with a huge white cross made from bed sheets.[23]

"Bombs gone!" came the cry, and the forty-three-pound food crates tumbled from the open bomb bay.

Down below, Cervantes could see hundreds of civilians rushing to collect the packages, even as more tumbled down on them from the sky like missiles, falling on top of them. There were German soldiers down there, too, with rifles on their shoulders, watching the Dutch and watching the passing bombers. Banking away and climbing, the 349th Bomb Squadron took up a course for the return to Norfolk. To Cervantes, this had been a bomb run like no other. He would do it twice more in the coming days.[24]

Ball-turret gunner Norman Coats from the 390th Bomb Group flew another Chowhound mission on May 3. Coats was to estimate that he waved to every single resident of Holland that day. He too saw the huge "THANK YOU" messages spelled out on the ground and the American flags and Dutch civilians pointing to him in his turret.[25]

Pilot Bob Miller of the 493rd BG was also flying Chowhound again on May 3. With Chowhound seemingly working like a well-oiled machine, the aircraft of Miller's group were now authorized to fly singly out of formation and choose their own way home. Like other B-17 pilots, Miller was becoming increasingly daring. His squadron had been briefed that morning not to fly in tight formation, but to make their drops one after the other in a single line ahead. Miller liked this much better, considering it the best way to carry out this type of work, taking the pressure off pilots. No longer did they have to be alert to avoid hitting other B-17s flying all around them or food containers falling from aircraft above. Now they could concentrate on making accurate drops.

Miller dropped his load at Vogelenzang airfield southwest of Amsterdam from just 300 feet, then turned his B-17 toward The Hague. A warm glow came over him as civilians below waved Dutch flags at him. And then he was flying over the Dutch capital, clearing a steeple by just five feet. Miller would convince himself that the building with the steeple that he almost flew into was the tower of the Peace Palace, home of the International Court of Justice. Symbolic, he thought, of this whole mission.[26]

Miller wasn't the only one making dare-devil maneuvers. Some B-17s were returning from Holland with foliage attached to wings and tail wheels after near misses with trees. Of course, most Chowhound pilots were just in their early twenties, and boys will be boys. One bomb squadron captain would issue a command telling his pilots to cut this out and not fly their B-17s as if they were fighter aircraft.

17

AUDREY HEPBURN'S BIRTHDAY PRESENT

THE LIBERATION OF HOLLAND

On Friday, May 4, 1945, living at her grandfather's villa at Velp with a host of refugees as house guests, Audrey Hepburn turned sixteen. She and her mother, both near to starvation, had heard of the radio reports that said the Allies were on the brink of liberating occupied Holland. But Audrey's birthday passed without any sign of liberation. And then, the next day, Audrey received a belated birthday present. At 8:00 a.m. on May 5, the tanks, jeeps and trucks of the 1st Canadian Army began rolling into German-occupied Holland. At last the Netherlands was again a free country. Audrey would later say that she whooped and hollered and danced with joy. Standing in the crowd watching the Canadian troops pass by as they advanced into occupied territory, she wanted to kiss every one of them.[1]

Sixteen-year-old Audrey was five feet six inches tall, but she weighed ninety pounds. Her starvation diet over the past seven months left her afflicted with anemia, jaundice and asthma. But with the Canadians came food. Truckloads of food and candy and cigarettes and things that the Dutch had not seen in years. Simple things like salt and sugar, which had become beyond luxuries in their absence from Dutch tables; they had become the stuff that dreams are made of. The next day, Audrey sat down to the most luxurious breakfast she could remember—oatmeal from the Canadians coated with sugar, also from the Canadians. Audrey cleaned her bowl. It was delicious but so rich that her system couldn't cope with it—the meal made her violently ill. But Audrey didn't mind. She would never forget that first meal as a free person once again.[2]

Several days later, the Canadian troops stationed in the area would set up a gasoline-powered electric generator in the village square at Velp, hooking it up to a movie projector. Audrey and her teenaged friends joined the rest of the people who packed the square that night to watch the first Hollywood movie screened in the town in five years.[3] Audrey never could remember which movie it was. Everything was too exciting, too heady. A good feed, a movie, and the gift of freedom. Now that was a heck of a way to celebrate a sixteenth birthday.

ON MAY 4, John Eyking, a Dutch child living in the coastal village of Beverwijk, northwest of Amsterdam, saw packages tumble from the belly of a Flying Fortress that zoomed by overhead. Eyking's father had a market garden where he had grown tulips, daffodils and hyacinths before the war, but he had sown it with grain, vegetables and fruit following the German occupation. The family had a few farm animals, too, and these were herded every night into a barn, where, since the start of the Hunger Winter, family members had taken turns standing guard over them with pitchforks to prevent their being stolen.

Now packages fell into the Eyking garden from the passing B-17. When the family ran to them and opened them, they found that the packages contained luxuries such as margarine, sugar, condensed milk and candy. Only months prior to this, the Dutch Resistance had set off a bomb in Beverwijk. Aimed at killing a German general when he passed in his staff car, it missed its target, but it had destroyed another military vehicle. In reprisal, occupation troops had dragged ten Dutchmen at random from their Beverwijk homes, lined them up against a wall, and shot them.

John Eyking's father, terrified that he would be shot if it became known that he and his family had eaten this American contraband that had fallen from the sky, had the family members hide the food from the air drop, promising them that they would enjoy a liberation feast the day the Germans in Holland surrendered. And that was just what they would do several days later.[4]

18

GRIF MUMFORD'S SPECIAL AIR DELIVERY TO A DUTCH SISTER

On May 5, Lieutenant Colonel Grif Mumford was piloting the lead B-17 on the 95th Bombardment Group's Chowhound mission to Utrecht. In the nose of the bomber sat lead navigator and Grif's best friend, Major Ellis B. Scripture. Both men had deserted their desks at 3rd Air Division HQ at Elveden Hall to volunteer to fly Chowhound—an operation implemented under their command. By the end of the operation they would fly several Chowhound sorties.

The usual squadron formation of sets of three B-17s abreast—a lead aircraft with a wingman to port and another to starboard—had been abandoned. Leading thirty-nine other B-17s from the 95th in single line ahead, Mumford was piloting a borrowed bomber as he followed the course set for him and the group by buddy Ellis Scripture. Such was the confidence that the 8th Air Force bomber pilots now had in their ability to make accurate, low-level drops—and the confidence their commanders had that the Germans would continue to adhere to their agreement and not fire on the B-17s—that the Forts were flying in to make their drops one at a time in a long line, as if on an invisible conveyor belt.

Mumford made a perfect approach to Utrecht's Valkenburg airfield, the most easterly of Chowhound's Dutch drop points and the closest to the German border. If Mumford kept flying due east, he would soon find himself over the German industrial city of Münster, where, in October 1943, five of twenty-two 95th BG B-17s had been shot down during a bombing raid—one of the most expensive raids, percentage wise, that the group was to fly during the war. Mumford had himself flown combat missions for close to two years, being one of the few original pilots of the group to survive being killed or captured on operations by the autumn of 1944. Promotion to a desk had probably saved his life. But he had missed the joy of flying. And, as chief air executive of the 3rd Air Division, Mumford had sent the men under him on the risky Chowhound missions. He was determined that he would never send his men where he wasn't prepared to go himself.

Now Mumford's load of humanitarian supplies was tumbling onto the small airfield outside Utrecht, and he gunned his Fort's four engines and gained height as Scripture gave him a course to a small village in eastern Holland over the intercom. Back at 3rd Air Division HQ at Elveden Hall, Mumford had been approached by a female aide to the current Air Division commander, Major General Earle Partridge, with a special request. Captain Cornelia Visman's sister had married a Dutch citizen and was living in a rural village in occupied Holland. Grif Mumford had a special delivery for Captain Visman's sister—a letter from one loving sister to another.

Approaching the village, Mumford and his crewmates could see that the local population had filled their square to celebrate the liberation of Holland. Three times Mumford flew over the square at several hundred feet as his crew enjoyed the sight of the cheering, waving crowd below. On the third pass, one of Mumford's crew sent a small package dropping from their B-17. Sinking to earth beneath a small parachute, the package contained Cornelia Visman's letter to her sister, weighted down by a large Hershey chocolate bar. A note attached to the package said: "Please deliver this letter and keep the chocolate bar." The package landed in a quiet park, away from the revelers. Following the war, Mumford learned from Cornelia Visman that her letter had been duly delivered to her sister. Who got the Hershey bar remained a mystery.[1]

Haven P. Damer's *No Credit* was one of the thirty-nine 95th BG bombers flying behind Grif Mumford's machine to Utrecht that day, and it too had a special delivery to make. By the time they flew this Chowhound run to Holland on May 5, things were very different for the *No Credit* crew from their first nerve-wracking flight four days earlier. No longer were they or their commanders worried about being shot at by the Germans; it was almost as if they were taking a flying vacation. For one thing, they had sightseers aboard—two captains who usually flew desks back at base and two line men from the ground crew.[2]

Unlike their May 1 flight, too, not only was their squadron flying in loose formation, but their load had also changed. By this time, Chowhound payloads of crates of K-rations were increasingly being augmented, and often replaced, by the burlap sacks being used by other Allied bombers. Unlike the K-ration packs with their ten different items, these sacks frequently contained a single item—it might be dried egg, milk powder, dried yeast, cheese, chocolate bars, margarine, dehydrated meat, tea, coffee, luncheon meat, salt, pepper or mustard. More than one Chowhound crewman would report seeing civilians who were white from head to foot as they gathered supplies on the ground—they had been hit by a milk powder sack, which burst over them.

Meanwhile, on the ground, Dutch youths would rush to a single sack that fell, late, from a B-17 as it passed overhead. Hoping for chocolate bars or coffee, they found to their disappointment that it contained pepper. These late drops of a sack or two from B-17s over remote locations had to do with the change in delivery method. Forty-three-pound crates of K-rations were relatively easy to dispense, but once the 8th Air

Force switched to carrying sacks instead of crates, it found that a sack or two would often become stuck and would have to be thrown or kicked free by a crew member hanging on for dear life in the bomb bay—there wasn't enough room in there to wear a parachute—to allow the bomb bay doors to close.

Albert VanWey, a radio operator aboard a B-17 of the 570th Squadron, 390th Bombardment Group, was one of those who found himself hanging precariously in a bomb bay, knocking sacks free.[3] Meanwhile, Ray Powell of the 100th Bombardment Group discovered that, after his B-17 had made its drop at Alkmaar airfield ten miles inland of the coastal city of Bergen, several sacks remained stuck, and he and other crewmen set about freeing them. After leaving the drop zone, Powell's aircraft flew over some isolated houses on the North Sea coast, where the occupants came out to wave at them and unexpectedly found themselves on the receiving end of the last sacks of the B-17's load.[4]

Ground crew also found the sacks much harder to load into partially open bomb bays—they would slip and slide and sometimes fall out. Some crew chiefs came up with a solution for this: a large canvas tarpaulin was loaded with sacks on the ground, and this was hauled up into the bomb bay. Another solution was the building of a wooden platform that was piled with sacks and then loaded into the bomb bay. The crew chief of the B-17 of Bernie Behrman, a top-turret gunner with the 569th Squadron of the 390th BG, was one of those who used this method.[5]

Max Krell, a pilot with the 96th Bombardment Group, had watched as one of these wooden platforms was constructed in the bomb bay of his aircraft in late April. On one side of the bomb bay, the platform, or temporary floor, was hung from the outer edges. The other side rested on the bomb shackles located in the middle of the bomb bay, next to the middle catwalk. The bomb bay doors would be opened electrically by the bombardier, after which a member of the crew had to manually release the platform, which dropped on one side, sending its load tumbling into the air. Several crew members then had to pull the dangling platform back up into the bomb bay by hand before the doors could be closed.[6] But as many aircrew were to find, use of such platforms didn't always prevent ration sacks from becoming caught up in the bomb bay once the platform had been released.

Despite the problems they were causing, these sacks were delivering vitally needed food in bulk—as the creators of K-rations had worked out, no one could live on ten-in-one rations for a prolonged period. Even so, some sack drops were misdirected or let go from too great a height. At Schiphol Airport, for weeks after the Chowhound drops, buildings would be streaked yellow from sacks of margarine that had burst on hitting them, while the smell of coffee was thick in the air from other sacks that had burst on impact.[7]

Approaching Utrecht on May 5 astern of Grif Mumford's Flying Fortress, Haven P. Damer eased his B-17 down to 400 feet for the now routine drop and throttled back the engines. At 135 miles per hour *No Credit* let go of its load right on target.

"Groceries away!" said the bombardier with a smile in his voice.

Once the bomb bay was emptied, the bomber banked away with its bomb bay doors slowly closing, and Damer commenced his usual low-level buzzing, weaving around windmills with their slowly turning sails, to the glee of passengers and crew.

"Good buzz job, skip," remarked his twenty-one-year-old radio operator, Paul Laubacher.[8]

Then Damer set a course for home, gaining altitude and heading southwest toward Antwerp. Now he noticed fields ahead ablaze with natural color. He realized that it was tulip time in Holland, and the fields were full of tulips in full bloom. In one of those fields Dutch farmers had cut tulips so that the flowers spelled out a giant message to the passing bombers: "THANK YOU YANKS." The message made all of *No Credit*'s crewmembers feel good about their Chowhound flights, and even better about what they were about to do next.[9]

Prior to this flight, pilot Damer had set a very personal little mercy mission in motion. He had asked each crew member to donate to a small "comfort" package that he put together, containing the sort of things he knew the people of Holland would not have seen in quite a while—chocolates, cigarettes, soap, gum, and so on. He'd even found a small parachute used for message drops, the same kind that Grif Mumford had used. Adding a note wishing the finder well, Damer had packed his little collection into a small box and tied it to the parachute. As the bomber flew toward the coast, radio operator Laubacher threw *No Credit*'s private contribution to the mercy mission from the aircraft, sending it sailing to earth with the crew's hopes that it would make someone happy.[10]

What the crew didn't realize was that by this time, *No Credit* had reached the Holland-Belgium border. Their package landed on Belgian soil just across that border, in the town of Ekeren not far from downtown Antwerp. That morning, five-year-old Mariette DeWeerdt was walking in her family's small field with her father, Jan, herding their four precious sheep, when she saw *No Credit*'s package come floating down from the heavens. With great excitement, father and daughter ran to the package and tore it open to find the little treasures it contained. The Belgians, like the Dutch, had had it tough during five years of German occupation since the Nazi Blitzkrieg of 1940, and it would be a long time before they would be able to buy the sorts of things that *No Credit* had sent them. Mariette DeWeerdt would never forget her surprise and joy at that moment of discovery.[11]

That same day, May 5, Hank Cervantes and his 100th Bombardment Group comrades were making their latest Chowhound delivery, this time to Bergen. Twenty-one aircraft from the group dropped close to forty tons of food on the IJmuiden military airfield south of Bergen that morning. Looking down from his pilot's seat, Cervantes would see a sight that would lodge in his memory forevermore. A mother was hugging her children. They were all looking up at Cervantes as he flew overhead, and the children were pointing to the enormous grins on the faces of Cervantes and his crewmates.[12]

At 10:00 that morning, 96th Bombardment Group pilot Delfred C. Kraske was making a Chowhound drop at Schiphol Airport. Kraske would always remember this drop, his first. A row of red-brick buildings four stories high ran along the eastern side of the runway. Dutch civilians hung from every window in those buildings, with many waving Dutch and American flags. The sight made Kraske and his crew proud to be American.[13]

Bob Belgam of the 390th Bombardment Group was another of the pilots who followed Grif Mumford to Utrecht's Valkenburg airfield on May 5. Like Haven P. Damer, Belgam had become an experienced hand at the low-level food drops; this was his third Chowhound sortie. Belgam duly dropped his load, then deliberately set his B-17 on a course for Amsterdam—to do a little sightseeing. Flying up a main avenue of Amsterdam at several hundred feet, Belgam gave elated Amsterdammers a fly-past as they filled the streets to celebrate the end of hostilities in their country. Belgam flew so low that his bomber was actually lower than some of the people watching from upper-story windows. Belgam's tail gunner yelled that, in their excitement, someone had just fallen out of a window looking down at them as they passed.[14]

By this stage, Belgam, like most American pilots flying Chowhound sorties, had lost all fear of being fired upon from the ground. They now considered themselves lords of the skies over Europe. After all, hadn't German troops in occupied Holland surrendered on this day, with the Canadian army now in charge throughout Holland? In fact, that was in theory only. On May 5 General Blaskowitz accepted Allied documents spelling out the unconditional surrender of German troops in Holland,

and Queen Wilhelmina went on the radio to announce the liberation of her country. But Blaskowitz didn't agree to the content of these documents until a formal ceremony at Wageningen the following day.

Most German troops in western Holland had yet to disarm, and Canadian forces would take days to reach every part of Fortress Holland and relieve surrendered German garrisons of their weaponry. They would not enter Amsterdam, for example, until May 10. A graphic illustration of the dangers that still faced Allied aircrew would come in Amsterdam days after the German capitulation when, on May 7, Waffen SS troops who had yet to give up their weapons opened fire on thousands of Dutch civilians celebrating the liberation in Dam Square.

As Bob Belgam flew home after his brazen and devil-may-care sightseeing deviation to Amsterdam, unaware that the SS below were in a trigger-happy mood, May 5 generated another report of Germans on the ground firing at Chowhound aircraft. The report came from a B-17 of Hank Cervantes's 100th Bombardment Group. The crew of the B-17 in question told of three German soldiers firing their rifles up at them as they flew overhead to make the Bergen airfield drop. The disgruntled Germans managed to hit the B-17, too—back at base at Thorpe Abbotts in Norfolk, holes caused by rifle bullets were found in the bomber although no critical damage was discovered.[15] It was clear that nothing could yet be taken for granted as far as Chowhound was concerned.

Norman Coats of the 390th Bombardment Group flew another Chowhound mission that day—the group's squadrons made drops at both Utrecht and Vogelenzang. After dinner back at base at Framlingham, the young air gunner attended a church service conducted by the station's USAAF chaplain. Coats came away from the service feeling pretty pleased with himself after the chaplain told the worshippers that they should consider it an honor to fly these Chowhound mercy missions to aid the starving Dutch people.[16]

LATE IN THE AFTERNOON of May 5, Colonel General Johannes Blaskowitz, accompanied by his deputy, General Reichelt, arrived at the battered De Wereld Hotel in the ruined Dutch town of Wageningen to formally sign the surrender of German forces in Holland.

Lieutenant General Charles Foulkes, commanding the 1st Canadian Corps, was signing for the Allies. Prince Bernhard was there, too. He'd driven from Apeldoorn in RK-1, with members of his staff following in RK-2, Arthur Seyss-Inquart's second Mercedes limousine, which had recently been seized by the Dutch. The prince even brought along his fluffy white terrier, Martin. Bernhard's secretary, Marie Marks, had come to watch proceedings, and the prince gave her the job of looking after Martin, warning her to keep a firm hold of the little dog, as Martin didn't like General Blaskowitz.

As a nervous, stilted General Blaskowitz arrived at the shell-shattered hotel for the surrender ceremony in his best uniform and shiny jackboots, and wearing a holstered pistol, Marie was so excited to see the Germans humbled that she let Martin slip from her grasp. The terrier ran straight to General Blaskowitz and bit him on the ankle of one shiny boot.[17] Despite this unexpected low-level attack, the general would accept the surrender document—once a typewriter was located to type it up—and sign it the next day.

Although hostilities had officially been terminated, the need for food relief for the Dutch people remained.

ON MAY 6, foul weather closed in over the RAF airfields in the central north and west of England, grounding the food flights by British and other Allied crews based there. But the USAAF bases in East Anglia remained clear, and the 8th Air Force alone carried on the mercy mission that day, with 380 B-17s dropping 703 tons of food at five locations across Holland.

Haven P. Damer's *No Credit* was back over Utrecht on May 6, making another food drop at Valkenburg airfield. The B-17 was once again carrying four sightseeing passengers. This time it was *No Credit*'s own crew chief and his deputy plus two other ground crew from another aircraft of their squadron. Three of the passengers had a great time, especially when Haven Damer did his usual buzz of windmills. The fourth was not so happy; *No Credit*'s deputy crew chief was airsick for almost the entire flight.[18]

The low-level buzzing of the Dutch countryside became a way for many Chowhound pilots to let off a bit of steam now that the pressure was off. Oscar Sinibaldi of the 385th Bombardment Group was surprised when his pilot Lee Marcussen got into the act. Older than the rest of his crew and so conservative that he did everything by the book, Marcussen amazed his colleagues by dropping down to a hundred feet or so after one drop and buzzing cattle, panicking them and driving them at a run into a canal.[19]

19

BOMBARDIER BRAIDIC'S
FATEFUL DECISION

The seventh day of Chowhound was to bring the first American casualties of the operation. It would also see one US airman spared by a twist of fate that he could not explain.

At USAAF air station number 119 at Horham in Suffolk, Tony Braidic was among the scores of young men of the flight crews of the 334th Squadron, 95th Bombardment Group, who gathered in their briefing room early on the morning of May 7 to learn about their latest mission. A bombardier, and a good one, First Lieutenant Braidic had completed his training at Drew Field, Florida, in the fall of 1944 and departed for England as part of a B-17 crew commanded by First Lieutenant Lionel Sceurman—or "Spider," as he was known to one and all. In January 1945 Braidic and the rest of Spider Sceurman's crew had arrived at Horham from the States flying B-17G number 48640 to join the 334th. Over the next few months, Braidic and his comrades completed six daylight bombing missions over Hitler's Reich.

Because of his skill, and because the war in Europe was not expected to last much longer, Braidic was then removed from the active duty list and reassigned to train for B-29 Superfortresses operating in the Pacific theater against Japanese targets. His place in Spider Sceurman's crew was taken by a new arrival, Staff Sergeant Dave Condon. But Braidic was still at Horham in late April when Operation Chowhound began, and he volunteered for the mercy missions.

Since the beginning of the month, Braidic had flown on four Chowhound missions in the B-17 piloted by Lieutenant Paul Crider. Now, in the early morning chill, Braidic waited with the remainder of Crider's crew to learn about their mission for the day. But before they were given this information, the briefing officers gave the crews some long-awaited news.

"The war in Europe's over, boys! The Krauts have signed an unconditional surrender!"

Cheers rent the air, caps were tossed high, men hugged each other and shook hands.

But their superiors followed this with more sobering news, telling the airmen that the German surrender would not take effect until 8:00 a.m. next day, May 8. In the meantime, it was business as usual for both sides. Meaning that the Germans were still armed and could potentially still fire on US aircraft flying over territory they occupied. With peace just hours away, no American wanted to be the last man killed in this war.

Once the boisterous crews had settled down, their briefing proceeded. It was to be another Chowhound day, with Hilversum their target and air corridors and drop zone similar to those of the past few days. As the crews dispersed to their aircraft, many went with a nagging worry. Up till now, most of the German forces in Holland had kept their word and had not fired on the hundreds of American aircraft flying Chowhound missions. But what if, soured by the order from their High Command to surrender and disarm the next day, some disillusioned, fanatical Nazi antiaircraft gunners decided to go out fighting, taking more than a few B-17 crews with them?

Around 7:00 a.m., Tony Braidic and the rest of Paul Crider's crew reached the flight line, where more than twenty B-17s of the 334th stood loaded and ready for their aircrews. Braidic was awaiting his turn to climb up into the belly of Crider's B-17 when he was approached by his old skipper, Spider Sceurman, accompanied by bombardier Dave Condon.

"Tony, why don't you come fly with me today?" said Sceurman. "I'd like to celebrate the end of the war flying with the same crew I started out with. Dave will change places with you. No one will know the difference." He added that no one was obeying the rules when it came to Chowhound.

Numerous pilots had been taking ground crew along for joy rides over Holland as they made their food drops, and on this very flight Sceurman was taking along five members of the group's photographic unit as passengers. This was all strictly against flight regulations, but with the war due to end in a matter of hours, no one was worrying about regulations.

Braidic hesitated before he answered.

In the pause, Dave Condon spoke up. "I'd be happy to swap with you, Tony."

Braidic liked Sceurman and had good friends among his crew—the same flyers he'd trained with back in Florida and with whom he'd put in six dangerous combat missions—copilot Jim Schwarz, navigator Russ Cook, radio operator Gano McPherson, armorer/gunner Norbert Kuper, tail gunner William Lankford and ball-turret gunner John Keller. In particular, the four lieutenants in the crew, Braidic, Sceurman, Schwarz and Cook, had spent a lot of off-duty time together at the Crown, a pub in the village of Redlingfield not far from the 95th Bombardment Group's airfield, and on visits to London. Yet, inexplicably, Braidic said no to the idea of rejoining Sceurman's crew for this historic last mission. Not even he could explain why. Perhaps it was loyalty to his new skipper, Paul Crider. But say no he did. Bidding Sceurman and Condon farewell, Braidic climbed the metal ladder into Crider's B-17 and took his place forward in the bombardier's position.[1]

Soon, belching smoke from their exhausts, all four engines of the B-17s were roaring into life, and one after the other the aircraft of the squadron taxied out to take their turn lifting into the sky. On a normal bombing mission, when the bombers were heavy with fuel and bomb bays were packed with tons of high explosive, the B-17s would struggle to get into the air. Occasionally, especially during adverse weather, one would crash before it even had a chance to take the war to European skies. But food weighs less than bombs. And the flight from the east coast of England to Holland and back would be a brisk commute compared to the long hauls into the far reaches of the Reich that the group had been flying up till now, a flight that would not eat up much fuel.

Crider's aircraft took its position in the squadron as it assembled above the Suffolk fields, and then the 334th turned east and flew out over the sea, bound for Holland, as other squadrons of the 95th Bombardment Group took up station all around them. Crossing the Dutch coast, the B-17s dropped down to 400 feet. Some pilots had become so brave after a week of unchallenged Chowhound flights that they would go as low as a hundred feet on this last morning over wartime Europe. As Braidic's bomber approached Hilversum—it was one of twelve from the 95th BG with Hilversum as its target that day—Crider relied on Bombardier Braidic to guide their aircraft on the last leg to the drop zone. Ahead, in single file, other B-17s of the group were letting go of their loads on and near the white cross, made from bed sheets, created by the Germans on the ground to indicate the drop zone. Food sacks streamed from bomb bays like confetti, falling without parachutes, hitting the ground and tumbling over and over or, especially if they contained margarine, occasionally splatting on the ground, or the "deck," as aircrew called it.

On earlier Chowhound runs Braidic had seen some bombardiers misjudge their drops, with precious foodstuffs ending up in flooded polders, the low-lying fields of Holland that had been deliberately inundated by the Germans to discourage Allied paratroop landings. But Braidic did another precision job, hitting fair and square on target with his cascading load of supplies. "Bombs away," he habitually informed Crider.

"Okay, let's go home," the pilot responded, resuming responsibility for the ship and their return home. But he was in no hurry to return to base. Banking the B-17 around in a gentle turn, Crider deliberately set them on a course for the Dutch cities of Rotterdam and then Amsterdam, still flying low. This leg was to be purely for sightseeing purposes. From his position up front, Braidic marveled to himself that this was his last mission of the war in Europe, as tulip fields, dikes, canals and windmills flitted by beneath him. And not a single German soldier did he see down there.

Back west they flew, to scud over the port of Rotterdam, looking down on docks devastated by Allied bombing and German explosive charges and a harbor littered with the wrecks of ships destroyed by both sides over the past five years. Then turning north to Amsterdam, where, to Braidic's amazement, thousands of Amsterdammers were packed into the city's main square. Many in the crowd waved to them like mad people as the B-17 skimmed over the rooftops. It would be shortly after Paul Crider's B-17 flew over that the SS opened fire on the crowd in Dam Square, cutting down more than a hundred people—nineteen were killed and 120 wounded. Unaware of the tragedy taking place back in Amsterdam, Crider flew south and took his crew over Antwerp in Belgium before finally turning west and crossing the North Sea to land safely at Horham after a long, languid flight.

All seemed well as the group's aircraft landed one by one and returned to their designated concrete hardstands out in the English meadows. Jeeps ran each crew back to the administration buildings. As Braidic jumped from a vehicle and walked up the slight incline to the single-story, tiled-roof station headquarters for the routine debrief, he received a startling piece of information from the member of the crew of another 334th aircraft just emerging from debrief.

"Spider's ship is missing."[2]

The news stunned Braidic. At his crew's debrief and following it, he anxiously sought information about Spider Sceurman and his friends in B-17G 48640. He eventually found a member of another crew who had seen Sceurman's B-17 halfway across the North Sea, struggling almost at wave-top height with its number-two engine on fire and trailing thick black smoke. Braidic's informant said there was talk of German 20 mm antiaircraft guns stationed at the IJmuiden airfield or the associated German navy E-boat and submarine base opening up on the airplane as it flew overhead. Another report would say that Sceurman's B-17 collided with an aircraft from the 385th Bombardment Group. Nonetheless, all B-17s of the 385th returned from their Chowhound sorties this day.

Come nightfall, Braidic rushed to the air station's hospital on learning that survivors from Spider Sceurman's aircraft had just been brought in. Out of thirteen passengers and crew aboard, there were only two survivors—copilot Lieutenant Jim Schwarz, and the bombardier, Staff Sergeant Dave Condon. Both were suffering from the effects of being in the bitterly cold North Sea but were otherwise unhurt. They told Braidic that their food drop had gone without a hitch. The Sceurman aircraft, like twenty-seven other B-17s from the 95th BG, had Utrecht, rather than Hilversum, as its target that day. Following the drop at Utrecht, Spider had followed Crider's example and flown northwest to give his normally earthbound passengers a sightseeing visit to Amsterdam. After waving to a lot of Amsterdammers, they'd followed a canal to the coast and then headed for home at 1,500 feet. Everyone on board was in such good spirits that when one of them began to sing the 1942 hit song "Deep in the Heart of Texas," they all joined in, clapping in time at the appropriate places.[3]

Midway across the North Sea, as copilot Schwarz was returning to his seat after a foray to the rear to see radio operator McPherson, he was alerted by gunner Kuper that their Fort's inner port engine was running rough. Back in his place he could see oil leaking all over the cowling of the engine. Before long, the engine burst into flames. Pilot Sceurman had put the airplane into a dive in an attempt to extinguish the fire, but when that failed, and with the interior of the B-17 quickly filling with smoke, he had leveled out at 500 feet and given the order to bail out. Sceurman then tried to keep the dying Fort airborne for as long as possible to give everyone a chance to get out.

Dave Condon said that as he strapped on his parachute, he saw navigator Lieutenant Russ Cook force open the forward escape hatch door, struggling against the pressure of the slipstream, and then jump for his life. One of the photographer passengers went out the escape hatch next, and someone opened the bomb bay doors to create another avenue of escape. But Condon paused to try to drag an inflatable life raft to the escape hatch door—he wanted to spend as little time as possible exposed to the freezing cold waters of the North Sea once he jumped. When a ball of flame rushed past him, he realized it was time to go. Out the hatch he went, leaving the life raft behind. Condon had pulled his ripcord the moment he left the aircraft, which was losing height fast.

"Seconds later I hit the water with a smack and went under," Condon explained. "When I surfaced I inflated my life vest but didn't unfasten my parachute harness because I thought I would be more visible that way."[4]

Before long, Condon had become entangled in the parachute's lines, so he decided to get rid of it after all, and he unclipped the harness and freed himself of it. Not long after, he saw a British Lancaster fly low overhead, heading for Holland, and waved, hoping he had been spotted. Sure enough, the Lancaster, from the RAF's 550 Squadron, caught sight of Condon's parachute in the water and saw him floating beside it. The British bomber turned, and began to circle, just 200 feet above the waves, dropping flares to identify the location. Thirty minutes after Condon hit the water, an American PBY-Catalina float-plane landed close to him, and he was hauled aboard. He was so cold that he passed out once in the rescue aircraft. Meanwhile, a searching RAF Walrus air-sea rescue amphibian spotted Jim Schwartz and one of the photographer passengers, and both were plucked from the freezing waters fifty-five minutes after bailing out. The photographer, unconscious and in the grip of hypothermia, didn't survive the flight to shore.

But Tony Braidic wanted to know what had happened to Spider and his ship. Condon and Schwartz told him that, four miles from the English coast, Spider had attempted to bring the crippled B-17 down on the water with great skill. But at the last moment the bomber's burning port wing had dropped and clipped the water. This had sent the B-17 cartwheeling across the wave tops like a giant Catherine wheel before it settled and sank, fast. The open bomb bay doors had allowed water to rush into the aircraft. Spider Sceurman had drowned, and his body, along with those of three others on the ill-fated airplane, had been recovered by a boat summoned to the crash scene by the Lancaster. Seven men from the flight were never found, dead or alive. The four bodies that had been recovered lay in the hospital's mortuary.

As midnight approached, celebrations for VE (Victory in Europe) Day started early at the Horham base. But Tony Braidic and a number of other aircrew from the 334th couldn't bring themselves to celebrate. They were shattered that their friends had died on the last day of the war. And Braidic was wracked with guilt—if he had accepted Spider Sceurman's offer and flown with him that day, he might have shared his fate. He was inconsolable even when friends pointed out that bombardier Dave Condon had been one of the two survivors—suggesting that, had Braidic been in his place, he too would have survived.

As the partying went on in the camp that night, Braidic was able to find a drunken mortuary technician who agreed to show the bodies of Sceurman and the three others to Braidic and several friends from the 334th, to allow them to say their final farewells. Braidic would later regret this. The sight of the dead men on the slab shocked him. Not that they were disfigured: Sceurman had received cuts to the head and shoulder when trying to escape through the shattered sliding window beside his pilot's seat, but he had ultimately drowned; his lifeless body had been found floating in the sea. The pilot looked as if he were asleep, and that seemed to make it worse to Braidic as he harked back to that morning and the look of disappointment on Spider's face when he'd said no to him. He recognized two of the other dead crewmen as his friends, navigator Russ Cook and armorer/gunner Norbert Kuper. The fourth man was a stranger to him—one of the photographic unit men who'd gone along for the so-called joy ride, the one pulled from the water along with Jim Schwartz.

"Was it an unconscious premonition that warned me to decline Lionel Sceurman's suggestion on that fateful day?" Braidic would later ask. "I shall never know."[5] In the early hours of the next morning, Tony Braidic awoke screaming. He'd had a nightmare in which he was drowning. The nightmare, and the screaming, would punctuate his nights for a long time to come. Braidic attended the burial of Sceurman and the others at the American Military Cemetery near the English university town of Cambridge. His Chowhound flight was his last operation in Europe. And Sceurman's B-17 was the last aircraft of the 95th Bombardment Group to be lost in the war. It was the only US aircraft lost during Operation Chowhound, and the eleven men who perished the only USAAF fatalities during the ten-day mercy mission.[6]

No convincing evidence would emerge that Sceurman's aircraft was hit by German fire over IJmuiden. For one thing, the German navy's E-boat crews there had handed their boats and heavy weapons over to local authorities as soon as the agreed-on May 5 surrender date had arrived. Gallivanting Canadian captain Farley Mowat even ended up taking one of the super-fast E-boats for a test drive. So it is unlikely that any German 20 mm guns were still manned at IJmuiden by May 7. And neither of the B-17's surviving crewmen, Schwarz or Condon, was aware of their aircraft taking a hit from flak before the inner port engine caught fire.

The loss of Sceurman's B-17 is generally put down to mechanical failure; unlike those B-17s genuinely hit by German ground fire on May 2 and 5 and the Lancasters of Australians Peter Collett and Alex Howell, which both received bullet hits in the early stages of Operation Manna.[7] And, of course, several reports of B-17s such as *Stork Club* being shot at from the ground during Operation Chowhound were recorded in the war diary of the 8th Air Force, and damage would be confirmed. But in the case of Spider Sceurman, his bomber would join the list of US aircraft lost to causes other than enemy action—for every six B-17s lost in combat, another was lost to accident or mechanical failure during the war in Europe.[8]

WHILE TONY BRAIDIC was mourning the loss of friends on the night of May 7–8, most of his 8th Air Force comrades were in a celebratory mood, knowing that the war in Europe was due to officially end the next day. On May 7, a total of 231 B-17s from seven bombardment groups had flown Chowhound missions. These were the last American flights of the operation.[9] Twenty-one-year-old Douglas S. Eden, lead bombardier with the 100th Bombardment Group, would be proud of the fact that, on his last run to Schiphol Airport, on May 7, he dropped his load all over several parked German transport aircraft, splattering them with food.[10]

With the Canadian army taking charge on the ground in what had been German-occupied Holland, increasing quantities of food supplies could now be brought into the Netherlands by sea and road convoys. But it was a slow process for those in northern Holland. The Canadian army would only reach the northernmost parts of the country in the second half of May. In the meantime, the distribution of thousands of tons of relief supplies was continued by thousands of Dutch civilian volunteers.

20

THE END

FOR SEYSS-INQUART AND THE WAR

On May 7, the day of Spider Sceurman's fateful flight and the day the SS massacred Dutch civilians in Amsterdam's Dam Square, Arthur Seyss-Inquart was in a German military staff car attempting to cross the Elbe River bridge in Hamburg, Germany. Two British soldiers from the Royal Welsh Fusiliers Regiment stepped out into his vehicle's path, leveled their weapons and forced the car to a halt.

Admiral Karl Doenitz, Hitler's appointed successor as Germany's head of state, was holding daily cabinet meetings at his headquarters at Flensburg in Schleswig-Holstein, close to the border with Denmark, which, like most of Holland, was still under German occupation. Doenitz was trying to keep up the pretense that Germany still had a working and workable government and was striving to keep the country from lurching into chaos now that Hitler was dead and Allied armies were advancing into the heart of the Nazi Reich from east, west and south.

Arthur Seyss-Inquart, appointed Germany's new foreign minister in Hitler's will, had been summoned by Doenitz to Flensburg. Doenitz himself had only fled there from Plons, a little farther to the south, on the night of May 2–3.

Seyss-Inquart had come to Flensburg at night from IJmuiden in Holland by sea, aboard a speedy E-boat of the German navy. E-boat was the Allied name for these craft. Called the *Schnellboot*, or fast boat (*S-boot* for short) by the Germans, these 100-ton, triple-engine torpedo boats could race along at 43 knots, leaving Allied warships in their wake. In going to Flensburg, Seyss-Inquart had hoped to get Doenitz to confirm his action in ignoring Hitler's scorched-earth policy and to perhaps appoint him to act as surrender negotiator with the western Allied powers in his capacity as Hitler's appointee as the new foreign minister.

Doenitz not only failed to confirm Seyss-Inquart's appointment as foreign minister in the new government, but he gave that role, among others, to his new chancellor, Lutz Graf Schwerin von Krosigk, who had been finance minister under Hitler. And Doenitz sent the new head of the German navy, Admiral Hans-Georg von Friedeburg, to negotiate surrender terms on his behalf, first on May 4 with Montgomery at his headquarters at Lüneburg Heath just to the south of Hamburg in Lower Saxony, and then with Eisenhower at Reims on May 7. Left with no role in Nazi Germany's last regime, but with Doenitz's agreement that the scorched-earth policy was not to be implemented, Seyss-Inquart had opted to return to Holland.

When later asked why he made this decision to return, he would say that he wanted to be with the German co-workers of his administration at the end and wanted to answer for that administration "in the hour of disaster."[1] He was also probably hoping for favorable treatment from Eisenhower if he was found in charge in Holland at war's end, as opposed to being just one of many Nazi personages arrested with Doenitz. When a storm confined Seyss-Inquart's E-boat to port, he abandoned his plan to return to Holland by sea and instead set off to make the journey by road. This brought Seyss-Inquart to the congested Elbe River bridge.

As the two British soldiers stopped his car, Seyss-Inquart protested that he had important work to do. "I'm going to Montgomery," he declared, without disclosing his true identity. Whether he had genuinely intended to go to Montgomery is unclear. Perhaps this was a last-minute change of plan in the face of the British troops. Or perhaps it was merely a ploy to get him past the checkpoint and allow him to continue on his way to Holland. There was nothing he could achieve by going to Montgomery. But that was his claimed intent.

Go to Montgomery? One of the British soldiers smiled wryly. "You bloody-well are!" he declared.[2]

Seyss-Inquart, his driver and two aides were taken to the newly established British military headquarters at Hamburg's once swish Atlantic Hotel. As they were being taken in the door for questioning, a Dutch captain passed them. Recognizing Seyss-Inquart, he alerted the British. The game was up for Six-and-a-Quarter. One of the two soldiers who had captured Seyss-Inquart had a very good personal reason to see the Reichskommissar clapped behind bars with the rest of the Nazi hierarchy and put on trial for war crimes. The soldier's name was Norman Miller, but in 1939 it had been Norbert Mueller, and he had been a fifteen-year-old Jewish boy from Nuremberg who had arrived in England with a load of other Jewish children. They had escaped Nazi Germany as part of the Kindertransport program in which almost 10,000 Jewish youngsters were evacuated to Britain from throughout Europe. Their escape had been engineered through the efforts of the British Jewish community and their supporters.

Among the last to successfully flee the Nazis under this program, Miller had been one of forty children who had escaped by sea from IJmuiden in Holland on May 14, 1940, the day the Netherlands fell to the invading German army. Norman Miller's family had not been so lucky. Remaining behind in Germany, Norman's entire family had perished at the Jungfernhof concentration camp at Riga in Latvia. Now Arthur Seyss-Inquart and other leading Nazis would be brought to account for the concentration camps, the death camps and the other horrors of the Nazi regime.

ON MAY 8, Seyss-Inquart was flown from Hamburg to Hengelo in the Netherlands, northwest of Arnhem and not far from the German border, then driven to nearby Delden and the HQ of the 1st Canadian Army, to be kept under guard by the Canadians as he awaited planned war trials of senior Nazis. His escort was commanded by Lieutenant Colonel George Ball from Edmonton, who had joined the Canadian army at war's commencement as a corporal with the Royal Canadian Mounted Police.

That same day, May 8, the members of the 8th Air Force, now stood down from European operations, partied to celebrate the end of the war in Europe. Grif Mumford and his good friend Ellis Scripture were in London that day. Come nightfall, Grif and Scrip saw the British capital's street lights turned on for the first time since the start of the war in 1939 as the entire city came out into the streets to celebrate VE day. Back at Mumford and Ellis's 3rd Air Division headquarters at Elveden Hall, radio technician Ted Lucey from the 95th BG's 336th Squadron joined other HQ staff for what Lucey was to describe as "the party to end all parties." Held in the stable yard and garden at the stately mansion, the party inevitably included a baseball game.[3]

Canadian Farley Mowat spent VE Day at his latest headquarters— the new HQ of the 1st Canadian Corps, which was located at the former German 25th Army HQ at Hilversum, where Mowat had dined on horse with General Reichelt only days before.

Not long after the liberation of Holland, Audrey Hepburn's half-brother Alex emerged from hiding; he spent VE Day back with his family. Weeks later, the family was rejoined by Audrey's other half-brother Ian, who had walked all the way from the factory in Berlin where the Nazis had forced him to work for three years. With her family back together again, and with their wartime home in Arnhem destroyed, Baroness Ella van Heemstra decided to move to Amsterdam to give daughter Audrey every opportunity to pursue a career as a dancer. To Amsterdam they moved, and from there, first as a dancer, then as a model and later as an actor, Audrey Hepburn would blossom into the star she became.

Physically and mentally affected by the experience of near starvation, Audrey would observe a birdlike diet for the rest of her days. Apart from several pregnancies, her weight would never exceed 103 pounds.[4] Audrey's body, and her career, were shaped by the Hunger Winter of 1944–45. Legendary French fashion designer Hubert de Givenchy came to know Audrey Hepburn at the very beginning of her acting career and went on to make all her clothes, for her film roles and for her personally—including the famed "little black dress" in *Breakfast at Tiffany's*. Her wafer-thin body was a perfect clothes horse for Givenchy's elegant creations. "How proud and happy I am to have been able to work with and embellish my dear Audrey," Givenchy would say.[5]

When casting for the 1959 movie *The Diary of Anne Frank* was under way, Audrey was offered a leading role and was given a copy of Anne Frank's diary to read. Annelies "Anne" Frank was a Jewish girl whose family and Jewish friends had hidden in an attic in Amsterdam for two years, beginning in 1942, before being betrayed to Arthur Seyss-Inquart's administration and arrested in August 1944. Anne and her family were transported by the Nazis to the Auschwitz concentration camp in Poland. Anne and her sister Margot were later transferred to the Bergen-Belsen concentration camp in Germany's Lower Saxony where, in March 1945, both died during a typhus epidemic—just weeks before British troops reached and liberated the camp. Audrey turned down the film role. She had found Anne Frank's diary too distressing, both because of the heartbreaking story it told and the memories it evoked of her own harrowing experiences during the German occupation of Holland.[6]

21

THE AFTERMATH

Admiral Doenitz and the members of the last German government to fly the swastika flag were arrested at Flensburg on May 23, 1945, and subsequently brought to trial in Nuremberg for war crimes. Germany now came under an occupation government of the Allied powers.

When Arthur Seyss-Inquart joined former Nazi colleagues in court, he failed to impress the judges at the Nuremberg Trials in 1946. While he and other surviving Nazi military and political leaders headed by Reichsmarshall Hermann Goering had been called to account, charged with crimes against humanity, a number—including Propaganda Minister Josef Goebbels, SS chief Heinrich Himmler and navy chief Admiral Von Friedeburg—had avoided trial by committing suicide. Seyss-Inquart's hopes that he would be given credit for facilitating the mercy mission of April–May 1945 that brought thousands of tons of food into occupied Holland by air, sea and road were misplaced. He was given only the briefest opportunity to mention the matter, and the court was uninterested in his claim that he had attempted to mitigate the excesses of the SS and SD in Holland throughout his time as governor. Seyss-Inquart was found not guilty of conspiracy to commit crimes against humanity, but he was convicted on all three of the other counts that he faced—Crimes against Peace, War Crimes, and Crimes against Humanity. Like Goering and many of the other surviving Nazi leaders, Seyss-Inquart was sentenced to hang.

Seyss-Inquart was rated second most intelligent of all the Nuremberg defendants by prison psychologist Dr. Gustave Gilbert, who gave Seyss-Inquart an IQ of 141 on tests he conducted with all the defendants. Seyss-Inquart was smart enough to know what was coming and accepted his fate after his sentence was handed down. "Well, in view of the situation," he said to Gilbert shortly afterward, "I never expected anything different."[1]

Hermann Goering, the most senior of the Nazi defendants at Nuremberg—Luftwaffe chief, former deputy to Hitler and at one time in charge of the German economy—cheated the hangman by taking poison concealed in his cell the night before he was due to be hanged. But Seyss-Inquart and nine other convicted Nazi war criminals, a mixture of generals and government ministers and administrators, were duly hanged on October 16, 1946, a little over two weeks after the death sentences were handed down, in the gymnasium of the Palace of Justice building at Nuremberg where they had been tried.

The bodies of Seyss-Inquart and the other Nazis executed that day were placed in plain coffins, each labeled with a false name. One was given a Jewish name, to the amusement of the troops carrying out the gruesome work. The coffins were then loaded into trucks and driven under high security to the Eastern Cemetery in Munich, where all of the bodies were cremated. The ashes of the war criminals were then taken secretly to a bridge over the Isar River, where they were scattered into the waters below so that no repository for their remains could ever become a shrine for Nazism or neo-Nazis.

Former Nazi armaments minister Albert Speer, with whom Seyss-Inquart had consulted in April 1945 about how to react to Hitler's scorched-earth order, was treated more leniently by the Nuremberg tribunal, being sentenced only to twenty years' imprisonment. Released in 1966, he wrote a memoir that became an international best seller. Grand Admiral Karl Doenitz, U-boat and German navy chief and Hitler's brief successor as Germany's head of state, was sentenced to just ten years in prison, being released in 1956.

German-born Prince Bernhard was extremely popular with the Dutch in the years immediately following the war, even more so once his wife became Queen Juliana in 1948 on the abdication of her long-serving mother, Queen Wilhelmina. In 1946 Bernhard was appointed inspector general of the Dutch navy, in addition to his role as inspector general of the army. In 1953 the Dutch air force was added to his area of responsibility, with his title changing to that of all-encompassing inspector general of the armed forces. Following the war he also became heavily involved in business, sitting on the boards of scores of corporations, including KLM Royal Dutch Airlines and Fokker Aircraft. In 1961 he cofounded the World Wildlife Fund (WWF), which was later renamed the World Wide Fund for Nature. The prince served as the WWF's first president.

Bernhard's younger brother, Aschwin, who had served on the German side during the war, survived the conflict and in 1949 settled in the United States, joining the staff of New York's Metropolitan Museum of Art as an expert in Chinese art and remaining with the museum until his retirement in 1973. After he developed Parkinson's disease, Aschwin was encouraged by Bernhard to resettle in Holland, which he did, dying in The Hague in 1988.

Bernhard was involved in several postwar scandals that soiled his reputation. One, in the mid-1950s, involved a manipulative spiritualist and faith healer, Greet Hofmans, whom Bernhard's wife, Queen Juliana, made her close confidante for nine years. So much did she come to rely on Hofmans for advice on all matters, the queen even allowed her to live at the royal palace. Considering Hofmans to have an improper influence over the queen, Bernhard sought the involvement of the government of the day, which set up a commission of inquiry headed by former prime minister Pieter Gerbrandy. That commission agreed with Bernhard's view of Hofmans, and the Dutch government had the woman officially banished from the Netherlands. Needless to say, this had a severely detrimental effect on the royal marriage, and it was not a surprise to many commentators when it later came out that Bernhard had fathered at least two illegitimate children during his marriage (born in 1952 and 1967).

There was worse to come. In 1976, it was revealed that Bernhard, as inspector general of the armed forces of the Netherlands, had accepted bribes of more than $1 million from the Lockheed Corporation in the United States. Bernhard later claimed that the money all went to the WWF. The scandal forced the prince to resign as inspector general and to step down from his board positions. The long-lasting scandal was also believed to have influenced Queen Juliana's decision to abdicate the Dutch throne in favor of her daughter Beatrix in 1980. Bernhard lived to the age of 93, dying in 2004. For all his adventures, and scandals, Bernhard was nonetheless much respected by the Dutch for his role during the Second World War. Despite the likelihood that he had been a German agent in Paris in the 1930s, everything points to Bernhard's having been genuine about becoming a Dutchman once he married Juliana, and all his activities and energies seem to have been directed to helping the Dutch in occupied Holland in 1944–45 for all the right reasons, even though he clearly lied to hide his Nazi past.

It is difficult to know whether Operations Chowhound and Manna would have gone ahead without Bernhard's nonstop attempts to push the Allied political and military leadership into committing to the mission. Certainly, the greatest praise should be reserved for Dwight Eisenhower, who drove the air-drop operations forward when his own superior, General Marshall, was clearly holding back on the idea and worrying about the Russian reaction. But there can be no doubt that Bernhard's earnest and tireless advocacy of aid for the starving Dutch gave Eisenhower the gumption to push ahead with the operation. And, as Andrew Geddes said, the efficient distribution of the food aid once it hit the ground was attributable in great measure to Bernhard. Perhaps, without Bernhard, Chowhound and Manna would still have gone ahead. Perhaps not. Or maybe, without Bernhard, the food drops would have come days later—too late for the very young and the very old in occupied Holland.

What no one in Holland disputes to this day is the psychological and physical impact that the Hunger Winter of 1944–45 had on the Dutch people. According to a Dutch government report presented at the Nuremberg Trials in 1946, an estimated 25,000 Dutch died from malnutrition through that winter—a figure with which Seyss-Inquart agreed at his trial. Meanwhile, more than 200,000 men, women and children suffered from hunger edema in occupied Holland. General Alexander Galloway, commander of the Holland District, was to say in a careful and considered report to his superiors shortly after the liberation, "The average loss of weight is over forty pounds. Half of the population in the big cities suffers from undernourishment. Fifteen percent lives at the brink of starvation. Only thirty-five percent is reasonably healthy."[2]

Many survivors of the occupation, such as Audrey Hepburn, would suffer physically and emotionally for the rest of their days. Some among the millions of affected Dutch would, like Audrey, eat like birds. Others would become compulsive eaters, consuming everything that was put in front of them—in case there was no food the next day, as had often been the case during the Hunger Winter. Others, until their dying day, would habitually hoard food, just in case the bad times returned. None would forget the Hunger Winter—or the food raining from the skies that signaled its end.

Between April 28 and May 4, 1985, the fortieth anniversary of Operations Chowhound and Manna was remembered in Holland with week-long celebrations and the unveiling of a special monument dedicated to all involved. Many former aircrew who had flown the mercy flights from a variety of nations, including the United States, Canada and Britain, were present for the commemoration. A number of those who had flown the missions only discovered the vast scope of Chowhound and Manna at those celebrations. "The Dutch people remembered so vividly after forty years," said a surprised Ellis B. Scripture, who was one of the Chowhound veterans to attend. "That visit to Holland will be the highlight in the lives of all the veterans and their wives for all time. None of us privileged to be present had ever seen such a display of genuine emotion and great national pride as we witnessed during that memorable week."[3] There was a similar commemoration in Holland in 2010, by which time many of the veterans, including Scripture and Grif Mumford, had passed away.

22

THE BEST THING WE EVER
DID IN THE WAR

More than 25,000 men from the 8th Air Force's 3rd Air Division, both air and ground crews, were involved in Operation Chowhound, which saw the division's B-17s fly 2,268 Chowhound sorties.[1] The division's lead navigator, Ellis B. Scripture, who flew several of those missions, was to say, "It was certainly a wonderful feeling to be able to do something constructive, instead of destructive, as we ended our flying service in the European theatre of operations."[2]

Pilot Hank Cervantes of the 100th Bombardment Group, who retired from the air force as a lieutenant colonel, flew twenty-nine missions in B-17s during the war. Twenty-six were bombing missions over German targets, the last of which took place on April 20. His final three missions were all Chowhound flights. He would later say, "Among all of my wartime experiences those three missions are among my most treasured memories."[3]

Mike Faley, 100th Bombardment Group historian, concurred. "Many who flew these [Chowhound] missions will never forget them and recall them being some of the proudest moments they experienced during the war."[4] Bill Richards of the 493rd Bombardment Group was to say, "It was a marvelous experience to bring people food instead of death and destruction."[5]

Many Chowhound aircrew would not realize until long after the war just how grateful the people of Holland had been, and continued to be, for their food drops. Some years after the war, a postcard would find its way to former 390th Bombardment Group radio operator Paul Laubacher in Oxnard, California. Laubacher had settled there after leaving the USAAF, working as a clothing salesman and raising seven children. Originally sent to pilot Haven P. Damer, the postcard was from the grandfather of Mariette DeWeerdt, who, as a five-year-old, had helped her father retrieve the package thrown from *No Credit* by Laubacher on May 5, 1945. On the postcard, Mariette's grandfather thanked the B-17 crew for "a generous gift fallen from heaven."[6]

Laubacher kept a copy of the postcard in his attic for years until a friend and fellow Ventura County resident, Rick Biddle, mentioned that he was planning a trip to Belgium. Pulling out the card, Laubacher said to Biddle, "Look these folks up, will you?"

Biddle did just that. He returned to Oxnard to tell Laubacher that the DeWeerdt family still lived in the same house in Ekeren, the Antwerp suburb where they had resided during the war, and had made him very welcome. Sitting out on patio chairs in the garden, they recalled the day in 1945 when *No Credit* sent them a small but precious gift from the heavens.

Some little time later, in October 1995, the by then sixty-one-year-old Laubacher received a letter from Mariette DeWeerdt. It was accompanied by photographs of Mariette and her family as well as a card decorated by Mariette in typical Belgian needlepoint. "My family and myself send you a thousand thanks for that beautiful day," Mariette wrote. "We still have today a very good memory of it." For the first time, forty years after the event, Paul Laubacher understood how big an impact *No Credit*'s little package had made on a family in occupied Europe. "It beats bombs," he told his local newspaper, the *Oxnard Star*, when it got wind of the story.[7]

Max Krell, a B-17 pilot with the 96th Bombardment Group, was to say, "After hauling bombs and being shot at by enemy fighters and anti-aircraft fire it was a great experience to see so many people being happy because we could bring them something to eat."[8]

Canadian Joe English from Calgary was the pilot of a Lancaster bomber of the RAF's 625 Squadron. He and his crew had just completed thirty bombing missions over German targets when they were assigned to the Dutch food drops in April 1945. "The food packs were the best kind of bombs we ever dropped," he would later say.[9]

A fellow Canadian pilot who took part in the food drop missions, Len Bawtree from Enderby in British Columbia, was to observe, "As far as I was concerned, we had one desire, and that was to free Europe. First it meant demolishing factories and other military targets. But when we started the food drops, it was to improve people's lives and give them back their freedom."[10]

Dwight D. Eisenhower and Walter Bedell Smith never received any formal recognition specifically for creating and driving what became Operation Manna and Operation Chowhound, and following the war neither man would speak publicly about the food drops to the starving Dutch. In 1947, a year before she abdicated, Queen Wilhelmina of the Netherlands presented Eisenhower with a gold-inlaid Honorary Saber, one of her country's highest and rarest military awards. Eisenhower's saber was engraved: "Grateful memory of the glorious liberation." In addition, both Eisenhower and Bedell Smith were made honorary knights of the Order of the Netherlands Lion by the queen. Yet, to both men, their actions to instigate the mercy missions of April–May 1945 had been the natural thing to do under the circumstances and were not worthy of any special mention.

Eisenhower and Bedell Smith also established a precedent for their successors at the most senior levels of American military command in Europe. They proved that, with sufficient aircraft and sufficient bravado, a massive airlift to supply millions of civilians surrounded by hostile forces could be made to work. Three years later, in 1948, as Soviet forces in Germany threatened to cut off Berlin from supply from the West, it was the Manna/Chowhound example that gave American planners the confidence to think they could make the Berlin Airlift work.

Eisenhower went on to become the thirty-fourth president of the United States in 1953, serving two terms. Walter Bedell Smith served as US ambassador to the Soviet Union between 1946 and 1948 (taking his secretary at SHAEF, Ruth Briggs, along with him on the Moscow posting). But Bedell Smith's term as ambassador was generally not considered a great success—the gruff, no-nonsense Bedell Smith rubbed his Soviet counterparts the wrong way in those early Cold War years. Bedell Smith made a more notable mark on history by serving as director of Central Intelligence from 1950 to 1953, turning the previously disorganized new Central Intelligence Agency (CIA) into an effective intelligence service. He then served as undersecretary of state during 1953 and 1954. Until his death in 1961, Bedell Smith worked for his wartime boss in a number of consultative capacities to the president.

Andrew Geddes, the Briton who drew up what became Operation Manna and Operation Chowhound on Beetle Bedell Smith's orders, gained a much higher profile for his work on the operations. He would be dubbed "the Miracle Worker" by the Dutch. Geddes was awarded the Legion of Merit by the United States government in recognition of his behind-the-scenes work for both D-Day and Manna/Chowhound. He remained with Britain's Royal Air Force until 1954, then worked in local government for many years. In 1986, Geddes was elected president for life of the Manna Association, an organization created to bring together the many thousands of men and women who had been involved in the creation and implementation of the miraculous plan that Geddes had conceived on the orders of Eisenhower and Bedell Smith. Geddes died two years later.

In April 2007, a memorial was opened to Geddes by the Dutch people. It takes the form of a hiking trail in the Rotterdam district of Terbregge, one of the drop zones for Operations Manna and Chowhound. The memorial trail, named the Geddespath in Andrew Geddes's honor, passes an earlier monument to Manna/Chowhound. Officially unveiling the trail in 2007 were Geddes's son Angus Geddes, a lieutenant commander in Britain's Royal Navy, and Geddes's grandson David Chiverton, a warrant officer with the Australian army.

Andrew Geddes considered Manna/Chowhound as historically important as D-Day, "[e]specially since we had so very little time to lay on the operation," he said in 1985.[11] The D-Day invasion of Normandy had been more than a year in the planning, while the Dutch food drops, involving upward of a thousand heavy bombers and tens of thousands of personnel, had taken less than two weeks to organize.

Other, less publicized memorials to Manna/Chowhound have emerged over the years, often in surprising places. Following the war, Peter Buttenaar, the Dutch boy who ran all the way home after being buzzed by the Lancaster bombers of Bob Upcott and Peter Collett on their way to test the food-drop scheme, migrated to Ontario, Canada. Not only did he never forget that day, or the food drops that followed, in adulthood Buttenaar set about researching the Manna/Chowhound missions. He discovered that the lead aircraft on the April 29, 1945, test flight was *Bad Penny*, and that its crew was primarily Canadian. Buttenaar became a successful property developer, and in the 1990s he opened a new residential development at Southampton in southwest Ontario. He called the main street of his development Lancaster Street in honor of the April 29 flight. He went further, naming other streets in the development after each member of the crew of *Bad Penny*—such was the importance that Buttenaar attached to the Dutch food drops of April and May 1945.

The local press in Ontario soon learned of the *Bad Penny* connection to the development, and before Buttenaar knew it, he was being put in contact with Canadian members of the crew. In 1996, Peter Buttenaar had an emotional meeting with pilot Bob Upcott and bombardier Bill Gray at a Lancaster bomber memorial at Jackson Park in Windsor, Ontario. Buttenaar was able to impress on Upcott and Gray just what a morale booster the food drops had been for millions of Dutch people in 1945. The three men stayed in contact thereafter.

The mercy missions Operations Chowhound, Manna and Faust remain among the least-known and least-celebrated military operations of the Second World War, with the complex series of events that saw them conceived and delivered known only to those involved. Yet as early as May 8, 1945, the world was told how a massive tragedy had just been averted in Holland as a result of those operations. Allied war correspondents who had flooded to Holland in the wake of the May 5 German capitulation there found civilians lying dead in the street from starvation, found the hospitals full of the dying, and malnourished babies with the gaunt "faces of old men."[12]

The correspondent for the *London Daily Herald*—Britain's, and the world's, biggest-selling daily newspaper just prior to the war—was to write, "Only a few realized how really serious was the urgency of rushing food to the Dutch and how close the Netherlands came to a catastrophe from which it might never have recovered. Eisenhower knew how serious the situation was, which is why he called the Food Conference of April 30 [Bedell Smith's Achterveld meeting with Seyss-Inquart], four days after the last rations had been distributed." The *Daily Herald* reporter was in no doubt: "The food reached the Dutch only just in time."[13]

Few of the participants in Operation Chowhound are still alive today, but they and their descendants should know that several generations of Dutch people cherish their memories of the food drops of April–May 1945. It meant more than just food to the 3.5 million Dutch under German occupation. The masses of low-flying aircraft, day after day, were a very visible signal that they had not been forgotten and that their five years under the jackboot were about to be terminated.

In the end, Chowhound was about hope. And the 8th Air Force men and women from across the United States and their fellow flyers from far-flung places around the world as varied as Britain, Canada and Australia delivered it in K-ration packs and burlap sacks. Many a Dutch person who lived through the Hunger Winter as a child will be able to show you a burlap sack, a yellowed K-ration box, or a very old, very stale cracker as evidence of the hope that was delivered from the skies to them, their families and their neighbors in those last desperate days of World War Two. They, their children, their grandchildren and the Dutch nation will be forever grateful.

NOTES

CHAPTER 1: NAVIGATOR ELLIS B. SCRIPTURE'S PRAYER

1. Scripture describes this and other missions in Hawkins's *B-17s Over Berlin: Personal Stories from the 95th Bomb Group (H)*. The author has elaborated by also basing the narrative on the accounts of other aircrew flying these missions detailed in the same work and in extracts from letters and diary accounts that appear in Onderwater's *Operation Manna/Chowhound: The Allied Food Droppings April/May 1945* and at the Manna/Chowhound website, http://operationmanna.second worldwar.nl.

2. Killen, *The Luftwaffe;* Fleming, *August 1939: The Last Days of Peace.*

3. Hawkins, *B-17s Over Berlin.*

4. Hauptmann (Captain) Luci Wolff, ex-Oberkommando der Luftwaffe (High Command of the German Air Force), interview with the author, 1978. In 1939, at the age of nineteen, Luci Wolff was conscripted into the Luftwaffe at her German hometown of Wismar on the Baltic, serving as secretary to the local Luftwaffe commander until being transferred in 1942 to the Air Ministry in Berlin. There, among other duties, she worked as secretary to Reichsmarshall Hermann Goering for several weeks while his regular secretary was on leave. Later that year she was transferred to the OKL to become secretary to General Otto Langemeyer, chief of the high command's transport and supply department. In 1943 Luci met a Luftwaffe night fighter ace who shared her last name, Major Heinz Wolff. They married shortly after. Major Wolff was shot down and killed two weeks later. Following General Langemeyer's forced retirement in the wake of the failed Stalingrad Airlift, Langemeyer was replaced by his deputy, Colonel Walter Jacobi. Luci Wolff worked for Jacobi until the OKL's capture by American forces at Berchtesgaden in Bavaria on May 1, 1945. Made a prisoner of war, she escaped from the American POW camp at Berchtesgaden with three other former OKL secretaries and walked across Germany to the home of relatives at Cuxhaven on Germany's North Sea coast. She later relocated to Hamburg. In the 1950s she migrated to Australia, where she Anglicized her name to Lucy Wolf. The author, a young advertising copywriter and freelance journalist at the time, interviewed Mrs. Wolf extensively in 1978 and wrote of her wartime experiences in articles that appeared in the *Tasmanian Mail* and Sydney *Sun* in June and July of that year.

5. Scripture includes this traditional Native American prayer, whose author is anonymous, in Hawkins's *B-17s Over Berlin*. The prayer can also be seen in Bentley, Best and Hunt, *Funerals: A Guide*.

CHAPTER 2: HITLER'S SECRET AGENT

1. Hitler was to himself describe this 1936 meeting and his reaction to it, to staff, six years later. His comments are reprinted in Hitler, *Hitler's Table Talk*.
2. Ibid.
3. Ibid.
4. Ibid.
5. Van Der Zijl, *Bernhard: A Hidden History*.
6. Waterfield, "Dutch Prince Bernhard Was Member of Nazi Party."
7. *Newsweek,* April 5, 1976.
8. Bernstein, *Elimination of German Resources for War.*
9. Bernstein, *Report of the Investigation of I.G. Farbenindustrie AG.*
10. Ibid.
11. "New Facts About Prince Bernhard PhD Annejet van der Zijl," Querido, Dutch publisher's website.
12. Waterfield, "Dutch Prince Bernhard Was Member of Nazi Party."
13. The file had been at Humboldt University all along, but, from 1945 to 1989, the archive was under the control of the Russian occupation government and then the Communist government of East Germany, neither of which allowed access. The file's document number is ZBII1849 Act 28.
14. Hatch, *HRH Prince Bernhard of the Netherlands: An Authorised Biography.* In 1945, when the Allied powers designated the SS a criminal organization, it did not include the Reiter-SS in that category, describing it as little more than a social club.
15. Quoted in Hoffman, *Queen Juliana, the Story of the Richest Woman in the World.*

CHAPTER 3: THE SUSPECT PRINCE IN THE WORLD OF JAMES BOND

1. Lycett, *Ian Fleming.*
2. Ibid.
3. Ibid.
4. Ibid.

CHAPTER 4: THE BRIDGE TOO FAR

1. Wilhelmina, *Lonely But Not Alone.*
2. Ryan, *A Bridge Too Far.*
3. Hawkins, *B-17s Over Berlin.*
4. Ibid.
5. Wilhelmina, *Lonely But Not Alone.*
6. Hawkins, *B-17s Over Berlin.*
7. Ryan, *A Bridge Too Far.*
8. Ibid.
9. Keogh, *Audrey Style.*
10. Jonkheer Ian Edgar Bruce Charles van Ulford.
11. Jonkheer Aarnoud Alexander Charles van Ulford.
12. Keogh, *Audrey Style.*

13. Ryan, *A Bridge Too Far.*
14. Ibid.
15. Ibid.
16. Johnson, *Wing Leader.*
17. Ryan, *A Bridge Too Far.*
18. Ibid.
19. Testimony of Seyss-Inquart at Nuremberg War Trials, *The Avalon Project: Documents in Law, History and Diplomacy, Nuremberg Trial Proceedings*, Volume 16.

CHAPTER 5: THE GERMANS GO ON THE OFFENSIVE

1. Keogh, *Audrey Style.*
2. Killen, *The Luftwaffe.*
3. Johnson, *Wing Leader.*
4. Galland, *The First and the Last: The German Fighter Force in World War II.*
5. Johnson, *Wing Leader.*
6. Price, *Luftwaffe Handbook, 1939–1945.*

CHAPTER 6: SURVIVING THE HUNGER WINTER

1. Onderwater, *Operation Manna/Chowhound: The Allied Food Droppings April/May 1945.*
2. Bijvoet and Hutten, *The Hunger Winter: The Dutch in Wartime, Survivors Remember.*
3. Ibid.
4. Ibid.
5. Ibid.
6. Ibid.

CHAPTER 7: AN OFFER FROM NAZI GOVERNOR SEYSS-INQUART

1. Galland, *The First and the Last: The German Fighter Force in World War II.*
2. Testimony of Seyss-Inquart at Nuremberg War Trials, *The Avalon Project: Documents in Law, History and Diplomacy, Nuremberg Trial Proceedings*, Volume 16.
3. Ibid.
4. Van der Zee, *The Hunger Winter: Occupied Holland 1944–5.*
5. Ibid.
6. Ibid.
7. Ibid.
8. Ibid.
9. Ibid.
10. Ibid.
11. Ibid.
12. Ibid.
13. Ibid.
14. From a Dutch Foreign Office report reprinted in part in Van der Zee, *The Hunger Winter.*
15. Van der Zee, *The Hunger Winter.*
16. Ibid.
17. Ibid.
18. Captain Luci Wolff, ex-Oberkommando der Luftwaffe (high command of the German air force), interview with the author, 1978.

CHAPTER 8: PRESIDENT "DUTCH" ROOSEVELT'S PROMISE

1. Freidel, *Franklin D. Roosevelt: A Rendezvous with Destiny*.
2. Franklin Delano Roosevelt Family, Business and Personal Papers.
3. FDR to Princess Juliana, May 20, 1944. President's Secretary's File.
4. De Jong, *The Netherlands and Nazi Germany*.
5. President's Secretary's File.
6. Richardson and Freidin, *The Fatal Decisions*.
7. De Jong, *The Netherlands and Nazi Germany*.
8. Van der Zee, *The Hunger Winter: Occupied Holland 1944–5*.
9. Ibid.
10. Ibid.

CHAPTER 9: "BEETLE" BEDELL SMITH'S PLAN

1. Ridder, *Countdown to Freedom*.
2. Ibid.
3. Ibid.
4. Van der Zee, *The Hunger Winter: Occupied Holland 1944–5*.
5. Ibid.
6. Ibid.
7. Onderwater, *Operation Manna/Chowhound: The Allied Food Droppings April/May 1945*.

CHAPTER 10: FARLEY MOWAT GOES BEHIND GERMAN LINES

1. Mowat, *My Father's Son: Memories of War and Peace*.
2. Ibid.

CHAPTER 11: THE ACHTERVELD AGREEMENT

1. Ridder, *Countdown to Freedom*.
2. Ibid.
3. Ibid.
4. The author has been unable to establish a first name for Stoeckle. Also, in two separate accounts, Geddes variously gives Stoeckle the rank of captain and major. The author suspects that where Geddes accorded Stoeckle the rank of major he may have been confusing him with Major Groebe, who attended the next Achterveld conference with Von Massow. Further, Geddes consistently gives Alexander-Ferdinand von Massow the rank of oberleutnant, or first lieutenant, through these conferences; however, there are indications that Von Massow may have been promoted to the rank of captain in 1942. Without confirmation of Von Massow's rank in 1945, for this narrative the author has retained the rank of ober-leutnant accorded him by Geddes.
5. Ridder, *Countdown to Freedom*.
6. Ibid.

CHAPTER 12: THE FIRST NERVOUS TEST FLIGHT

1. Details of the crewmembers' thoughts, actions and observations come from *A Bad Penny Always Comes Back*, "Bios," "Radio Operator Remembers," "and 'Dutch Treat," http://badpennybook.com.

2. Ibid.
3. Ibid.
4. Ibid.
5. Ibid.
6. Ibid.
7. Ridder, *Countdown to Freedom.*
8. Ibid.
9. Captain Luci Wolff, ex-Oberkommando der Luftwaffe, who had been with Goering on this occasion, related this event to the author in a 1978 interview.
10. Onderwater, *Operation Manna/Chowhound: The Allied Food Droppings April/May 1945.*
11. Ibid.
12. *A Bad Penny Always Comes Back.*
13. Ibid.
14. Mowat, *My Father's Son: Memories of War and Peace.*
15. Ibid.
16. Ibid.

CHAPTER 13: IKE'S HATCHET MAN TELLS THE NAZI GOVERNOR STRAIGHT

1. Onderwater, *Operation Manna/Chowhound: The Allied Food Droppings April/May 1945.*
2. The 16-hour work day was calculated by author Cornelius Ryan, based on the Prince's detailed diaries, and included in a footnote in *A Bridge Too Far.*
3. De Guingand, *Operation Victory.*
4. Bedell Smith, *Eisenhower's Six Great Decisions, 1944–45.*
5. Testimony of Seyss-Inquart to the Nuremberg War Trials, *The Avalon Project: Documents in Law, History and Diplomacy, Nuremberg Trial Proceedings,* Volume 16.
6. De Guingand relates this part of the exchange in *Operation Victory.*
7. Bedell Smith, *Eisenhower's Six Great Decisions.*
8. Ibid.
9. Van der Zee, *The Hunger Winter: Occupied Holland 1944–5.*
10. Ibid.

CHAPTER 14: THE US 8TH AIR FORCE PREPARES FOR CHOWHOUND

1. Based on the recollections of Henry L. 'Hank' Cervantes at Manna/Chowhound website, http://operationmanna.secondworldwar.nl.
2. Ibid.
3. Onderwater, *Operation Manna/Chowhound: The Allied Food Droppings April/May 1945.*
4. Ibid. The same source reveals that ground crew of one British squadron covered the ends of their machine guns with plastic as a reminder to their air gunners that they were not to be fired.
5. Ibid.

CHAPTER 15: MAY 1, 1945

1. Onderwater, *Operation Manna/Chowhound: The Allied Food Droppings April/May 1945.*
2. Ibid.

3. Ibid.
4. Based on Krell's recollections, which appear at the Manna/Chowhound website, http://operationmanna.secondworldwar.nl.
5. Based on diary extracts of *No Credit*'s radio operator Paul Laubacher, which appear on the Manna/Chowhound website, http://operationmanna.worldwartwo.nl.
6. Onderwater, *Operation Manna/Chowhound.*
7. Based on diary extracts of *No Credit*'s radio operator Paul Laubacher, which appear on the Manna/Chowhound website, http://operationmanna.worldwartwo.nl.
8. Onderwater, *Operation Manna/Chowhound.*
9. Based on Krell's recollections, which appear at the Manna/Chowhound website, http://operationmanna.secondworldwar.nl.
10. Onderwater, *Operation Manna/Chowhound.*
11. Based on Coats's diary extracts, which appear on the Manna/Chowhound website, http://operationmanna.worldwartwo.nl.
12. Based on Hall's recollections, which appear on the Manna/Chowhound website, http://operationmanna.worldwartwo.nl.
13. Geddes relates this story in Ridder, *Countdown to Freedom.* He refers to Von Massow's brother the general as "Kurt" von Massow, but the general's name was actually Gerhard-Albrecht von Massow, and he was usually referred to as Gerd.
14. Ridder, *Countdown to Freedom.*

CHAPTER 16: GERMANS OPEN FIRE ON CHOWHOUND BOMBERS

1. Van der Zee, *The Hunger Winter: Occupied Holland 1944–45.*
2. Based on Sinibaldi's recollections, which appear on the Manna/Chowhound website, http://operationmanna.worldwartwo.nl.
3. Onderwater, *Operation Manna/Chowhound: The Allied Food Droppings April/May 1945.*
4. Based on Sinibaldi's recollections, which appear on the Manna/Chowhound website, http://operationmanna.worldwartwo.nl.
5. Based on Coats's diary extracts, which appear on the Manna/Chowhound website, http://operationmanna.worldwartwo.nl.
6. Onderwater, *Operation Manna/Chowhound.*
7. Ibid.
8. Ibid.
9. Ibid.
10. Ibid.
11. Based on Miller's diary extracts, which appear on the Manna/Chowhound website, http://operationmanna.worldwartwo.nl.
12. Ibid.
13. Onderwater, *Operation Manna/Chowhound.*
14. Ibid.
15. J. Vrouwenfelder, quoted in Onderwater, *Operation Manna/Chowhound.*
16. Ibid.
17. Onderwater, *Operation Manna/Chowhound.*
18. Ibid.
19. Ibid.
20. Ridder, *Countdown to Freedom.*
21. Based on Cervantes's recollections, which appear on the Manna/Chowhound website, http://operationmanna.worldwartwo.nl.
22. Ibid.

23. Ibid.
24. Ibid.
25. Based on Coats's diary extracts, which appear on the Manna/Chowhound website, http://operationmanna.worldwartwo.nl.
26. Based on Miller's diary extracts, which appear on the Manna/Chowhound website, http://operationmanna.worldwartwo.nl.

CHAPTER 17: AUDREY HEPBURN'S BIRTHDAY PRESENT

1. Keogh, *Audrey Style.*
2. Ibid.
3. Ibid.
4. Bijvoet and Hutten, *The Hunger Winter: The Dutch in Wartime, Survivors Remember.*

CHAPTER 18: GRIF MUMFORD'S SPECIAL AIR DELIVERY TO A DUTCH SISTER

1. Hawkins, *B-17s Over Berlin: Personal Stories from the 95th Bomb Group (H).*
2. Based on diary extracts of *No Credit*'s radio operator Paul Laubacher, which appear on the Manna/Chowhound website, http://operationmanna.worldwartwo.nl.
3. Onderwater, *Operation Manna/Chowhound: The Allied Air Droppings April/May 1945.*
4. Ibid.
5. Ibid.
6. Based on Krell's recollections, which appear on the Manna/Chowhound website, http://operationmanna.worldwartwo.nl.
7. Onderwater, *Operation Manna/Chowhound.*
8. Based on diary extracts of *No Credit*'s radio operator Paul Laubacher, which appear on the Manna/Chowhound website, http://operationmanna.worldwartwo.nl.
9. Ibid.
10. Ibid.
11. "One Man's War: After 50 Years, Sweet Memory," *Oxnard Star.*
12. Based on Cervantes's recollections, which appear on the Manna/Chowhound website, http://operationmanna.worldwartwo.nl.
13. Onderwater, *Operation Manna/Chowhound.*
14. Ibid.
15. Ibid.
16. Based on Coats's diary extracts, which appear on the Manna/Chowhound website, http://operationmanna.worldwartwo.nl.
17. Van Der Zee, *The Hunger Winter: Occupied Holland 1944–45.*
18. Based on diary extracts of *No Credit*'s radio operator Paul Laubacher, which appear on the Manna/Chowhound website, http://operationmanna.worldwartwo.nl.
19. Based on Sinibaldi's recollections, which appear on the Manna/Chowhound website, http://operationmanna.worldwartwo.nl.

CHAPTER 19: BOMBARDIER BRAIDIC'S FATEFUL DECISION

1. Braidic tells his story in Hawkins, *B-17s Over Berlin: Personal Stories from the 95th Bomb Group (H).*
2. Ibid.

3. Morris and Hawkins, *The Wide Blue Yonder and Beyond: The 95th Bomb Group in War and Peace.*
4. Onderwater, *Operation Manna/Chowhound: The Allied Food Droppings April/May 1945.*
5. Hawkins, *B-17s Over Berlin.*
6. The other USAAF passengers who died were Staff Sergeants Edward Bubolz, Robert Torbor, Gerald Lane and Joseph Repiscak, and Private First Class George Waltari.
7. No RAF, RCAF (Royal Canadian Air Force) or RAAF (Royal Australian Air Force) aircraft were lost during Operation Manna. A Lancaster did suffer serious wing damage when it collided with a radar tower over southeast England while flying a Manna sortie, but its pilot managed to nurse the bomber back to its base and make a successful landing.
8. Freeman, *The Mighty Eighth in Colour*, gives the six-to-one figure.
9. There would be 145 Manna flights by RAF Lancasters the following day before the entire air-drop operation was brought to a close.
10. Onderwater, *Operation Manna/Chowhound.*

CHAPTER 20: THE END

1. Testimony of Seyss-Inquart at the Nuremberg War Trials, *The Avalon Project: Documents in Law, History and Diplomacy, Nuremberg Trial Proceedings*, Volume 16.
2. Van der Zee, *The Hunger Winter: Occupied Holland 1944–5.*
3. Hawkins, *B-17s Over Berlin: Personal Stories from the 95th Bomb Group (H).*
4. Maychick, *Audrey Hepburn: An Intimate Portrait.*
5. In a 1999 Introduction to Keogh's *Audrey Style.*
6. Maychick, *Audrey Hepburn.*

CHAPTER 21: THE AFTERMATH

1. Gilbert, *Nuremberg Diary.*
2. Onderwater, *Operation Manna/Chowhound: The Allied Food Droppings April/May 1945.*
3. Morris and Hawkins, *The Wide Blue Yonder and Beyond: The 95th Bomb Group in War and Peace.*

CHAPTER 22: THE BEST THING WE EVER DID IN THE WAR

1. Onderwater, *Operation Manna/Chowhound: The Allied Food Droppings April/May 1945.*
2. Hawkins, *B-17s Over Berlin: Personal Stories from the 95th Bomb Group (H).*
3. Based on Cervantes's recollections, which appear on the Manna/Chowhound website, http://operationmanna.worldwartwo.nl.
4. "Chowhound," 100th Bomb Group Foundation website, http://100thbg.com.
5. Onderwater, *Operation Manna/Chowhound.*
6. "One Man's War: After 50 Years, a Sweet Memory," *Oxnard Star.*
7. Ibid.
8. Based on Krell's recollections, which appear on the Manna/Chowhound website, http://operationmanna.worldwartwo.nl.
9. Barris, *Days of Victory: Canadians Remember, 1939–45.*
10. Ibid.
11. Onderwater, *Operation Manna/Chowhound.*
12. "Holland Was Saved Just in Time," *London Daily Herald.*
13. Ibid.

BIBLIOGRAPHY

BOOKS

Barris, Theodore. *Days of Victory: Canadians Remember, 1939–45*. Toronto: Thorne Allen, 2005.

Bedell Smith, Walter. *Eisenhower's Six Great Decisions, 1944–45*. New York: Longmans, Green, 1956.

Bentley, James, Andrew Best, and Jackie Hunt. *Funerals: A Guide*. London: Hodder and Stoughton, 1995.

Bijvoet, Tom, and Anne van Arragon Hutten. *The Hunger Winter: The Dutch in Wartime, Survivors Remember*. Penticton, Canada: Mokeham, 2013.

Cremer, Peter Erich. *U333, The Story of a U-Boat Ace*. London: Triad, 1986.

De Guingand, Sir Francis Wilfred. *Operation Victory*. London: Hodder and Stoughton, 1947.

De Jong, Louis, et al, eds. *The Netherlands and Nazi Germany (Erasmus Lectures 1988)*. Cambridge, MA: Harvard University Press, 1990.

Droge, Peter. *Bernhard, Master of Spies: The Intelligence Career of Prince Bernhard*. Amsterdam, Vassallucci, 2002.

Fleming, Nicholas. *August 1939: The Last Days of Peace*. London, Davies, 1979.

Freeman, Roger Anthony. *The Mighty Eighth in Colour*. London: Arms and Armour, 1991.

Freidel, Frank. *Franklin D. Roosevelt: A Rendezvous With Destiny*. New York: Little Brown, 1990.

Galland, Adolf. *The First and the Last: The German Fighter Force in World War II*. London: Methuen, 1955.

Gilbert, G. M. *Nuremberg Diary*. London: Eyre and Spottiswoode, 1948.

Guinness, Rupert. *The Flying Grocer*. Sydney: Random House Australia, 2007.

Hatch, Andrew. *HRH Prince Bernhard of the Netherlands: An Authorised Biography*. London: Harrap, 1962.

Hawkins, Ian L., ed. *B-17s Over Berlin: Personal Stories from the 95th Bomb Group (H)*. Washington, DC: Potomac Books, 2005.

Hitler, Adolf. *Hitler's Table Talk, 1941–1944*. Oxford: Oxford University Press, 1988.

Hoffman, William. *Queen Juliana, the Story of the Richest Woman in the World*. New York: Harcourt, Brace Jovanovich, 1979.

Johnson, John E. *Wing Leader*. Feltham, Middlesex: Hamlyn, 1979.

Keogh, Pamela Clarke. *Audrey Style*. New York: HarperCollins, 1999.

Kershaw, Robert J. *It Never Snows in September: The German View of Market Garden and the Battle of Arnhem, September 1944*. Cambridge, MA: Da Capo, 1996.

Killen, John. *The Luftwaffe*. London: Sphere, 1969.

Lycett, Andrew. *Ian Fleming*. London: Phoenix, 1996.

Manrho, John, and Ron Pütz. *Bodenplatte: The Luftwaffe's Last Hope; The Attack on Allied Airfields New Year's Day, 1945*. Mechanicsburg, PA: Stackpole, 2010.

Maychick, Diana. *Audrey Hepburn: An Intimate Portrait*. New York: Birch Lane, 1993.

Morris, Rob, and Ian Hawkins. *The Wide Blue Yonder and Beyond: The 95th Bomb Group in War and Peace*. Washington, DC: Potomac Books, 2012.

Mosely, Leonard. *The Reich Marshal: A Biography of Hermann Goering*. London: Macmillan, 1977.

Mowat, Farley. *My Father's Son: Memories of War and Peace*. Boston: Houghton Mifflin, 1992.

Onderwater, Hans. *Operation Manna/Chowhound: The Allied Food Droppings April/May 1945*. Leicester, England: Midland Counties Publications, 1991.

Price, Alfred. *Luftwaffe Handbook, 1939–1945*. London: Ian Allen, 1977.

Richardson, William, and Seymour Freidin, eds. *The Fatal Decisions*. London: Michael Joseph, 1956.

Ridder, Willem. *Countdown to Freedom*. Bloomington, IN: Author House, 2007.

Ryan, Cornelius. *A Bridge Too Far*. New York: Simon and Schuster, 1974.

Stanley, Peter. *Commando to Colditz: Micky Burns Journey to the Far Side of Tears—The Raid on St. Nazaire*. Sydney, Australia: Pier 9, 2009.

Taylor, James, and Warren Shaw. *A Dictionary of the Third Reich*. London: Grafton, 1987.

Van der Zee, Henri A. *The Hunger Winter: Occupied Holland 1944–5*. London: Norman & Hobhouse, 1982.

Van der Zijl, Annejet. *Bernhard: A Hidden History*. Amsterdam: Querido, 2010.

Wilhelmina, Queen of the Netherlands. *Lonely But Not Alone*. Translated by John Peereboom. New York: McGraw-Hill, 1959.

Zuehlke, Mark. *On to Victory: The Canadian Liberation of the Netherlands, March 23–May 5, 1945*. Vancouver: Greystone, 2010.

NEWSPAPER, MAGAZINE AND JOURNAL ARTICLES

Barris, Ted. "Manna from Heaven." *Legion Magazine*, May 1, 2005.

Cook, William R. "The Final Flight of B-17G USAAF s/n 44-48640." *Air Classics Magazine*, Issue 6, 1995.

"Holland Was Saved Just in Time." *London Daily Herald*, May 8, 1945.

Newsweek, April 5, 1976.

"Obituary, HRH Prince Bernhard of the Netherlands." *The Telegraph*, December 4, 2004.

"One Man's War: After 50 Years, a Sweet Memory." *Oxnard Star*, November 14, 1995.

Seigel, Jessica. "An Interview With Audrey Hepburn." *Chicago Tribune*, January 20, 1992.

Waterfield, Bruno. "Dutch Prince Bernhard Was Member of Nazi Party." *London Telegraph*, March 5, 2010.

LETTERS

Franklin Delano Roosevelt Family, Business and Personal Papers, Roosevelt Library, Hyde Park, New York.

President's Secretary's File, Roosevelt Library, Hyde Park, New York.

US GOVERNMENT REPORTS

"Elimination of German Resources for War." Washington, DC: War Department/ Government Printing Office, December 1945.
"Report of the Investigation of IG Farbenindustrie AG." Prepared by the Division of Investigation of Cartels and External Assets. Washington, DC: War Department/ Government Printing Office, November 1945.

WEBSITES

A Bad Penny Always Comes Back. http://badpennybook.com.
Operation Manna/Chowhound. http://operationmanna.secondworldwar.nl.
95th Bomb Group Heritage Association. http://95thbg.org.
100th Bomb Group Foundation. http://100thbg.com.
"New Facts about Prince Bernhard PhD Annejet van der Zijl." *Querido.* http://querido .nl/web/Nieuws/Nieuwsartikel/Nieuwe-feiten-ore.
"The Seyss-Inquart Judgment." Nuremberg Trial Proceedings, Volume 16. *The Avalon Project: Documents in Law, History and Diplomacy.* Yale Law School. http://Avalon. law.edu/imt/judseyss.asp.

INDEX